"So You Think I Drive a Cadillac?"

Welfare Recipients' Perspectives on the System and its Reform

Karen Seccombe
Portland State University

Allyn and Bacon

Boston ■ London ■ Toronto ■ Sydney ■ Tokyo ■ Singapore

Series Editor, Social Work and Family Therapy: *Judy Fifer*
Editor-in-Chief, Social Sciences: *Karen Hanson*
Series Editorial Assistant: *Jennifer Muroff*
Marketing Manager: *Susan E. Ogar*
Composition Buyer: *Linda Cox*
Manufacturing Buyer: *Megan Cochran*
Cover Designer and Administrator: *Jenny Hart*
Production Administrator: *Rosalie Briand*
Editorial-Production Service: *Spectrum Publisher Services*
Electronic Composition: *Cabot Computer Services*

Library of Congress Cataloging-in-Publication Data

Seccombe, Karen, 1956–
    So you think I drive a Cadillac? : welfare recipients'
perspectives on the system and its reform / Karen Seccombe.
      p. cm.
    Includes bibliographical references and index.
    ISBN 0-205-28312-8
    1. Poor women—United States. 2. Welfare recipients—United
States. 3. Public welfare—United States. I. Title.
HV1445.S39 1998
362.5'8'0973—dc21   98-29817
                                            CIP

CONTENTS

PREFACE

I have always been self-conscious about social inequality. Growing up in a region of rich and poor neighboring communities, at a very tender age I couldn't help but notice the glaring contrast between those who have "more" and those who have "less." It prompted me to think intellectually about the causes and consequences of inequality. How is our sense of self shaped by the material goods around us? I didn't know that there was a formal discipline that pondered such questions—sociology—or a profession organized to help the casualties of inequality—social work—until much later.

This book provides insight into what it is like to be poor and live on welfare. In this era of controversial welfare reforms, we hear from lawmakers or policy "experts," but rarely from the voices of poor women themselves. We do not hear what the sting of poverty feels like, or how single mothers cope with the stigma and stresses of raising children on meager welfare benefits or low-wage earnings. Nor do we know the meanings that women attach to the label of "welfare mother." Underneath the statistics and the theories are real live human beings who are trying to make sense of their lives. Although rates, correlations, and causal models are important for understanding poverty and social inequality, the old adage that "social statistics are humans with their tears washed away" also rings true. This study has been conceptualized and designed with an interpretative sociological framework that emphasizes the centrality of subjective meaning and its importance and connection to the larger social structure.

Welfare reforms, both recent and those in the past, are based on patriarchal understandings of women and their roles within the family and the paid labor market. Women's roles are now in a state of flux, and poor women are no longer excused from work in order to care for their children. Our society values their cheap market labor more than it values their labor in the home. We demand that they fill the growing number of low tier service sector jobs that pay only minimum wages and offer no benefits, such as health insurance or subsidized child care, and ignore the fact that employment of this nature does nothing to lift women and children from poverty. Because of the insecurity of these jobs, poor women have on-again off-again bouts with welfare. Our society is frustrated with these repeat spells of welfare use, and therefore has imposed strict time limits and work requirements. However, the real problem with welfare has little to do with lazy women, or the structure of the welfare system. Instead, the real problem with welfare is that the structure of low-wage work is so tenuous and insecure that it cannot support a family in any decent manner. The "welfare problem" is best conceptualized as a "work problem." Until we improve the structure and conditions of low-wage work, poverty will never be reduced or ameliorated, and welfare will continue to be difficult but necessary fact of life for millions of poor families.

Acknowledgments

I am fortunate to have had many family members, good friends, and helpful colleagues surrounding me throughout the three years spent on this project. Collectively, they have inspired and motivated me, and have supported my inquiry into the concerns of poor women struggling to raise their families within the confines of welfare and low-wage work in the United States.

Let me first thank Stephen Roguski, who read every word in this book many times over, and graciously accepted the near-daily task of challenging and encouraging me in this endeavor. His skill at canvassing the Internet was invaluable. Many of his ideas are interwoven with mine within these pages, and I am most grateful for his contributions.

Other family members also supported me, made me smile, and in multiple ways contributed to a better book: Derek, Morgan, Jazz, and the late Stevie. These two- and four-footed creatures, who often joined me on long walks while I digested ideas, added to my sense of wonder about life, and provided the daily distractions that kept me well grounded.

Several graduate students assisted in the collecting, transcribing, and coding of these data. Without their assistance, this project would not yet be complete. Thank you to Cheryl Amey, Sylvia Ansay, Kim Battle Walters, Goldie MacDonald, and Janice Weber for their helpful contributions in these processes, and to Meg Galletly for her valuable contributions to the library research.

I'd also like to acknowledge the help of friends and colleagues Katherine Allen, Leonard Beeghley, Felix Berardo, Joe Feagin, Sally Gallagher, Masako Ishii-Kuntz, Delores James, Gary Lee, Janet Lee, Beth Norrell, Karen Pyke, Leslie Richards, Connie Shehan, Alexis Walker, and Becky Warner, who faithfully read drafts, lent me their ears, gave me critical advice and feedback on these chapters and the book writing process more generally, and taught me about the meaningful role that qualitative research can play in understanding social phenomena and informing policy debates. I hope the final manuscript gives justice to their valuable contributions.

Thanks are also due to the manuscript reviewers for their valuable feedback and suggestions: Shirley M. Clark, Chattanooga State Technical Community College; Jean E. Daniels, California State University–Northridge; Ronald B. Dear, University of Washington, Seattle; Andrew Dobelstein, University of North Carolina, Chapel Hill; Michael Jacobsen, University of North Dakota; Donald G. Magel, University of North Alabama; Michael Reisch, University of Pennsylvania; Satish Sharma, University of Nevada–Las Vegas; and Steven Soifer, University of Maryland at Baltimore.

Who could possibly be expected to finish a book without the playful interruptions that become all the more imperative when you are tied-down to your computer? I profoundly thank the people of Ketchikan, Alaska, for providing the scenic wonder and good cheer that made this writing endeavor downright enjoyable. I credit my running team, Runs in Her Stockings, and particularly Michelle Troli, Linda Millard, and Marta Poore, for teaching me to go from 3 to 13 miles in one year flat. And where else can you, in between pages, sneak in a kayaking trip alongside Orca whales, porpoises, and "Alaskan-sized" salmon, all the while seeing black bear along the shore and eagles overhead? I have a special appreciation for neighbors Susan and John Dickinson, who welcomed us to their community with open arms. I am grateful to the University of Florida and the National Science Foundation for allowing me to have a sabbatical in one of the most spectacular places on earth.

Last, but emphatically, I want to express my deep and sincere gratitude to the 47 women whose stories are told here. You generously opened up your lives to scrutiny, and I hope that I have conveyed your messages with the warmth, empathy, and vigor that they deserve. You are truly remarkable women, and I thank you for your keen insight into the welfare system. As a token of my appreciation, a portion of the royalties from this book will be given to those programs, services, and charities that have helped you along the way. This book is dedicated to you.

1 Introduction

Putting a Face on Welfare

The house was located on a dead-end street and was difficult to find. Luckily, I left in plenty of time, and found the house with five minutes to spare. It was a very modest home, but well cared for, as though the resident took tremendous pride in maintaining it. Someone living there was obviously a gardener; there were many potted flowers and plants on the porch and walkway. I thought of my mother, an avid gardener. As my thoughts drifted, I surveyed the neighborhood of junked cars, broken children's toys, dilapidated houses, and scrawny dogs roaming loose, and a chill woke the vigor within me for the task at hand. I was prepared and anxious to hear the muffled voices of women straining to be heard.

The front door was wide open, and Sheila was waiting for me to arrive. She warmly, but nervously, invited me into her home. She was a short woman, white, and looked older than her 40 years, with her graying hair pulled back. Her eyes were friendly, but reserved. We sat in her small living room, which contained a worn couch, a rocking chair with its cushion covered by a towel, a small television set, and an old fashioned record player with many LPs and a large stack of "45s" sitting on a rack next to it. Hanging on the walls were over a dozen photos and paint-on-velvet pictures of Elvis Presley. I later learned that her primary hobby was collecting Elvis mementos, and most of the records were his early recordings. I had a wave of nostalgia.

Two preschool children were resting on the couch and slept through most of the interview. Sheila told me that they were her grandchildren, two of the "lights of her life," and the children of her 25-year-old married daughter. She was baby-sitting the children today. Sheila also had a daughter, Melanie, aged 12, who she spoke of with love, pride, and fierce protectiveness. For Melanie's care, she receives $241 a month in Aid to Families with Dependent Children (AFDC) and $212 in food stamps from the State of Florida.

Sheila described her daily routine: She gets up at 5:00 A.M. every morning to get started on her housework before she gets her daughter up for school. She spoke of going to night school two evenings a week to work toward attaining her graduate equivalency diploma (GED). Other than cleaning her house, taking care of Melanie, visiting her grown daughter Jamie and Jamie's husband, occasionally baby-sitting her grandchildren, and attending night school, Sheila is a loner. "When you got a bunch of people together, you got problems," she tells me. She has few friends, rarely socializes, and considers her daughters, son-in-law, and grandchildren her only real family, despite a husband from whom she has been separated for 14 years and a large extended family, all of whom live 200 miles away. For Sheila, 200 miles might as well be a world away. She fled abuse and an intolerable family situation. She is on her own, and her world revolves around taking care of her youngest daughter. Melanie's father has never contributed financially to Melanie's support, nor has he been involved emotionally in her life.

> He's never offered to even take care of Melanie at all. Even when we lived in the same town, he didn't have that much to do with her, except, say, when it was for his benefit. She's 12 now, and we went to court. He ain't paid a dime, he ain't trying to pay a dime, and they ain't doing nothing to him. Putting it straight, I just haven't had good luck with men. Let's put it that way. Everybody makes mistakes [laughter], but I ain't making mine over no more. I'm tired of doing the same old thing. And I don't associate with my family. The only family I have are my daughters and my two grandbabies. That's it. When I need help, I go to her [oldest daughter]. Her and her husband. Other than that, if they can't help me, then I just do without. Because they are the only ones I'll ask anything from.

When Melanie comes home from school in the afternoon, they rarely go out again, except for Sheila's night class. Both are shy, have few friends, and do not like to socialize. Sheila told me that Melanie is self conscious about being poor, and never invites anyone from school to come into their home. Instead, in the afternoon, Melanie tends to her homework with Sheila's supervision, completes her chores, and they watch television together. Sheila crochets or listens to her Elvis records to pass the time when she's not busy cleaning house or cooking supper. They live a quiet and very private life.

> People make comments at her school, you know. That's why she, Melanie now, that's why she's a loner too. When she comes in that door, she don't go back outside. This afternoon she's going off for the weekend with her older sister. That's about as far as she goes . . . people say, well, you can get up, you can do better for yourself, you can get a job, and this and that. They ain't never been in a situation like I've been. I mean, when you get in between a rock and a hard place, and you got a child to care of, you do what you got to do. But what goes around, comes around. So, one of these days, with all their smart comments, they might find themselves in a worser predicament than some of us have been in.

According to Sheila, there is always a stressful undercurrent in their lives. Will they have enough money to live on this month? Despite the best of planning, something "out of the ordinary" always occurs that taxes their budget. Can they afford Melanie's school field trip? She has outgrown her shoes—can they afford a new pair? Winter is approaching, and they both need coats. Sheila always feels this stress gnawing at her, and believes it is affecting her physical health. She has seen several doctors to find out what is ailing her, to no avail. Some days she doesn't "even feel like getting out of bed."

Sheila dreams of getting a good job someday. She bubbled with enthusiasm as she told me of a job that she applied for at the Post Office that paid over $8.00 an hour. In order to get the job, she might have to take a test, and this concerned her. Sheila's reading, writing, and math skills are low, typical for someone who has not completed high school. She worries that she will not qualify for a job like this. But she is not afraid of hard work; she's spent most of her life working as a maid in hotels or cleaning private houses. Despite long hours, these jobs never pulled her out of poverty. Sheila was born poor, and has been poor all her life, living along side the other 39 million poor Americans (U.S. Bureau of the Census, 1997a). At present, she and Melanie receive $241 in welfare and $212 in food stamps each month. It is a hardship, but at least the income is secure, she told me. She fears the insecurity of minimum wage jobs. The take-home pay may be more than welfare, but they don't provide health insurance. She's concerned that her food stamps will be eliminated. In addition, there is always the dread of being laid off. If she lost her job, it would take another month or two to get back on welfare, she told me, and it would be difficult to support her daughter in the meantime.

Sheila is feeling the pressure of the changes in the welfare system:

I'm supposed to have a job by January 1. That's what all this schooling is supposed to be for. Plus I got applications out on my own. I got one at the post office, and I got one out at the mail room out on 441, Pic and Save [discount store], Winn Dixie [grocery store], Alachua General [hospital]. I'd like to work in a hospital, you know, like in the housekeeping department. Cleaning, that's more my line because I know what I'm doing. I don't need someone to tell me how to clean. I've been cleaning since I was seven years old. If I ain't learned it by now, then I'll never learn. But it's hard to get a job. There aren't that many jobs out there for people who ain't finished school. Now they want a GED, or they want this, they want that. I've been going to this Career Connections thing to help me find a job, but going from 9 to 3, plus night school, when do I have time to do my own cooking and cleaning? Why do they want to make us old women do the things that they should be making those 15-, 16-year-old girls do? Now, if I were 15 or 16 years old, I wouldn't have one complaint about this Career Connections, this and that. But I'm 40 years old. I mean, give me a break! But as far as the GED part, yes, I want to do that even if they stopped my welfare tomorrow. I'm getting my GED! I'm determined. I'll be there ten years probably before I get that GED, but I'm going to get it, and it's going to hang right there on that wall.

Sheila was the first woman I interviewed, and the first to pose these questions and concerns to me. But she was not the last. These were common concerns that ran in each and every woman's story.

Patrice, a 25-year-old African American woman, is also a "typical" welfare recipient, if there is such a thing. But unlike Sheila, she has finished high school, and was taking classes towards becoming a Licensed Practical Nurse, until her unplanned pregnancy and its complications, which required complete bed rest, forced her to quit. Nonetheless, she now works for a local hospital providing personal care in private homes, such as assisting bedridden patients with cooking, personal grooming, and housecleaning. She works part-time, and her income is low. She therefore continues to receive a partial welfare benefit for her two preschool age children. Patrice is proud of her education and work experience:

> I went to traveler's school, so I have experience in the traveling field, and I took business management for a short while. I was a teacher's aid for a year and a half, so, you know, I have experience here and there. I can type. I can do a variety of things. But I prefer working with people, like in nursing, over all the rest.

Patrice reveals the complexities and ironies in life. Events do not always go according to plan. Even the best of intentions, and relationships with men that were thought to be solid, can sometimes fall through. She shares her perceptions of women's experiences with men, their children, and the welfare system, and notes how they cope with seemingly discouraging situations.

> **PATRICE:** Well, if you sit around moping about your condition, that's not going to better the situation. All you're going to do is become depressed, and then you become more vulnerable to different things and people will take advantage of you. So you have to keep your head on right and think positive.
>
> **INTERVIEWER:** Do you think that happens to a lot of women?
>
> **PATRICE:** I really do. Well, it's like this. Being a young lady, I think a lot of women date a guy for years. And then you get pregnant. You expect him not really to marry you, but to be there for you and the child, but they jump up and leave. I believe women get depressed because of the fact that you got to just totally give up your life. Like me, I was in nursing school, and I was doing great. I came pregnant, so I got depressed because the guy left me after all those years. I had to resign in my eighth month of pregnancy. But I was working then too, because I was trying to maintain my rent and my car, you know. I think a lot of women become discouraged and depressed because what you are expecting in life—all your dreams and fantasies become nightmares. The guy leaves you, and then you know you got to turn to welfare, which everybody thinks is bad because, you know, it's taxpayer money. People be criticizing you. Then you have to stand in these long lines to get

stamps. Then you have to be criticized on a daily basis. And it's just discouraging. Then you have to go for your appointments, sometimes, there for two or three hours before your worker calls you. They just blobber your business out real loud in the lobby [laughter]. You got to be embarrassed. You look around, you know? Then you have to go into the health department, and everybody looks pitiful. You don't have the proper clothes to dress, you know, maternity wear. You be depressed. Then you be vulnerable to the situation. The first guy—well maybe not the first—but a guy promises you the world, and you are weak to the situation. You don't think your own situation is going to ever get any better, and then you end up in the same situation all over again if you don't be smart. But after two mistakes—I won't say mistakes because I love my children—but after two downfalls, you know, with men, I've learned [laughter].

INTERVIEWER: Do you think this happens to a lot of women who are single moms?

PATRICE: Yes, I know, as a matter of fact, because a lot of my friends, we sit and talk when we aren't too depressed. We sit down and talk about it, and we've pretty much shared the same experience. You get pregnant for a guy you thought you knew; somebody you dated for years. Then he jumps up and leaves you and ends up marrying somebody they don't know for nothing but a couple of months. And you be depressed and have all the children and all the aggravation. You know, when the kids get sick, regardless of what you want to do, you got to stay up with them. And then the next morning when you're working, you've got to get up and report to work. Your employers don't want to hear that your child was sick and you kind of need to be flexible. And if you're at school, you've got to take days off when your child is sick. You got to be running from doctor's appointments, you know? Then you worry about the welfare office on your back. So, if you get depressed, you can't let your depression explode. You got to keep it under control because you got these children.

INTERVIEWER: Why do you think the guys leave at that point?

PATRICE: Well, I feel that a lot of men are scared of commitments and responsibilities. A child is a lot of responsibility. But the guys, they were older than I am by almost ten years, so I thought they would know their roles. But no. They probably felt that their life would have to stop. They couldn't do the things they wanted to do. But, as a mom, I had to give up everything, you know, stay home and take care of the children. I had to give up school, everything. But it's their responsibility too, their role. Not only are they hurting you, they are hurting the children because there are so many under-privileged kids getting into different things, drugs, and gangs and stuff because they don't have a positive male role model. They just have mom, and being a single parent I can't stay home and be with them 24 hours, seven days a week. I have to work to support me and them because they're my family. I think it's wrong because it puts me as a mom, me and other single moms, on the line because we have to give up our lives. You can't date freely because you've got children around. You don't know who is sick, you know, like a child molester. You really got to know the guy. And then you got to make sure they are going to take to your children, and how your children like them. But I'm going to do the best I can. I'm going to provide for them, you know. I'm going to think positive and I pray and ask the Lord to assist me with, you know, raising children alone.

This is a book about welfare. It contains the intimate stories of women who receive Aid to Families with Dependent Children (AFDC), the staple of public welfare prior to welfare reform. AFDC, and subsequent Temporary Assistance to Needy Families (TANF), provides cash payments to poor families with dependent children when the children are deprived of the support of one parent. For the sake of ease, I refer to these programs as "welfare," even though, in reality, they are only two of many programs lumped under that heading. The women interviewed graciously disclosed the experiences that led them to welfare; their appreciation for and frustration with the system, and the ways in which they cope with the frustration; their hopes, dreams, and plans for themselves and their children; and their ideas on welfare reform.

Equally important, this is a book about women. I examine the ways in which women are marginalized in our economic system, dependent in social relationships, and stigmatized for needing government aid to care for their children. These in-depth interviews reveal some of the consequences that this may have for women. The participants in this research come from all walks of life. Some of these women have been receiving welfare since childhood; others grew up in upper-middle class families. Some bore children out of wedlock; others had children within the confines of a marriage they thought would last forever. They are a diverse group and, on first glance, would appear to have little in common with one another. But, as their stories unfold, many common themes become apparent. What they have in common includes broken or intermittent relationships with men, and struggles to provide the financial security and physical and emotional care that children need. They serve as both mothers and fathers to their children, often unexpectedly.

Critical and Feminist Frameworks

I began this work because I wanted to better understand the lives of ordinary poor women on welfare and to share that information with others. I wanted to listen to their life stories: listen to the issues that engage them, the struggles that consume them, and their dreams and visions of the future that drive them. My fundamental goal is to help us better understand the lives of poor women who receive welfare by providing critical and feminist frameworks to understand their experiences. A critical perspective means that we do not blindly accept commonly touted explanations for the way things are. It requires that we examine the assumptions, values, and ideologies that are used to justify our attitudes toward women on welfare and the organization of the welfare system. Power relationships are at the heart of critical theory, which suggests that social and political arrangements often favor the dominant group, or the elite within society. Yet these arrangements may be presented as "normal" and as reflecting the best interests of all members of society, rich and poor alike. Members of society internalize this "status quo"—the ideologies become common sense and have shared meanings. For example, the ideology that welfare is "a narcotic, a subtle destroyer of the human spirit," as claimed by former President of the United States Ronald Reagan in his 1986 State of the Union Address (cited in Rank, 1994, p. 19), has widespread appeal, whereas other evidence that contradicts this view is routinely dismissed.

A feminist framework uses gender as a central lens and as a key variable in the current controversy about welfare. Feminist research is based on the belief that women continue to be devalued and oppressed and, as a result, their experiences have been neglected or distorted by science. Reconstructing knowledge designed to empower women and challenge the status quo is at the heart of feminist research and is my ultimate purpose (Cook and Fonow, 1986; Thompson, 1992). In this book I use a feminist framework to present research that is both *on* and *for* women. Research on women hopes to unmask biases and expand our knowledge about women. My goal is to sensitize people to the reality of women's lives. Research for women is "consciously aimed at emancipating women and enhancing their lives" (Thompson, 1992). In particular, it embeds personal experience in a broader social context. The rich personal experiences of all women are grounded in a social, historical, cultural, and political context. Women have certain experiences because society is organized by gender. Research for women illuminates far beyond simply filling in the gaps of our knowledge about women; it emphasizes the importance of context, social processes, and subjective experience.

I acknowledge that some recipients of cash assistance welfare programs are men, but I suggest that welfare is a "women's issue" for two reasons. First, only eight percent of households that receive cash assistance contain two parents; by far the most prevalent household is one in which a never-married or a divorced mother is the sole "head of household" (U.S. House of Representatives, U.S. Committee on Ways and Means, 1996). Second, and perhaps even more important, welfare is a women's issue because many women are simply one man away or one crisis away from welfare themselves. In reality, many middle and upper-middle class women are more vulnerable than they reveal. Statistics show that women are not a particularly wealthy group of individuals. Fifty-seven percent of employed women earned less than $15,000 in 1995 (U.S. Bureau of the Census, 1997b, Table 732, p. 473). Despite working, many women would quickly become impoverished if they lost the support of a spouse, experienced a crisis such as an injury, an illness, or experienced even a short-term lay-off or reduction in work hours. These disastrous events are rarely planned, but they can happen to any and all women with only minimal notice. Certainly, men are vulnerable as well, but women's wages are generally so much less than men's that they walk the fine line between subsistence and impoverishment. Moreover, women's economic status is often more tentative than is the case for men. This is particularly true if a woman is not employed and is deriving her economic status through her partner, as is the case with more than one-third of women with children under the age of six (U.S. Bureau of the Census, 1997b, Table No. 631, p. 404). But even when they are employed, women face unique challenges in the gendered workplace. Lower wages for work of comparable worth, occupational segregation, and unequal returns on education are ties that bind women together, regardless of whether women acknowledge them. For many affluent women, this insight is particularly troubling. It breaks down the barriers that society tends to impose between "us," defined as anyone who is not on welfare, and "them," and asks that we acknowledge our common experiences as women that transcend social class or race.

We also know, however, that there is no single meaning or given experience of being a woman. Feminist theories acknowledge difference in women's experiences. A woman is never really only a woman; many other structural and social features shape the lived experience of being female. For example, social class as well as race and ethnicity shape experiences of women. The experience of growing up poor and black in the rural south, as vividly described by Anne Moody in *Coming of Age in Mississippi* (1968), differ from the experiences portrayed by Dorothy Allison in *Bastards Out of Carolina* (1992), a story of a white girl's experience growing up in rural southern poverty. Womanhood is not a static or unidimensional status. It is, instead, shaped by social, historic, and cultural surroundings that influence the ways in which women experience, interpret, and construct their reality.

Yet there are some shared patterns of meaning and some commonalities of experience that can be noted. We live in a patriarchal society in which male dominance is maintained and supported through law, religion, culture, and societal norms. For example, women, as a collective group of people, are more likely to be economically dependent on others; they are more likely to be poor; they are more likely to hold low-wage work; and they are more likely to be a single parent to children than are men. Moreover, women around the world are routinely subjected to physical and sexual violence, simply because they are women. One of the "necessities" of patriarchy, according to Dorothy Miller in *Women and Social Welfare* (1992), is the need to separate the sexes, thus devaluing and controlling women. From the Chinese ritual of footbinding to the epidemic of female genital mutilation affecting more than 100 million women today (Daly, 1978; Greenhouse, 1994; Mackie, 1996), women are routinely raped, beaten, and tortured because of patriarchal norms. In her provocative book, *Against Our Will: Men, Women and Rape* (1975), Brownmiller suggested that the threat of rape, as well as the act itself, perpetuates and enhances patriarchy by limiting women's freedoms and encouraging their dependency on men for protection.

Gender is both an interactional and a political process, and is at the center of this analysis. This is one of the challenges of this book: To analyze women's experiences with welfare in a way that captures their individuality, but also recognizes the shared patterns of meaning and their commonalities of experience as women within the social structure. They are active participants in creating meaning of the welfare experience, developed through interaction with their families, friends, and with acquaintances, such as the staff in the welfare office. Moreover, they create meaning through their interactions with strangers in such public places as grocery stores, where they immediately become identified and labeled as "welfare mothers" when using their food stamps.

Specific Contributions of This Study of Lived Experience

Women who receive welfare are a distorted and stigmatized group. They are seen as "different," and as something "less than" the more affluent. They are not viewed as whole human beings, with a full range of needs and experiences. Rather, we compartmentalize and focus on narrow aspects of their lives such as their checks, their alleged fraud, or whether there is a man in the house. As Dorothy Miller (1992) argues, women on welfare are "manless" and therefore constitute a threat to the patriarchal order. They therefore must be punished and controlled so that their numbers will not multiply. This is accomplished in our social welfare system through such mechanisms as inadequate benefit levels and by stigmatizing recipients. A strong negative imagery has been created with respect to welfare mothers, and their supposed subcultural experiences.

Both men and women buy into these negative images of women on welfare. Women fail to see welfare as an issue of importance to all women, and do not recognize that they too could be poor and on welfare if for a possible, albeit unfortunate, turn of events. Women, like men, draw sharp class lines around themselves—lines that, especially for women who are dependent on men for their class position, are relatively arbitrary and possibly tenuous. They blanket themselves in their class position, denying their commonalities with other woman. A schism occurs based on class position. This lack of a "gender consciousness" is divisive. I hope to increase women's collective feeling by peeling away the mostly negative opinions of the "welfare mother" and, through their stories, uncover the meaning of motherhood, family, welfare, work, and dependency in their everyday lives. Negative opinion falls away easily in light of a balanced rendering of perspective and factual data.

As I explore women's experiences with welfare, I capture the shared meaning of motherhood within our society. This book illustrates that poor women share many of the same struggles and concerns about their children and about their lives as do others who are more affluent. They are passionately concerned about being good mothers—a job that they consider the most important job of all. They strive to promote the well-being of their children in multiple ways. They fear for the safety of their neighborhoods. They want to get out of the housing projects, which they say are crime-ridden and filled with despair. They dream of their own homes surounded by a picket fence. They search for jobs, particularly one that pays them enough money to be able to provide basic necessities for their families, such as food, adequate shelter, health insurance, and clothing. They want to be able to offer their children some semblance of a middle-class lifestyle, such as name-brand athletic shoes or cable television, considered paramount for their children's self-esteem. These are shared goals. Thus, one theme of this book is that *nonpoor women have more in common with poor women than they probably realize, and may care to know*. Without making heroes of the women interviewed, I show that the distinctions between "us" and "them" are largely arbitrary, and are artifacts of having or not having enough money to cushion the blows dealt in life.

Understanding these similarities and the lived experience of poverty and welfare can inform our discussions of welfare reform, and perhaps create a more rational, humane, and empowering policy. I uncover the oppressive features of welfare in the lives of the women who use it, and provide new insights into a workable alternative. A second theme of this book is that *current reforms are predicated on changing assumptions of appropriate women's roles within the marketplace and within the family, and beliefs that poor women enjoy the "free ride" they get from the welfare system at taxpayer expense*. Both of these assumptions reveal patriarchal dictums that women must be under the control and supervision of men. The policy relevant question should not be "How can we simply and expeditiously move more women off of welfare?" but rather, "How can we improve women's lives so that they will no longer be poor and need welfare in the first place?" These are two different issues. Forcing women off welfare into low-paying, dead-end jobs without critical health insurance or other benefits may be fruitful for creating a reserve and cheap labor force desired by a capitalist economy, but it does little to improve the lives of women and their children.

This leads to my third theme, *that the real "welfare problem" has little to do with the welfare system at all, but instead lies in the insecurity of low-wage work*. Until we strengthen the bottom tier of our employment structure so that these jobs provide more security through higher wages, critical benefits, and dependable hours, women who have families to support will be hesitant to take them. This does not represent a failure on the part of the welfare system. It represents a failure on the part of our government to ensure the quality and security of work. The thought is abhorrent, but welfare, with all its limitations, provides more security to vulnerable families than does employment within the lowest tiers of our labor market. It is therefore not surprising that poor women who strive to be good mothers choose welfare over work. It may be irresponsible to do otherwise.

The specific contribution of this research is unique and moves us beyond current political or social treatises. My fourth theme is straightforward, yet often overlooked: *Social policies designed to ameliorate poverty and human suffering will be more successful if we take into account the specific needs that poor women themselves articulate*. We need to begin with the participants' understandings and meanings of poverty and welfare (Blumer, 1969). An interpretation derived from those with direct experience with the welfare system is a highly effective way to better understand the strengths and limitations of our current system, and to gain insight into those who rely on it. Used in conjunction with the myriad of quantitative studies that examine trends in welfare use, in-depth interviews can infuse new ideas in the discussion, and answer old questions in new and creative ways. Consider, for example, the numerous quantitative studies that suggest the primary reason that women stay on welfare, or return to welfare quickly, is a lack of childcare. The lack of childcare slots has been identified as a critical social policy problem, and has been taken into consideration under President Clinton's welfare reform plan. These interviews, however, revealed that the issue is more complex. Namely, the reason that some women do not use childcare is not simply because it is unavailable, but because they do not *trust* strangers taking care of their children. As one woman told me, "I'm not putting my daughter in daycare until she's old enough to tell me what happened there!" Paranoia? Not necessarily, given the high percentage of girls and women who have been sexually and physically abused. Simply creating more childcare slots is admirable, but it alone will not resolve the issue of trust. Thus, qualitative studies like this one can increase our understanding of welfare from the vantage point of the recipients themselves.

Welfare and Public Policy

Welfare recipients are denigrated because welfare itself is considered to be the scourge of public policy. It is liked by neither Democrats nor Republicans, conservatives nor liberals. It is criticized by all sides, and is considered an extravagant and costly program that is spiraling out of control, and is responsible for a sizable component of our federal deficit. In reality, however, total AFDC expenditures actually decreased from $22.2 billion in 1992 to $22.0 billion in 1995. These expenditures are a small component of the overall social welfare budget, constituting only one percent of the federal government's total spending (Congressional Digest, 1995; U.S. House of Representatives, U.S. Ways and Means Committee, 1996, Table 8-26, p. 470). Moreover, the purchasing power of benefits has eroded over the past decades, when inflation is taken into account, from $676 in 1970 down to $373 in 1993 (Congressional Digest, 1995). This represents a 45 percent reduction in real purchasing power.

Although money is often cited as the source of these tensions, American values of financial independence and hard work are usually at the heart of welfare hostilities (Herbert, 1996; Meyer, 1994). The welfare system has been accused of encouraging long-term dependency among women, family break-ups and illegitimacy, while discouraging work incentives and motivation. Dick Armey, a member of the U.S. House of Representatives, argues that welfare stimulates poverty rather than reduces it. He suggests that welfare makes marriage economically unsound for low-income parents; that women marry welfare instead of their children's father (Armey, 1994). A public display by John Mica, member of the House of Representatives (R–Florida), during the debate on welfare cuts took a feverish pitch as he held up a sign that read, "Don't feed the alligators." He explained, "We post these warnings because unnatural feeding and artificial care create dependency. When dependency sets in, these otherwise able alligators can no longer survive on their own." He then noted that although "people are not alligators . . . we've upset the natural order. We've created a system of dependency" (Pear, March 25, 1995). This line of thought closely parallels that of Charles Murray, who, in his famous book *Losing Ground* (1984), says that welfare breeds dependency. Murray has successfully persuaded many people that welfare contributes more harm than good to society.

The real problem with welfare is that our society no longer feels comfortable paying mothers to stay home and take care of their children. More than two-thirds of married women with dependent children are now employed outside the home, representing a dramatic change from when welfare was originally created. In fact, married women with children are as likely to be employed outside the home as are their single counterparts (Bianchi and Spain, 1996). This dramatic change in the behavior of married women with children has contributed to our rethinking of welfare. As mothers' employment becomes the rule rather than the exception, people question the value of paying single mothers to stay home with their children. They ask, is it necessary to subsidize poor and single mothers so that they do not have to work outside the home, when most middle-class mothers are employed? Ignored in the discussions are the differing circumstances between the two groups. Poor single mothers must be both mothers and fathers to their children. They have no one else to rely on to share the financial and emotional strains that accompany parenting. And without money to cushion the difficulties of life, their strains may be substantial. It is therefore unfair and inappropriate to assume that poor single mothers and middle-class mothers are on a level playing field.

On August 22, 1996, President Clinton signed a bill before him to eliminate AFDC and to revamp welfare "as we know it." From the Personal Responsibility and Work Opportunity Reconciliation Act (P.L. 104-193), TANF was created. This critical welfare reform legislation went into effect as federal law on July 1, 1997, and set lifetime welfare payments at a maximum of five years, with the majority of able-bodied recipients being required to work after two years. Other changes under this reform included childcare assistance, at least one year of transitional Medicaid, the required identification of the children's biologic fathers so that child support can more easily be pursued, and the requirement that unmarried minors live at home and stay in school in order to receive benefits. Furthermore, more power is granted to states and less power resides in the federal government. Washington DC provides fewer mandates and instead allows more local and state authority in deciding how best to meet the needs of their impoverished residents. Some hail this as a boon to local control; others fear that poor states have little to offer their poorest residents, and consequently will either eliminate some families who were previously deemed eligible or else siphon off money from other state funded programs such as education or job training programs (Carney, 1995). According to the Congressional Budget Office, nearly $55 billion in cuts may occur to low-income programs over the next six years (cited in Super, Parrott, Steinmetz, and Mann, 1996). Although since 1996 some of these cuts have been restored (Center for Law and Social Policy, 1997).

Two important assumptions underlie these reforms, and they shed light on the suspicion and contempt we have for women who need government assistance. First, we as a populace apparently no longer believe that the most important job of single mothers is to care for the emotional and physical needs of their children. Instead, single mothers should now be wage-earners first and leave the care-taking to someone else, rather than vice versa. The norms and expectations for motherhood have changed. Single mothers no longer constitute a category of "worthy poor."

Second, reforms are based on the belief that recipients do not want significant changes made in the structure of the welfare system, and therefore we must force these changes on them. Welfare reforms, therefore, have been developed within a context of antagonism—that we must force recipients to get off the public dole whether they want to or not.

Many states are enacting welfare reform policies that are *more* stringent than those imposed by the federal government. For example, as of February 1997, 40 governors submitted state welfare plans to the federal government and the Department of Health and Human Services have certified 37 of these plans as complete. Of these, 18 states, or 45 percent of those that have filed welfare plans, set time limits on welfare that are more strict than the five-year lifetime limit proposed by the federal government. Indiana and North Carolina, for example, have two-year limits. Sixteen states, or 40 percent of those filing plans, have adopted more stringent work requirements than mandated by the federal government. Florida, Tennessee, and Texas expect welfare recipients to go to work immediately. At least 19 of the 40 states that have filed plans say they will impose family caps and refuse to increase benefits to women who have additional children while receiving public assistance. Two states, New York and Ohio, plan to implement drug testing among welfare recipients. At least 20 states plan to deny welfare to people convicted of felonies involving the possession, use, or distribution of narcotics (*Gainesville Sun*, Feb. 23, 1997).

One year after signing reform legislation, President Clinton hails welfare reform a resounding success by citing statistics suggesting a 1.4 million-person drop in welfare use. "I think it's fair to say the debate is over. We know that welfare reform works," he said in a recent speech in St. Louis (Broder, August 17, 1997). This statistic, however, only indicates that the number of people on welfare fell. It tells us nothing about whether welfare reform "works" in the sense of fostering self-sufficiency, independence, and self-esteem. Furthermore, it tells us nothing about whether poverty itself has declined. Meaningful evaluations of policy changes take years, or even decades. "You can't tell whether welfare reform is working simply from caseload numbers," argues Wendell Primus, a welfare expert who quit the Clinton Administration in protest over President Clinton's signing of the welfare legislation. "Those figures do not tell how many former recipients moved from welfare to work, or simply from dependency to despondency. You have to look at where these people went," he suggested (Broder, August 17, 1997).

Where Are the Voices of Welfare Recipients in the Discussion?

One fact is particularly glaring and troublesome. The participants of social welfare programs have had little input into the welfare reform process. Their needs, desires, and suggestions have not been uniformly sought. Why? Because numerous stereotypes persist regarding "able-bodied persons" who receive welfare. Mothers who are without husbands to support them and their children are suspect and viewed as potentially undeserving, depending on the reason that they have no husband. Social Security's insurance program provides a considerably higher benefit to children whose fathers had died than welfare provides to children whose fathers deserted

Stigma

them. Although the need is the same, the reason for that need determines the amount of cash assistance that they receive. We have created a stratified system in which social insurance programs are given respect, whereas public assistance programs are deeply stigmatized. No one who receives benefits from social insurance would dare to say they receive "welfare," despite the fact that both were created and exist under the Social Security umbrella.

Welfare recipients are a stigmatized group, "reduced in our minds from a whole and usual person to a tainted, discounted one" (Goffman, 1963: 3–4). The attributes assigned to welfare recipients are less than positive and are familiar to us all. Recipients are thought of as being lazy, unmotivated, as cheating the system, and as having additional children simply to increase the amount of their benefit. Famous author and welfare critic George Gilder, in a recent article in the *American Spectrum*, stated that, "on the whole, white or black, these women are slovenly, incompetent, and sexually promiscuous" (1995: 25).

These perceptions do not simply reflect ignorance or randomly misguided information. Rather, they developed in relation to our long-standing values and beliefs: That the individual is primarily responsible for his or her own economic conditions; that work is good and idleness is a vice; and that social services are likely to dull initiative and hard work. Much of the underlying belief about women on welfare is that these women are looking for a free ride at the expense of the American taxpayer (Davis and Hagen, 1996). Unlike years gone by, women are no longer excused from work in order to care for their children. Staying home to nurture and tend to dependent children is only appropriate if you have the financial means to do so. If you do not have the means, then remaining at home to care for children now constitutes idleness.

Lost in the discussions of laziness, fraud, and dependency are the significant number of women who are eligible for public assistance but do not receive it; who choose not to receive all the programs they are eligible for; and the women who voluntarily leave programs before their eligibility terminates. Instead of focusing on ways to make welfare more inclusive, we are instead afraid that "handouts" will encourage dependency. Welfare programs stigmatize those who receive assistance in order to minimize the likelihood that those currently receiving aid will get too comfortable, and to make a statement to onlookers that aid comes at an emotionally expensive price.

A National Profile of Welfare Recipients

A wide body of research using large and nationally representative samples draws into question or refutes the popular folklore surrounding lazy "welfare queens." Who then, does receive welfare?

According to the Green Book by the Committee on Ways and Means, U.S. House of Representatives, in 1995, 4.9 million families, or 13.6 million individuals received AFDC. Of these recipients, nearly three-quarters, or 9.3 million, were dependent children under the age of 18, accounting for nearly 14 percent of the total child population in the United States. It is therefore fair to say that the "typical" welfare recipient is a child. Nearly 13 percent of these children live in poor two-parent households but receive welfare because of an unemployed or incapacitated parent. In the vast majority of cases, children who receive welfare live in single-parent households with a mother who has never married (56 percent), is divorced (27 percent), or is a widow (2 percent). The majority of these children are far too young to contribute to their financial support: 46 percent of these children are under the age of six, and another third are between the ages of 6 and 11. However, it should be noted that not all poor children receive welfare: only 60 percent of poor children are eligible or otherwise receive welfare benefits (U.S. House of Representatives, Committee on Ways and Means, 1996: Tables 8-27, 8-28, pp. 471, 473).

Despite the fact that the majority of those who receive welfare are children, the available data on welfare recipients are focused largely on parents rather than their children. Table 1.1 describes selected characteristics of welfare recipients throughout the United States for the years 1986, 1990, and 1994.

As shown in Table 1.1, the average number of people in families who receive AFDC is 2.8, down slightly from 1986. Families on welfare are not large; 43 percent have only one child, and nearly three-quarters of recipients have no more than two children. Less than 10 percent of families have four or more children.

Few current welfare recipients are teenagers, despite portrayals in the media to the contrary. However, the percentage of welfare recipients under age 20 has risen from 3.3 to 6.3 between 1986 and 1994. Nearly half of recipients are in their twenties, and another third are in their thirties. Only 11.5 percent of recipients are age 40 or older.

Stigma

Popular folklore also suggests that most welfare recipients are African Americans. This, however, is not correct, as the proportion of AFDC recipients who are African American and white is nearly equal. Together these two groups comprise nearly three-quarters of recipients. Hispanics account for another 20 percent of recipients, up from 14 percent in 1986. This may reflect immigration patterns, as recent immigrants are disproportionately from Latin America and are likely to be poor. Native Americans account for 1.3 percent and Asians 2.9 percent of welfare recipients, respectively.

Unfortunately, data on the level of education obtained by mothers is incomplete. Among those cases in which their educational level is known, more than one-third have not completed high school. Nearly half of the women whose education is known have a high school degree, and 8.2 have attended or completed college, a figure that has doubled since 1986.

As one would expect, most women who receive welfare are unemployed. Only eight percent, or roughly one woman out of twelve, are employed, and most of these women work part-time. Only 3.3 percent of welfare recipients nationwide work full-time; however, they continue to receive a partial welfare benefit because of their low wages relative to their economic needs.

We also know that recipients' stays on welfare are not as long as often imagined by program critics. The median number of months on AFDC during the most recent stay is 22.8 months, down from 27 months in 1986. Most episodes of AFDC use last

TABLE 1.1   Characteristics of AFDC Recipients, 1986, 1990, 1994

	1986	1990	1994
Average Family Size (Persons)	3.0	2.9	2.8
Number of Child Recipients (Percent of AFDC Cases)			
One	42.7	42.2	42.6
Two	30.8	30.3	30.0
Three	15.9	15.8	15.6
Four or More	9.8	9.9	9.6
Age of Mother (Percent of Mothers)			
Under 20	3.3[1]	7.9	6.3
20-24	33.6[2]	23.8	24.6
25-29	20.0[3]	24.6	22.6
30-39	30.1	32.0	34.9
40 or Older	13.0	11.7	11.5
Race (Percent of Parents)			
White	39.7	38.1	37.4
Black	40.7	39.7	36.4
Hispanic	14.4	16.6	19.9
Native American	1.3	1.3	1.3
Asian	2.3	2.8	2.9
Other and Unknown	1.4	1.5	2.1
Education of Mother (Percent of Mothers)			
8th Grade or Less	4.8	5.8	4.0
1–3 Years High School	14.3	16.5	17.6
High School Degree	17.3	19.3	21.1
Some College	3.4	5.7	7.7
College Graduate	0.5	0.4	0.5
Unknown	59.7	52.3	46.0
Mothers Employment Status (Percent)			
Full-time Job	1.6	2.5	3.3
Part-time Job	4.2	4.2	4.6
Median Months on AFDC Since Most Recent Opening	27.0	23.0	22.8

[1]In 1986, this was "under age 19."

[2]In 1986, this was "19–25."

[3]In 1986, this was "26–29."

Source: Information from Table 8-28 and from the 1996 *Green Book*, U.S. House of Representatives, Committee on Ways and Means, pp. 473–474.

less than one year (56 percent), and the proportion of recipients with shorter stays has been steadily increasing since the 1980s. Recipients are on the program for short spells while they amass the skills and resources needed to survive financially on their own.

Yet, it is important to note that there is considerable movement on and off welfare among many women. While, for some, welfare is a temporary and short-term phenomenon, there are a sizable number of women who return to welfare soon after leaving the system. Those who leave welfare because of employment tend to remain off somewhat longer than do those who leave for other reasons. Fifty-eight percent of those who exit AFDC come back to it within two years; 69 percent return within four years (Committee on Ways and Means, U.S. House of Representatives, 1996: Table 8-44, p. 503). Consequently, when totaling all of the stays on welfare, in 1994, nearly half (48%) have received benefits for more than five years (Committee on Ways and Means, U.S. House of Representatives, 1996: Table 8-47, p. 506). Those who are likely to use AFDC longer than average during their lifetimes are persons who have less than 12 years of education, have no recent work experience, are under age 24, are black or Hispanic, have never married, have a child younger than age three, or have three or more children (Committee on Ways and Means, U.S. House of Representatives, 1996: Table 8-48, p. 507).

Why do women return to welfare? Several researchers have posed this question, and have looked at the factors that are associated with returning to welfare or remaining off welfare for good. Results from quantitative studies suggest that the most important factors influencing repeated use are "those factors that shape a woman's income packaging strategy and determine her economic security," such as her education, age, number of children and their ages, and recent work experience (Harris, 1996; Petersen, 1995). Although conclusions are not unanimous, it does appear likely that women who have lower levels of education; those who are younger; women who have many children, particularly children under the age of six; and women who have little recent work experience are more likely to return to welfare after leaving it, and are likely to remain on welfare for longer periods of time overall. Qualitative studies elaborate on these ideas; it appears that many women cannot sustain low-wage jobs without benefits attached to them, such as health insurance or childcare, for long periods of time. Whether this implies that they are lazy, unmotivated, and dependent on welfare, as critics would suggest, is obviously a matter for further study as well as interpretation. These interviews reveal that most women are sufficiently motivated to leave welfare. Their obstacles are not their own laziness or other personal shortcomings. Rather, they are on welfare largely because of an entanglement of constraints, relationships that have gone sour, a dearth in their levels of human capital (e.g., education, job skills), insufficient social support systems, and a lack of jobs that provide the security that families need.

Given the high rates of recidivism, some recipients have been accused of being "dependent" on the system. There is widespread concern over the intergenerational transmission of welfare. A review of seven studies conducted between 1986 and 1989 (Moffit, 1990) reports that their results provide consistent evidence of a strong corre-

generational?

lation between parents' use of welfare and the later behavior of their daughters. Daughters from welfare families are more likely to use welfare themselves later than are daughters whose parents did not use welfare. A correlation, however, does not assume causality. The studies do not answer the question of whether growing up with welfare causes a daughter to later use it as well. Many other possible explanations for the observed correlation are possible. Children from homes that use welfare generally have fewer parental resources available to them, live in poorer and more dangerous neighborhoods, and go to inferior schools. Thus, deficiencies in social capital, human capital, or fewer jobs in the impoverished neighborhood could be responsible for the correlation. However, it's important to recognize that 41 percent of women who are considered at present to be "highly dependent" on welfare (defined as receiving at least 25 percent of average family income as cash welfare payments) received no welfare in their household when they were children, and most of the remaining women considered "highly dependent" on welfare received aid for only a short period (Table 8-51, p. 512).

Gottschalk and Moffitt (1994) suggest that the best way to conceptualize "welfare dependence" is to examine the total time spent on welfare over a given period of time. Using data from the Panel Study of Income Dynamics (PSID) for the years 1974–1987, they found that dependence has not grown significantly in the population as a whole, with the exception of younger women. They propose that the increase in total time on welfare and total percentage of income dependence can be explained by the drop in age at first entry onto welfare, and not from an increase in welfare episode duration.

I maintain that the term "welfare dependency" is a misnomer, because few women are really "dependent" on the system as the term implies. Instead, the rich data from these in-depth interviews reveal an elaborate system in which women attempt to build a respectable and meaningful life for their children and for themselves. As you will see, they use their meager welfare benefits, as do women with greater incomes, to secure food, shelter, clothing, and to try to buy some semblance of a middle-class lifestyle. But because neither their welfare benefits nor their earnings are sufficient to pull them out of poverty, let alone allow for a middle-class lifestyle, they reconstruct intricate webs to help them live and survive. Orchestrating this type of life is stressful. The lucky ones have family and friends to rely on; the unlucky ones do not.

Terri Lynn is one of the luckier ones. I spoke with her, and her sister, one rainy winter day at their mother's house. Although her extended family is not large, she relies on them daily for her housing, childcare, and transportation. She is a 24-year-old African American woman and mother of a six-year-old daughter who shares close bonds with her mother, sister, brother, and aunt. She currently lives with her sister in her rent-subsidized apartment while she saves money from her job to enable her to get her own apartment. She says that this living arrangement is preferable to her previous arrangement. Her former apartment cost $215 a month, and often was without heat or the water was turned off because the landlord failed to pay the bill. During these times Terri Lynn and her daughter would take the bus over to her mother's house and shower, cook, and perhaps even sleep there.

Terri Lynn is employed as a night cashier at a bowling alley across town. She continues to receive a partial welfare payment because the hours are sporadic and, at minimum wage, her income does not lift her above the eligibility limits for aid. "But I wish I wasn't getting none of it," she told me. She's tried to get off welfare by taking computer classes at a for-profit business school in town. But after graduation, without experience, and without their help in finding employment, she could not find anyone to hire her. Instead, she found the job at the bowling alley and slowly works to pay off her tuition debts. Luckily for Terri Lynn, her mother or sister baby-sit her daughter for free, a savings of several hundred dollars per month. On her income and her small welfare grant, Terri Lynn would not be able to pay them or anyone else to take care of her child. She does not own a car, and neither does her mother or sister, so she relies on the bus to get to work. For Terri Lynn, transportation logistics are a nightmare. The bus ride takes over an hour and a half each way. Thus, between working and commuting, her daughter often spends 11 hours a day with her childcare provider, in this case Terri Lynn's mother or sister. She is thankful she does not have to leave her with a stranger, and in an unfamiliar place, for such long periods of time. When she works late into the night and the bus has stopped running, she usually takes a taxi cab back to her mom's house, where her daughter is sleeping. The cab costs her $6.00, and cuts into a sizable portion of her minimum wage earnings. She cannot afford to take the cab all the way back to her own house on the other side of town.

> I leave here at 3:45, and get downtown at 4:15. Then I wait until 4:30 to catch the #7 bus. And then by the time I get there it's 5:05. And then I have to walk on down there, and I get there at 5:30 on the dot. But after work at 1:00 in the morning, I have to catch a cab because the bus has stopped running. So I catch a cab to my mom's house where she [daughter] is sleeping. I sleep there too, and then I get up real early so that we can catch the early bus back to my house so I can get her [daughter] ready for school. See, and by then I have to take her to school because she'd done missed the school bus. After that I go back home and try to get some rest, and then, after school, I go back and pick her up. We take the bus back to my mom's house so she can watch her, and then I go to work again. So, I be running back and forth all day long.

Sometimes her brother is able to pick her up from work late at night, and take her and her daughter directly home, which makes their morning routine considerably easier. She told me, in no uncertain terms, that this assistance from her family was invaluable to her. Without it, she would not be able to work. Her daughter's father, in contrast, provides no emotional or financial support.

> **TERRI LYNN:**   Her dad never gave me nothing. I had to beg him to buy one bag of Pampers for her when she ran out once and I didn't have no money. He's called her maybe three times since he was out of jail. Now she asks, "When is my daddy coming?" What can I tell her? I don't know. I told him that he needs to straighten himself out and spend

more time with her because she wanted to see him. Now that he's been out of jail he was supposed to come see her, but he hasn't gotten her yet. I guess he thinks I'm supposed to bring her to him, but I'm not going to bring her to him. I don't have a car.

INTERVIEWER: Does he pay any child support?

TERRI LYNN: No. But right now they are getting on the people who aren't paying. They are cracking down real hard on them. They want to know when was the last time you seen him, the name and address. And I have his social security number.

SISTER: My son's father isn't paying because I don't know his address. And he's using a different name instead of his name. He don't take care of him either. He's got four kids, two in Tampa, and two here, and they are five months apart. My son, and another girl's son. I have to call him to come see him. And that ticks me off. I have to do it by myself. When I see him, I have to cuss him out. To come and see him, and to give me money. When I come around that corner, he has to run because he's going to get cussed up. He came the other night when I was watching TV, and he gave me some money, but he wanted something too, if you know what I mean. He wanted me to kiss him and stuff.

Terri Lynn has received welfare since her daughter was born six years ago. Is she "dependent" on the system? By traditional definitions of welfare dependency, yes. However, a cogent argument can be made that Terri Lynn's family provides at least as much assistance to her, if not more, than does the state. A closer look reveals a portrait of a hard working young woman who is doing her best to improve the life conditions for herself and her daughter. Yet, despite working hard, what are Terri Lynn's chances of beating poverty? Unless her income nearly doubles from her current minimum wage, her chances of pulling herself and her daughter out of poverty are slim at best. This is not because of her own laziness, personal inadequacy, or lack of family support, but because of structural features of the social system that snowball against poor women. Given the largely grim statistics of women's under-employment in general, what are the odds that a 24-year-old woman with a high school diploma, who is without reliable transportation, who needs childcare, and whose only work experience is in the service sector, will soon land the $8.00 to $10.00 per hour job needed to lift her out of poverty? Moreover, why does her daughter's father not contribute to her support? Can we really expect Terri Lynn, alone, to provide for all her daughter's emotional and financial needs without any help from the government?

Who Are the Participants in This Study?

Sheila, Patrice, and Terri Lynn are among 47 women who were willing to be interviewed for this book. They live in several small and medium-sized communities in

Florida. They were first introduced to this project at the county welfare office, as were most of the others, as they came to pick up their food stamps. Others were friends of those who were initially interviewed. Sheila, Patrice, Terri Lynn, and the other women generously volunteered their time and energy to this project without pay or other compensation. They invited us into their homes, where they embraced the opportunity to reveal to me and three graduate students, Kim, Cheryl, and Sylvia, the ways in which they live, negotiate, and survive welfare. The interviews were often lengthy, up to several hours in some cases, as women disclosed the joys and frustrations with their children, with their extended families, with employment, and with the welfare system. They told us about the experiences that led them to welfare; about the individual and structural constraints on their lives and on their opportunities for upward mobility; they told us of their coping and survival strategies; the stigma they face; their future goals; their attitudes toward other recipients; and their concerns with governmental aid, the welfare system, and welfare reform.

My intention was to obtain narratives about welfare from a diverse group of women. Because the goal of this project is to discover meaning rather than simply to measure the distribution of attributes across the population, it was important to obtain a sample that elucidates particular population types. Therefore, respondents represent a variety of traits or conditions found among welfare recipients, such as variation in race or ethnic background, age, number of children, and housing type. This diversity is important in order to approximate variations in the welfare experience.

The demographic characteristics of the 47 women interviewed are reported in Table 1.2, and are reasonably representative of welfare recipients in the area from which they came. Eighteen respondents were white and 29 were African American. Although this over-represents the proportion of African Americans on welfare in the United States overall, it does reflect the race and ethnic background of welfare recipients from the interview region.

The respondents ranged in age from 19 to 48, with a mean age of 29.9 years. Most women were young, with more than half under the age of 30. Most respondents (N = 28) had never been married, whereas the remainder were either divorced or separated. Families who receive welfare tend to be small, on average. These mothers had an average of 2.3 children who lived with them.

Only nine of the respondents reported to have less than a high school education. Eighteen respondents had completed high school or received a GED, whereas nineteen had taken some college or vocational course beyond high school, most often at a community college. These were often sponsored by the welfare department itself, either "Project Independence" (a version of the national Job Opportunities and Basic Skills Training Program [JOBS] program) or "The Family Transition Program" (FTP) (a county-wide welfare reform experiment). Both programs were designed to provide job skills and educational benefits to welfare recipients. At the time of the interview, nineteen women reported to be currently in school, either working on their GED, taking community college or university courses, enrolled in private vocational training, or were part of an education and training program sponsored by the district welfare office.

TABLE 1.2   Descriptive Characteristics of Sample (N = 47)

	N	Percent	Range	Mean
Age			19–48	29.9
Under 21	2	4		
21-29	24	51		
30-39	10	21		
40 and over	7	15		
Missing	4	9		
Race/Ethnicity				
African American	29	62		
White	18	38		
Marital Status				
Single	28	60		
Divorced	13	28		
Married/Separated	4	9		
Missing	2	4		
Children in Household			1–5	2.3
One	12	26		
Two	16	34		
Three	12	26		
Four	5	11		
Five	2	4		
Employment Status				
Not Employed	37	79		
Part-time	7	15		
Full-time	3	6		
Education				
Not a High School Grad	9	19		
High School Grad/GED	18	38		
Some College/Vocational	19	40		
Missing	1	2		
Currently Enrolled in School				
Yes	19	40		
No	28	60		
Subsidized Housing				
Yes	29	62		
No	18	38		

Expectedly, most respondents were not employed outside the home for pay, although some worked in the informal sector by baby-sitting or hair styling. These jobs were usually sporadic, and were not a dependable source of income. Generally, income from informal jobs was not reported to the welfare department. Seven other women were "officially" employed part-time, and three worked nearly full-time outside the home for pay. The most common type of work found was in the fast-food industry. Notoriously low-paying and without fringe benefits, incomes from their service sector jobs were not sufficient to pull them above the poverty line, and therefore they continued to collect a partial welfare benefit.

The majority of respondents (N = 29) lived in subsidized housing. Some of these women lived in large, often multistoried "projects." These tended to have inexpensive rent, sometimes only costing $10 to $20 per month. Most of these apartments were, however, in a substantial state of disrepair, with paint peeling both inside and out, screens ripped or missing from windows, carpet that was well worn and drapes that were torn and tattered. Other women we interviewed lived in private apartments or single-family houses with reduced rent. These were far more desirable, although more expensive, and were usually located in "mixed" neighborhoods with others who were not on welfare. The waiting list for this type of subsidy was considerably longer than for the wait to move to the large housing projects. Other women paid full price for their housing, sometimes doubling up with family members or friends to make ends meet.

Conclusion and Organization

Using critical and feminist lenses with which to examine the narratives of welfare recipients, this is both a book about welfare and a book about women's lives more generally. Poor women on welfare are stigmatized; this book calls into question the negative connotations associated with women who use welfare. What unfolded from the narratives were stories about hardship, faith, and hope that were not systematically different from other women who are more financially well-off. It reveals that, in many ways, poor mothers are strikingly similar to mothers who are more affluent. They share many of the same goals, hopes, and dreams for themselves and for their children. But trying to attain these with a limited income is a constant struggle. I learned about the mechanisms that poor women need to improve their lives and lift themselves from poverty. This book explores the intricate web of informal and formal support that women need for living and surviving on welfare, and I analyze the coping strategies used by women and their children. These insights can inform and guide the way we amend the welfare system and restructure work in the lowest tiers of our economy. These, I suggest are more fruitful than simply asking, "How do we reduce the number of women on welfare?" Lifting women from poverty and eliminating them from welfare are two separate issues. Unfortunately, it is the latter concern that is most often addressed in welfare reforms.

Chapter 2 begins with the questions "Why are people poor?" and "Why are they on welfare?" My goal is to put these questions into the larger framework of understanding how we have historically and how we today explain and legitimize social inequality. These sets of beliefs are important because they filter social perceptions and provide the cognitive structure in which to interpret the causes of poverty and welfare use. However, these explanations are not gender neutral; instead, they marginalize or ignore women's experiences within such domains as family and intimate relations, and within the domain of work.

Chapter 3 examines recipients' experience with stigma and discrimination. Themes of laziness, often racially charged, emerged frequently. How do they cope with or manage this stigma of being "a welfare mom"? As social worker Frederick B. Mills reminds us, the stigma paradigm hinges on the concepts of dependence promiscuity, illegitimacy, and addiction (1996). These stereotypes are widespread, including among welfare recipients themselves. They have important implications and serve as political tools that trivialize the plight of poor women, and consequently keep meaningful work and welfare reforms from occurring.

Chapter 4 focuses on what Scott and Lyman (1968) have labeled as "accounts"— the justifications or excuses people use to account for their own poverty and welfare use. In this chapter, I examine the economic and relationship factors that caused them to enter the welfare system for the very first time. Through their narratives, I illuminate the ways in which their histories and experiences, such as their education, work experience, and their relationship with the fathers of their children, in conjunction with the social structure, have influenced their economic circumstances. We can see that, for many women, their use of welfare is a result of an age-old reliance on men that has gone awry, and a result of a social system that refuses to pay a living wage. We explore the incongruence between their accounts of their own welfare use and their perceptions of other recipients.

Chapter 5 explores the ways in which women on welfare manage their lives on a day-to-day basis. What is it like to live and provide financially for one's family from a welfare grant? What decisions need to be made on a regular basis? After accounting for inflation, the average monthly welfare benefit has declined nearly 50 percent since 1970; thus budgeting to make ends meet requires creativity and flexibility. Families on welfare suffer from a cultural dissonance: They are aware of consumptive patterns in the United States, but they unable to participate. Recipients describe day-to-day living and the process of surviving the welfare system while keeping their children safe and out of danger as extremely challenging and stressful.

Several important studies identify that women on welfare do not subsist on their meager welfare grant alone. Instead, they must rely on formal or informal sources of assistance to augment their check. *Chapter 6* explores the ways in which recipients rely on informal supports, such as family, friends, and children's fathers, to make ends meet and to manage the stress. Most women revealed that this help was extensive and valuable, and admitted that they could not care for their families adequately without it. It also examines the formal supports that women rely on to make ends meet, such as charities or food banks, and the "hidden" income and gifts they receive and rely on. How important are these to women? How do they assemble a "survival package" to live and cope with welfare? Their stories offer a striking portrayal of the ways in which impoverished families construct relationships so that the effects of poverty can best be eased.

Recipients are often portrayed by the media as people who like the welfare system and take delight in receiving monthly benefits from it. Yet, the women interviewed here portray a markedly different point of view. *Chapter* 7 focuses on recipients' perceptions of the strengths and weaknesses of the welfare system. Criticisms of welfare were vast and widespread. Women spoke with a heightened sense of concern and passion as they relayed their firsthand experiences with a system they deemed as frustrating, demoralizing, and in need of considerable change and repair. Because welfare policies vary significantly by state, I examined welfare reform in one particular state—Florida, where the women who were interviewed reside. Respondents shared their ideas on what the role of the federal government should be in helping poor people. They commented on three critical reforms: (1) time limits for receiving aid; (2) work requirements; and (3) family caps, which limit or deny additional aid for children born to women already receiving welfare. Furthermore, they shared their perspectives of what meaningful reforms would entail.

Chapter 8 examines the challenges faced by women as they leave the welfare system. Although human capital enhancement programs would be helpful to some women, the difficulties they are likely to face as they transition off of welfare because of TANF time limits, extend far beyond increasing their education or job skills. The structure of the labor market, including a lack of unskilled jobs, low pay, the increasing number of temporary positions, and the lack of health insurance among low-tier jobs, has a profound affect on their likelihood of success in finding and maintaining work.

Chapter 9 revisits the themes introduced in Chapter 1. It concludes that welfare is not simply about providing money for women who are too lazy to work. Welfare provides security for single mothers and their children, and other vulnerable groups in society. The way to resolve the "welfare problem" is to intervene in the structure of low-tier work in the United States, not to force families off of assistance. Until the structure of work in the bottom tier is deliberately made more secure by humane and rational government intervention, many single mothers will not risk their children's health and well-being by accepting low-wage, exploitive, and unreliable employment.

CHAPTER

2 Historic and Persisting Dilemmas

How Do We Explain Poverty, and What Should We Do about It?

Why are people poor? Why are they on welfare? These seemingly straightforward questions have a multitude of contradictory and conflicting answers. Opinions about welfare and welfare recipients reflect general beliefs that people hold regarding not only poverty, but also wealth in our nation.

This chapter provides a summary of the frameworks Americans use to explain and legitimize poverty and social inequality. It offers a glimpse into the historic and persisting dilemmas that plague our nation. Most of the current opinions are derived from age-old questions and answers about poverty and the distribution of wealth more generally. They reflect longstanding questions about if, how, and under what circumstances we should care for others who cannot or do not seem able to care for themselves. They reflect our views about human nature, about the importance of hard work and our dislike of idleness, and our expectations of appropriate roles for men and women in society (Trattner, 1989).

Our history of rugged individualism, a spirit of Calvinism, and the idea that hard work will reap results set the backdrop for the development of our social welfare system in this country. Poverty was considered part of the natural social order, and was not necessarily taken as a defect of the social structure. Fueled by social Darwinism, the competitive struggle to secure one's economic status allowed the "fittest" to win out over others. Government should not hamper this competitive struggle, we reasoned. Borrowing from Poor Laws of England, we distinguished early on between the "worthy poor" (e.g., the disabled, the aged), and the "nonworthy poor" (e.g., the able-bodied). Our social welfare system developed within this framework of duality and continues to operate in this fashion today. Our system has been referred to as "reluctant," indicating our generosity towards the worthy poor while demonstrating callous disregard for others (Jansson, 1988). Thus, current decisions about who constitutes the worthy poor and at what level should they be taken care of reflect our longstanding debates.

The "welfare problem" has been, and is today, defined primarily in terms of the moral values of work (Handler and Hasenfeld, 1991). The most consistent part of our evolving welfare policy is to reinforce the work ethic. Traditionally, American social policy attempts to encourage people to work, not to choose welfare. Only those people who cannot work are deemed worthy to receive assistance. Thus, our approach to welfare has been to make the conditions of assistance less desirable than lowest wage work (Katz, 1986). But some welfare critics suggest that this is no longer the case; instead, welfare has become a more desirable alternative than low-wage work (Gilder, 1981; Mead, 1986; Murray, 1984, 1988). Our attitudes toward single mothers reflect these concerns. The 1986 *Report of the White House Working Group on the Family* claimed that welfare "provides valuable temporary help to a family, yet that same help in effect replaces the breadwinner . . . enables mothers to raise children without the help of father or a job" (1986: 32). Historically, our policies ponder whether single mothers, as a group, are worthy of assistance. Should we pay them to stay home to take care of their children, or should we require them to work? Does government assistance undermine their incentive to work, encourage loose morals, and undermine their willingness to enter marriage, and thus perpetuate their poverty?

History of Aid to Families with Dependent Children

Welfare programs such as Aid to Families with Dependent Children (AFDC), at least in theory, were created and designed to help protect women and their children who were seen as more vulnerable than men to conditions of poverty, and thus potentially deserving of assistance. The concept of "Mother's Pensions," the forerunner of the AFDC program, arose during the Progressive Era (1896–1914) to provide greater government responsibility for the well-being of poor women and children—particularly those who were white, and who were widows. Some reformers were particularly concerned over: (1) the 5.3 million women who were working for wages outside the home were taking jobs away from men, (2) the large numbers of children residing in orphanages because their mothers could not support them or care for them while they were employed, and (3) the increasing rate of delinquency among children left at home unsupervised (Abramovitz, 1996a,b; Gordon, 1994; Mink, 1995). The future of our nation, and proper citizenship, depended on the proper upbringing of children by their mothers, reformers clamored. Mothers' Pensions were designed as payment for the services of motherhood, thus giving it legitimacy, and attempting to remove the stigma associated with public aid.

In reality, however, Mother's Pensions continued the traditional charity models of assistance. Benefits were low, and the emphasis was placed on moral reform. They strongly enforced patriarchal norms about women's moral character. In exchange for aid, poor mothers were forced to conform to rules and policies designed to weed out the suspected fraud, and to ensure that women followed strict gender role norms. For example, agency caseworkers monitored the women for signs of drinking, poor housekeeping, improper childrearing techniques, and relationships with men. Foreign-born women were urged to assimilate and to adopt white, middle-class values; reformers generally held the view that immigrants were inferior to the native born (Abramovitz, 1996b).

Modern day welfare emerged from these values of moral reform. AFDC, or "welfare" as we have come to call it, was created in 1935 as Title IV of the Social Security Act, a critical piece of legislation produced during the New Deal, when millions of families were suffering financial hardship. Approximately one-quarter of the workforce lost their jobs during the Great Depression. Homelessness, hunger, malnutrition, and begging were widespread. Private charities and churches stepped up their efforts to help the needy, but the problem had become so rampant that their efforts could not keep pace with the need. Under President Franklin D. Roosevelt, a wide variety of safety net programs were created to assist vulnerable populations. The Social Security Act established several key Social Security and unemployment programs, including Aid to the Blind (AB) and Old Age Assistance (OAA) programs. This important piece of legislation transferred responsibility for social welfare from individual states to the federal government.

Originally called Aid to Dependent Children (ADC), its focus was to keep single mothers from being dependent on their children for labor and income, and to keep both mothers and children out of the work force. It was "designed to release from the wage-earning role the person whose natural function is to give her children the physical and affectionate guardianship necessary not alone to keep them from falling into social misfortune, but more affirmatively to make them citizens capable of contributing to society" (Committee on Economic Security, 1985: 5–6). Welfare was to be synonymous with well-being, prosperity, good health, and good spirits, and therefore faced relatively little opposition in Congress. It was considered a pro-family program: It kept mothers in the home so that they could care for, nurture, and protect their children. Mothers were not expected to work and raise their children at the same time (Abramovitz, 1996a).

ADC was a fundamental departure from the inequitably distributed Mother's Pensions, which served almost exclusively white widows. ADC recipients included mothers who were abandoned, divorced, never married, or mothers whose husbands were unable to work. ADC was, theoretically at least, supposed to provide help to African American as well as to white women. Fourteen percent of all children who received ADC in the 1937–1938 fiscal year were African American, a figure far below true need, but at least represented an improvement over Mother's Pensions (Sterner, 1943). However, as Quadagno (1994) points out, ADC and other components of Social Security were marked with racism. To keep African Americans from receiving benefits, many states, particularly in the south, tightened their eligibility requirements so as to exclude them.

Although ADC's goals were admirable, it fell short of significantly reducing poverty in many respects. For example, although it was a means-tested "federal" program, ADC gave individual states great authority over eligibility and benefit levels. Southern congressmen fought to limit federal control and would only support ADC if the states were allowed to establish their own eligibility requirements and benefit levels (Quadagno, 1988, 1994). This resulted in dramatic statewide differences in the level of benefits. For example, in 1939 ADC benefits ranged from an average of $2.46 per child per month in Arkansas to $24.53 in the state of New York (U.S. Social Security Board, 1940). Southern states rationalized their lower-than-average benefit levels by declaring that black families needed less than did white families (Abramovitz, 1996b). Benefits continue to vary dramatically by state today. Although the median state average in 1996 was $312 for a two-person family, usually mother and child, a two-person family received $96 in Mississippi, and $821 in Alaska (U.S. House of Representatives, Committee on Ways and Means, 1996, Table 8-13, pp. 439–441). Cost of living differentials do exist in the United States; however, they are not large enough to warrant differences in benefits of this magnitude. Even when food stamps are taken into consideration, the combined AFDC and food stamp grants vary twice as much as the cost of living among states (Peterson and Rom, 1990).

Moreover, upon its creation, ADC benefits were considerably less than those provided for adults receiving OAA and AB, even though recipients of these latter two programs were less likely to have children in the home. Initially, ADC did not include money for the child's caretaker—generally the mother. Moreover, the program continued the practices commonly employed with Mother's Pensions of using aid to enforce behavioral standards and cultural norms. Home visits and periodic eligibility checks were routine measures used to scrutinize women's parenting, domestic, and sexual behaviors. Most state programs distinguished between deserving and undeserving mothers, closely perpetuating the old model associated with Mother's Pensions.

Congress amended ADC in 1939, and transferred the assistance given to widows to the Social Security's Old Age Insurance (OAI) program. The movement of widows out of ADC resulted in its further stigmatization. Marital status became a defining characteristic of ADC recipients; it was increasingly viewed as a program for children born to "unworthy" women who were never-married or were separated or divorced. At the same time, many African American widows and widows from other racial or ethnic minority groups were unable to receive benefits under the newly restructured OAI program because their husbands did not qualify for Social Security benefits. Thus, these widows had no choice but to turn to ADC. These policy changes have contributed to the enduring hostility surrounding "welfare" as a program for unworthy women.

ADC continued to be amended, and a relative was allowed to be included with a dependent child as a recipient. The number of persons receiving ADC continued to grow as the program was expanded, and by 1950, there were approximately 1.6 million recipients. Still, not all single mothers received these benefits. Only 25 percent of single mothers and children received ADC, while the remaining 75 percent did not.

The 1950s have been characterized as a decade of economic optimism. A post–World War II recession was averted, in part because of the generous monetary and educational provisions of the GI Bill, and because of the enormous backlog of demand for major consumer goods unavailable during the war. There was a new faith in the vigor of the economic system during the 1950s. People were optimistic after the war. Perhaps because of this, the potential for affluence was seen as being available to all people, and an attack on ADC began to take shape. The populace largely failed to acknowledge that other, more popular programs were also forms of "welfare": the

Mental Health Act, the Hill–Burton Hospital Act, the GI Bill, and Veterans' Administration (VA) housing loans are just a few of the programs that benefited many middle-class citizens. Despite providing for the security and welfare of its citizens, these programs, as did other programs under the Social Security Act that targeted the elderly or widows, were able to avoid the stigma of being categorized or labeled "welfare."

During the 1950s, the composition of various social welfare programs began to radically change. ADC, with a focus on mothers and children, began to overshadow other programs, such as those serving the elderly. Poor mothers with children quickly and dramatically increased from half to nearly three-quarters of the entire public assistance population between 1950 and 1960. These changes reflect normal population growth, changing family structures, labor market dislocations, the success of Social Security in reducing poverty among the elderly, and gender and racial discrimination. The costs of ADC alone increased more than 90 percent to more than $1 billion during this period (Axin and Levine, 1975, p. 235). As a reaction to this growth, the public focused on rising costs of the program and the moral fitness of welfare mothers. Punitive state policies were enacted to remove people from ADC. State residency requirements were enforced, names of welfare recipients were publicized, and entire caseloads were closed with recipients required to reapply with new application investigations (Axin and Levine, pp. 235–236). Politicians and the media blamed the expansion of ADC on the immoral behavior of poor women and the availability of assistance. They were frequently touted as being lazy, unmotivated, immoral, and fraudulent, spending money on lavish cars, jewelry, and clothing. Racist attitudes prevalent in the United States continued to plague ADC. African Americans were overrepresented among ADC recipients given their size in the population, as were never-married mothers, and the public was outraged that their tax dollars were being spent on undeserving groups within the population. Sympathy was replaced with increasing criticism. "Suitable home" and vague moral fitness criteria for ADC were expanded and used with a vengeance. Mothers who applied for aid were threatened with child removal; caseworkers informed them that a negative assessment might force the welfare office to remove their children and place them in institutions or foster homes (Abramovitz, 1996a).

Feminist welfare state theorists suggest that the heightened hostility towards ADC and its recipients was motivated by several forces (Abramovitz, 1996a,b; Gordon, 1994; Miller, 1992). First is the competing demand for women's unpaid labor in the home and cheap labor in the labor market. After World War II, the occupations that relied heavily on women's labor and low wages were expanding, while at the same time the number of women employed outside the home was shrinking. The effort to remove women from their wartime employment so that jobs could be returned to men after the war had been successful, albeit perhaps too successful. As Betty Freidan notes in her book *The Feminine Mystique* (1963), during the 1950s women dreamed of husbands, children, station wagons, and houses in the suburbs. Most did not dream about full-time employment. Women's average age at first marriage dropped to 20 years, the lowest in more than 100 years (Saluter, 1989), and the number of married women in the labor market plummeted. In the early 1950s, The Women's Bureau was reporting severe shortages of typists, stenographers, nurses, social workers, teachers, and medical aides (Kessler-Harris, 1982). Consequently, welfare benefits became all the more stigmatized or restricted in order to encourage more women into the labor pool. This was particularly seen in the south, where, for example, Louisiana refused ADC to "employable" mothers with young children, especially during the harvest season, as did Georgia when extra pickers were needed in the tobacco and cotton fields (Abramovitz, 1996b). Forcing women on welfare to work, or discouraging them from getting aid to which they were entitled, helped fill jobs at the bottom rungs of the employment sector—jobs that men did not want, and would then be left unfilled.

Second, feminist welfare theorists suggest that welfare critics also targeted poor women's marriage, sexuality, and childbearing patterns. The divorce rate skyrocketed to levels unprecedented after World War II. Hasty "shot-gun" marriages were short-lived, and the divorce rate climbed to 16 divorces per 1,000 married women aged 15 and older, double the rate before the war (Singh, Mathews, Clarke, Yannicos, and Smith, 1995). Nonmarital births also increased, almost tripling for white women, and increasing, although somewhat less, for African Americans. These changes in family structure have been blamed for the breakdown in "family values"—an emotionally charged term heavy with moral overtones about a woman's proper role. Women who had children outside of the confines of marriage were looked down on with disdain. Only women who lived under the safe confines of a husband-as-breadwinner escaped widespread scrutiny. Working mothers were criticized for neglecting their children's needs. They were accused of contributing to juvenile delinquency, truancy, and child abuse. Women receiving ADC were also harshly criticized. They were blamed for a wide variety of social ills, and were viewed as contributing to a climate in which juvenile delinquency, truancy, and child abuse flourished. Because widows, considered among the worthy poor, were separated out into another less stigmatized program, ADC recipients were subject to tremendous moral criticism. Policies designed to enforce behavioral, sexual, and gender norms once again flourished and were incorporated with gusto. Recipients were subject to "midnight raids" and other intrusions into their lives so that authorities could try to catch men staying over at recipients' homes. Some states would penalize a woman for having a relationship with a man who was not the father of her children. Arkansas, for example, denied aid to mothers in a "non-stable, non-legal union." Alabama eliminated 25 percent of their welfare clients by cutting off women who were "going with a man." Michigan cut aid to families with "male boarders" (Abramovitz, 1996b).

The 1960s contained both some gains and setbacks for the ADC program. On one level, several events occurred during the 1960s that are credited with an increased concern, compassion, and a "rediscovering" of poverty. First, a series of recessions and periods of high unemployment occurred in the late 1950s and early 1960s. The economy bounced back after each of these periods, but with less energy after each time. Second, the extent of poverty was exposed during the 1960s, due in part to books or essays such as Michael Harrington's *The Other America* (1963). In this popular book, Harrington vividly reported the poverty experienced by millions of America's forgotten people in geographically isolated pockets of our country. Third, the Social Security Administration had developed an official poverty index and, thus, the number of poor people and groups in the United States could be systematically counted and compared from year to year. Fourth, the Civil Rights movement brought increasing attention to the racism and poverty experienced by African Americans and other minority groups. And finally, the shift in the composition of public assistance rolls that began in the 1950s continued and showed no signs of abatement in the 1960s. "Welfare" was increasingly becoming synonymous with impoverished divorced and never-married women and their children who received ADC.

When elected in 1960, President John F. Kennedy stressed the issues of poverty, unemployment, and rehabilitation of the poor, and so began a major effort to reduce the number of poor in the United States. He believed that people were poor because they lacked adequate human capital, such as education, job skills, and experience in the labor market, and that they needed social services to help them succeed. He therefore argued for greater resources, such as education and job training programs, so that the poor could eventually pull themselves out of poverty. Moreover, as a believer in the Culture of Poverty perspective, he was concerned with the subcultural values and norms that he believed develop among the poor. He saw these values as anti–work oriented and dependency focused. President Kennedy sought to create programs that would focus on instilling positive attitudes among poor children that would eventually allow them to become more economically mobile and eventually join the ranks of the middle class. Given the expanded family focus, the name of the program changed to Aid to *Families* with Dependent Children (AFDC). The 1962, amendments to the Social Security Act, referred to as the Social Service Amendments, increased federal funding for social services, "services in addition to support, rehabilitation instead of relief, and training for useful work instead of prolonged dependency . . . to maintain family life where it is adequate and to restore it where it is deficient," claimed President Kennedy (cited in Bander, 1975: 380).

The assassination of President Kennedy did not stop his ideals from materializing. President Lyndon B. Johnson shared Kennedy's vision of reducing poverty, fueled in part by the annual government reports that were now effective in counting the numbers of poor persons and identifying sociodemographic groups that were particularly vulnerable: children, the elderly, large families, single mother families, rural families, and minority group members. Like President Kennedy before him, he believed the government had a critical role in reducing the incidence of poverty and the suffering experienced by millions. In his State of the Union Address in 1964, President Johnson announced that "this administration today, here and now, declares unconditional war on poverty in America. . . ." In this War on Poverty, President Johnson called for a wide array of legislation for children and adults designed to provide them with the tools, resources, and human capital to lift themselves from poverty. The underlying assumption of the War on Poverty in the 1960s was that poverty is largely the result of inadequate education, job training, and marketable skills. This approach, known as "human capital enhancement," posited that the numbers of poor could be significantly reduced with adequate training programs to increase the level of "human capital" that could be exchanged for wages in the job market. If we could train everyone for a job, and then find them one, poverty will be ameliorated or significantly reduced, human capitalists argued. This logic was beginning to be extended to single mothers. Shouldn't they too be required to work, some people questioned?

During President Johnson's administration, programs were created that focused on job training, education, improving health and providing jobs, such as the Economic Opportunity Act, Head Start, Medicare, and Medicaid. Volunteers in Service to America (VISTA) was designed to help rehabilitate slums and other impoverished areas. Not all programs were created at the federal level; Johnson's War on Poverty also shared a concern that programs should be structured and carried out, at least in part, on the local level. Federal dollars were often targeted to these local efforts. These programs received extensive media attention, leading the public to believe that these efforts would eventually move women off of welfare and out of the ranks of the impoverished.

During this national War on Poverty, the United States was also involved in another war—that in Vietnam. As the Vietnam War escalated, attention and dollars were diverted from needs at home. The war in Vietnam, demographic changes, the growth in the Civil Rights movement and its white backlash, and the expansion of welfare benefits contributed to what became known as a "welfare crisis." By the late 1960s and early 1970s many Americans had grown tired and weary of the clamor for social change, and had grown resentful of the concerns afforded the poor, ethnic minorities, and other disadvantaged groups. Because of changing eligibility rules, such as allowing women on AFDC to work, allowing some two-parent families to be eligible for aid, and extending benefits to children between the ages of 18 and 21 who were still in school, the number of families receiving welfare continued to rise. The number of welfare recipients soared from 3.5 million in 1961 to almost 5 million in 1967, causing costs to jump to $2.2 billion (Abramovitz, 1996a). Welfare programs, AFDC in particular, came under swift attack again. Politicians and the media referred to these as bloated programs, claiming that they had become too large and needed to be reformed.

At the same time, many social changes of the 1960s and 1970s became increasingly legitimized. In particular, with an increasing number of women with children in the paid labor force, a large number of people questioned whether poor mothers really constitute a category of the "worthy poor" any longer. By 1975, 52 percent of married women with children between the ages of 6 and 17 and 37 percent of married women with children under age 6 were employed outside the home (U.S. Department of Labor, 1994). Employment among mothers was becoming increasingly commonplace among all income groups. The belief that women belonged at home with their children was fading from the dominant paradigm. Consequently, politicians began to question the appropriateness of paying single mothers to stay home and take care of their children. They suggested that welfare benefits had become too attractive to women; that benefits had increased faster than wages, and thus more women were opting to receive AFDC rather than to work in the paid labor market. "For the hardcore welfare recipient, the value of the full range of benefits substantially exceeds the amount the recipient could earn in an entry-level job. As a result, recipients are likely to choose welfare over work, thus increasing long-term dependence," proclaimed the self-appointed experts, as they discussed the motivation of recipients (Tanner, Moore, and Hartman, 1997).

President Richard M. Nixon mirrored these views. He expressed concern about the rising welfare caseloads, increased costs, welfare fraud, federal involvement in services to individuals and communities, and elitist government bureaucrats. He initiated a series of programs called "the New Federalism," designed to make the federal government smaller and to provide more autonomy to states and localities. Yet, ironically, President Nixon's chief welfare proposal was designed to do the exact opposite of this. It shifted the burden of payment from the state to the federal government.

Named the Family Assistance Plan (FAP), President Nixon's proposal guaranteed that every unemployed family of four would receive at least $1,600 a year from the federal government. The working poor would be allowed to keep benefits until their earnings reached approximately $4,000. Only then would their benefits be discontinued. The FAP contained several other critical features or clauses, most notable, perhaps, is that women with children older than three years would be required to work or would be placed in a job training program.

Nixon's FAP sparked controversy immediately. Some regarded it as a fair and workable plan that would get control over the burgeoning AFDC program. Critics denounced the program, noting that the minimum benefit of $1,600 was still $2,000 below the federal government's own poverty line for a family of four. Some questioned whether single mothers of preschool age children should be required to work outside the home. Others raised concerns over whether the labor market could actually absorb the additional workers.

Quadagno (1994) suggests that the FAP contained an internal contradiction about women's roles because it encouraged single mothers to work, while it encouraged married mothers to stay home. Furthermore, FAP contained few programs to really help poor women improve their job skills or to assist them in finding jobs. Nor did it provide much support for child care. Rather, the employment component was primarily geared toward men. Commenting on the training programs, the director of the Office of Economic Opportunity (OEO) said:

> In general, we would support giving higher priority to the training and employment of men than women. Given the greater employment opportunities for men generally available, they are more likely to achieve self-sufficiency. Moreover, training and employment will often be much more expensive for women, if child care must be provided. (cited in Quadagno, 1994, p. 126)

In 1970, the FAP passed the House by a vote of 243 to 155. But because of the controversy surrounding the FAP, it remained bogged down in a Senate committee until it expired. It was never enacted. Instead of FAP, a multitude of relatively poorly funded work programs were created during the 1960s, 1970s, and 1980s: The Work Incentive Program (WIN), which was later replaced by WIN II; the Job Training Partnership Act (JTPA); President Carter's Better Jobs and Income Program; and the more recent 1988 Family Support Act and Job Opportunities and Basic Skills Training Program (JOBS). Each program received tremendous popular press and blaring headlines, such as, "The Most Sweeping Revision of the Nation's Principal Welfare Program" (Szanton, 1991). Yet most programs helped only a small fraction of the millions of poor families. At the high point of the WIN program, less than 20 percent of AFDC recipients were actively involved in the program; while funding under the more recent JOBS program covered only 13 percent of recipients (Welfare to Work, 1993). As Berrick (1995) notes, these figures rarely make headlines:

> So, instead, low-income women have continued to apply for and to use welfare and do not appear to be responding to public officials' generous offer of education and training. In turn, the public has grown increasingly frustrated with welfare women's intransigence, blaming them for not trying hard enough. (p. 11)

One of the most dramatic responses to these frustrations with welfare and its recipients occurred during the administration of Ronald Reagan in the 1980s, when several hundred thousand families were eliminated from AFDC eligibility. President Reagan's position on government involvement was very clear: He denounced big government; he believed that a strong business climate would provide prosperity for Americans; he felt that Americans were paying too much of their income in taxes; and he distrusted social welfare programs. He was heavily influenced by his social conservative mentors such Martin Anderson (1978), George Gilder (1981), Charles Murray (1984), and Lawrence Mead (1986), who authored books proposing significant retrenchment of social welfare programs. They suggested that welfare policies themselves exacerbate poverty and welfare use through creating a disincentive to work and thereby promoting laziness. Charles Murray, for example, in his book *Losing Ground*, argues that more generous welfare benefits make work and marriage unattractive to women. As "midnight raids," and "man in the house" rules were deemed illegal, and as welfare benefits approximate the pay of low-wage work, women are rewarded for choosing idleness, single-parenting, and out-of-wedlock childbearing. These behaviors, in turn, perpetuate poverty, according to Murray. Consequently, the primary way to correct this behavior and reduce poverty is to eliminate, or significantly scale back, the AFDC program. Mead (1986) refers to welfare recipients and other poor people in an unflattering light, "in general, low income and serious behavior problems go together" (Mead, 1986: 22). President Reagan agreed that social welfare programs encourage laziness and long-term dependency on the system. A popular anecdote was his story of a Chicago welfare queen with "80 names, 30 addresses, 12 Social Security cards, and a tax-free income of over $150,000" (cited in Lipset, 1990, p. 136).

Spending for all social welfare programs, broadly defined, actually decreased from 57.4 percent to 47.9 percent of total government spending between 1980 and 1986. Decreases occurred at the federal, state, and local levels (cited in the Ronald Reagan Home Page: Social Spending, 1997). AFDC was not the only program that was reduced. A wide array of programs serving the financial, social, and health needs of the poor and low income were either reduced, eliminated, or had ceilings applied to their growth. Adversely affected programs included food stamps, Medicaid, school lunch and other nutritional programs, family planning programs, subsidized housing, legal aid, and drug abuse counseling. Welfare expenditures were cut dramatically, down almost 30 percent per person, on average (Ellwood, 1988, p. 41).

With the election of George Bush as President, the philosophy toward the welfare system remained relatively consistent to that of Ronald Reagan. He argued that the best way to overcome poverty is through individual hard work and initiative, rather than through government sponsored programs. He stressed volunteer charity, school vouchers, and enterprise zones, and complained that the federal government should back away from welfare. Instead, states and local communities should establish standards and programs. Yet, despite Bush's rhetoric, the number of AFDC recipients continued to rise.

By 1996, under President Bill Clinton's administration, approximately 14 million persons, or nearly 5 million families with children, received AFDC (Committee on Ways and Means, U.S. House of Representatives, 1996, Table 8-27, p. 471). This was once again a critical time for social welfare programs in the United States as they emerged as a prominent target for reform. Welfare programs, AFDC and its recipients in particular, have been targeted as a primary cause of a variety of social ills. Some suggest that policymakers "rediscover" welfare when they cannot explain or reverse troubling social, economic, or political trends:

> Poor women and welfare come under attack either because it interferes with the dynamics of the free enterprise system or because it undermines the traditional family structure. During such periods of "panic," welfare and women receiving it are bashed in order to divert attention from the true causes of the nations' ills. It is these concerns, rather than making life better for poor women and children, which have been the driving force behind welfare reform for the past 150 years. (Abramovitz, 1996b, 15)

Policymakers have long since abandoned the idea of really helping the poor improve their economic situation significantly, and have instead focused on reducing welfare "dependency" (Bernstein, 1993). Ameliorating poverty through human capital enhancement, or any other method, is no longer the primary issue, as it was during the War on Poverty era. Instead, the paramount concern has become how to reduce the number of people who receive welfare assistance. Given the dominant views that the costs of welfare are unacceptably high and that welfare breaches cherished American values, the goal of government reform efforts has simply become to reduce the welfare caseloads. Reforms are not necessarily designed to reduce the number of people impoverished, or reduce the effect that poverty has on individuals and families.

Recent Attempts at Welfare Reform

Several recent attempts have been made to reduce the number of people on welfare, with only scant attention paid to whether these reforms will actually reduce the level of poverty in the United States. In 1992, lawmakers in New Jersey and Wisconsin passed welfare reform packages commonly referred to as "Bridefare." These reforms were designed to reduce welfare use among women by encouraging them to marry. Arguably fueled by conservative ideologies that are concerned with the presumed breakdown of family values, "Bridefare" extends AFDC eligibility to married women while restricting benefits among those who are single. Only women who agree to live within the confines of legal marriage could be eligible for full welfare benefits. The intent is to reverse what politicians have defined as a transfer of power and authority away from men in traditional family settings to the welfare state (Thomas, 1995).

New Jersey in 1993 and Arkansas in 1995 enacted another attempt at state level welfare reform, referred to as "Family Caps." These two states deny higher cash payments to women who have additional children while on welfare. Proponents suggest that a cap would remove financial incentives for AFDC recipients to have more children outside of marriage. Opponents, in contrast, argue that it is a misperception that women who receive AFDC have additional children in order to get more money. They point out that additional births do not dramatically increase the size of the welfare check; checks increase $24 to $147 per child, depending on the state.

Finally, the most critical and far reaching of these recent reform efforts can be attributed to President Clinton's sweeping welfare reform legislation. Bill Clinton has long advocated reforming the welfare system, including during his terms as governor of Arkansas. He maintained that the federal government should institute a comprehensive series of reforms in order to prevent long-term dependence on the system. He stressed that the focus of welfare should be in getting people back to work, as employment "gives hope and structure and meaning to our lives" (Clinton, 1997a). Towards this end, he argued that an assortment of services, including health insurance, should be made available to support lower wage workers. Without these services, welfare recipients have little inducement to forgo welfare for work, he argued. As he stated in a 1994 speech about welfare reform:

> . . . There are things that keep people on welfare. One is the tax burden of low wage work; another is the cost of child care; another is the cost of medical care . . . today you have this bizarre situation where people on welfare, if they take a job in a place which doesn't offer health insurance, are asked to give up their children's health care, and go to work. . . . That doesn't make any sense. (Clinton, 1997a)

The welfare reform legislation introduced by a Republican-led Congress, and eventually signed by Bill Clinton in 1996, was a long way off from his original rhetoric of strengthening poor families. It was an election year, and early on it looked like it could be a close race between President Clinton and a Republican challenger. Clinton's Republican opponent could make the most of the fact that Clinton had twice vetoed Republican initiated welfare reforms that came to his desk. He failed to sign them because he believed that they were too punitive and failed to provide adequate support to families.

But this time, when the revised legislation came to his desk, the election year pressure was insurmountable. Clinton signed welfare reform legislation into law, promising to make the needed changes to the legislation later. He claimed that the legislation met his general criteria for moving people from welfare to work, offered benefits such as child care and health care (albeit only temporarily), and would further enforce child support payments on the part of absent parents. Although he felt that this third attempt would produce legislation more towards his liking, he also acknowledged, "some parts of the bill still go too far, and I am determined to see that those areas are corrected" (Clinton, 1997b). In particular, he voiced concern over the deep cuts in nutritional assistance for working families with children and the exclusion of benefits for legal immigrants.

Public Law 104-193 abolished the AFDC program, and replaced it with a new program called Temporary Assistance to Needy Families (TANF). Under AFDC, all families that met federal eligibility criteria were entitled to receive cash assistance. Under TANF, eligibility will primarily be determined by state rules. No families are automatically entitled to assistance. The new law, under general federal parameters, requires states to examine whether to provide benefits, for whom, and for how long. These state-based decisions are complex because of federal mandates, fiscal constraints at the state level, conflicting goals of TANF, and the myriad of exemptions to work requirements or time limits that may be granted because of extenuating circumstances. For example, the new law retains a federal requirement that those receiving assistance must assign their child support rights over to the state. As in the past, in order to receive assistance, recipients must cooperate with the state in establishing paternity (if this is in question), obtaining a support order, and enforcing that order. The mother must appear at all relevant court–administrative agency hearings, and turn over to the state any child support payments received directly from the father. Only with "good cause" (i.e., the child was conceived as the result of a forcible rape or incest; pursuing support could result in physical or emotional harm; adoption was under consideration or was pending) could she be exempt from these requirements. However, now that states have more control in providing welfare assistance, they are free to supplement or amend these requirements and their possible exemptions. This has the potential to either help or to harm women and their children, depending on how individual states choose to resolve the interface between family law and assistance (Roberts, 1997).

Some of the most critical features of the TANF program, and the most controversial, are those related to work requirements and time limits. Federal law mandates that lifetime welfare payments can total no more than five years. Able-bodied recipients must work after two years, with few exceptions granted. In most cases, there is a two-year limit for TANF out of any 60 consecutive months. Two-parent welfare families are targeted as the first to be cut off of welfare assistance. By October 1, 1997, a little over one year after welfare reform became law, 75 percent of two-parent welfare families were mandated by the federal government to either have jobs or be in job training programs. In the first real test of welfare reform, approximately half the states fell short of these employment goals—goals that, in retrospect, many people are suggesting were unrealistic (Deparle, 1997). This first failure to meet employment goals is being held up for its symbolism. Work requirements among two-parent families, on first glance at least, should be relatively easy to fulfill. It requires a total of 35 hours per week between two adults, and while one is working, the other should seemingly be able to provide childcare. If the difficulties of employing two-parent households have been so seriously underestimated, then what does that suggest about the other, more challenging cases involving single parents? Despite the severity of federal guidelines, states are free to impose stricter time-limits and work requirements, which many have elected to do.

The Balanced Budget Act (BBA) of 1997 made a number of changes to the TANF program by partially restored funding for several of the most extreme cuts enacted in the 1996 welfare law. As a result, changes include such provisions as: (1) An increase of $3 billion over a two-year period to help states pay for a variety of employment related activities aimed towards persons with significant work barriers; (2) victims of family violence may be exempt from TANF work and time-limit provisions, and further study of domestic violence will be undertaken by the Government Accounting Office; (3) it restores Social Security Income (SSI) benefits to many disabled elderly legal immigrants; (4) several of the restrictions on food stamp eligibility will be waved for adults aged 18–50 who are not caring for minor children; and (5) a $20 billion child health block grant is designated to provide health insurance over the next five years to many of the 10 million uninsured children in the United States (Center for Law and Social Policy, 1997).

Some analysts fear that this is the end of the social safety net for vulnerable individuals and families. They wonder what will happen to the many poor people who won't be able to find work, for one reason or another, when they reach the government's time limit. They question whether jobs are available for all the people now on assistance without a massive job creation effort. They lament that even the lucky people who do find employment will most likely be paid wages that fail to bring their incomes above the poverty line. They are concerned that job training will be superficial in nature, and will not really be effective in increasing recipients' employment prospects. They want to know who will care for the children of parents who cannot afford to pay for child care on their own. And they wonder how will the health care needs of the influx of low-income workers and their children be met after their transitional Medicaid expires.

These are critical matters because, despite a multitude of welfare reforms in the 20th century, they have never been adequately addressed. Past reforms have been primarily symbolic efforts to appease the public over "what to do with" the large and growing number of women and children who are poor and need assistance. Policy makers wring their hands in anguish as their poorly funded efforts do little to reduce the large numbers of women needing aid. Democrats and Republicans alike find welfare to be the scourge of government policy—it's that nasty little problem that won't go away. Welfare recipients, as beneficiaries of this much-maligned program, become the focus of intense hostility. Most people think that government spending on welfare should decrease rather than increase (Dowd, 1994), less than a third believe that welfare recipients truly need the assistance, and more than two-thirds believe that recipients are cheating the system (*USA Today*, 1996). In the early 1990s, California Governor Pete Wilson proposed a 25 percent cut in AFDC benefits for recipients' within the state. He trivialized the effect of such a drastic cut, suggesting that it's impact might mean that welfare recipients "would have less for a six-pack of beer" (Bristro-Brown, 1991). Implicit in his comments are the assumptions that welfare benefits are too high, that women waste welfare benefits and are fraudulent.

The more recent reforms are not isolated incidents. They are grounded in the historic and persisting questions and dilemmas: Why are people poor? Why are they on welfare? Under what conditions are people worthy of assistance from the government? We pose these questions in the generic; but it is crucial to remember that the vast majority of those affected are women. Welfare programs reflect our ambivalent attitudes towards "manless women" (Miller, 1992)—women who have children and live outside the traditional family structure. Current reforms are only the latest in a long series of efforts in "regulating the lives of women" (Abramovitz, 1996a). As social worker and historian Mimi Abramovitz writes,

> In sum, AFDC, like its predecessor, the Mothers' Pension Program, substituted itself for the male breadwinner to make the "deviant" husbandless family approximate the "normal" one. In so doing, the state assumed more direct responsibility for reproduction in female-headed households and continued to punish women viewed as out of role. (1996a: 341–342)

Explanations of Poverty and Welfare Use

Several frameworks have been offered as a way to catalog explanations about poverty, welfare use, women's roles, and beliefs about government responsibility. If we think of these perspectives as residing on a continuum, we find *Individualism* and *Social Structuralism* at each end. The Individual perspective focuses on the achievement of the person, arguing that we are ultimately responsible for our own economic position, whereas social structuralism would stress that the inequality found in social institutions such as the labor market, families, and government affect our economic positions. Other perspectives, such as the *Culture of Poverty*, or *Fatalism*, combine features of these two perspectives to explain the ways in which our social structure shapes individual action.

These perspectives are, on first glance, gender neutral. They refer to attributes of the individual or of the social structure that supposedly transcend gender. However, I suggest that they are not gender neutral, but rather represent the male experience. Claims of "gender neutrality" are simply another way of marginalizing or ignoring women's contributions or experiences. For example, what is defined as "achievement," so important to those espousing individualism, is gendered. The result of a woman's hard work and the fruits of her labor may look considerably different from her male counterpart's. During much of our history, and for many women today, having a successful marriage and raising and nurturing children are the pinnacles of "achievement." Women have not been socialized to define success through an occupation or income, as is the case for men. Consequently, women who fail to seek employment, who are not driven by occupational roles, or who prefer to stay home to care for their dependent children should not be interpreted as failing to meet some generic criteria for "achievement." It would be unfair to render them as lazy or unmotivated. Therefore, it is critical that we provide a fresh perspective by acknowledging the ways in which gender interacts with our explanations of social inequality, poverty, and welfare use.

Individualism

A local newspaper recently ran an article describing the consequences of welfare reform in the lives of recipients (Chandler, January 8, 1997). One woman in particular was profiled: Kathy Sanding received AFDC for two years after bearing a child conceived during a rape. When interviewed, the 26-year-old mother was only one semester away from receiving an associate of arts (AA) degree from a community college, and had hoped to transfer to a nearby university for a four-year degree and study to become a teacher. Despite her 3.4 grade point average, and making the dean's list, the state of Florida's welfare department informed her that, within two months, federal and state welfare guidelines under TANF would require her to be either employed, actively searching for a job, or to be involved in vocational training. If she did not comply, she would risk losing her cash assistance, food stamps, and Medicaid coverage. She was told that going to a community college, with the goal of transferring to a four-year university, is not classified as either "work" or "learning a trade" according to the work-oriented policies enacted by the Florida legislature. Although this young woman is determined to get her AA degree, she now doubts that she can pursue a bachelor's degree from a university. Her dreams of becoming a teacher have been dashed by Florida's welfare reform policy. She knows that, like many other former welfare recipients, she will now likely end up working in a low-paying job in the expanding Florida service sector, most likely the fast food industry, earning near minimum wage. In her own words, she says,

> I think they should let people who are going to school continue until they've finished. I feel like I've busted my butt trying to have integrity; to do what the welfare system intends for me to do. Now the government has taken away my dreams and aspirations for having a successful life and changed them into having a mediocre or just poverty level life. (Chandler, January 8, 1997)

The story in the local newspaper was designed to provide an inside look at the way that welfare reform has eclipsed the dreams of at least one hard-working, achievement-oriented woman. Yet, for many, the article did not evoke sympathy. The tension and hostility felt towards welfare recipients runs deep, as was evidenced by a letter to the newspaper's editor soon after the original article was printed (*The Gainesville Sun*, January 22, 1997):

> First, I commend reporter Chandler on her superb ability to write an article that is able to put the welfare situation in such a sympathetic light for the recipients. I, however, tend to sympathize with the taxpaying public that has been burdened by this system for too many years now. . . . I do not feel it my responsibility to put her through school when I cannot afford to put members of my own family through school.
> . . . I worked a full-time and a part-time job to put myself through night school. I am also one of the millions of people in this country who have "a mediocre or just poverty-level life," whose hard-earned tax dollars Miss Sanding seems to feel are there to make her endeavor easy.

I do not blame Miss Sanding for her attitude. The government has created and nurtured this attitude in the American people for too long, and the blame lies primarily there. I do, however believe that articles of the nature of this one . . . are irresponsible and insulting to the millions of people in this country who have had the fortitude and perseverance to take the hard road to accomplish their dreams of attaining higher education.

. . . The time has come for those people that have had a free ride for so many years to get down in the trenches with the rest of us and take responsibility for their own lives and livelihoods.

This letter to the editor of the newspaper expresses the sentiment of Individualism. It suggests that individuals are largely responsible for their own economic position in society; that opportunities are available to all who are willing to work hard and who are sufficiently motivated. Because virtually everyone has an equal opportunity to acquire the skills, traits, and training needed for upward mobility, those that fail to "make it" have largely themselves to blame. The Individualistic perspective is reflected in our country's response to the poor throughout most of our history. Tales of Horatio Alger types abound—the "rags to riches" stories—the moral being that anyone can pull themselves up by their bootstraps with hard work, sweat, and motivation. Welfare recipients are a particularly blatant example of those who have failed to "make it" and therefore reside in the bottom of the economic hierarchy. They are at worst lazy and unmotivated, and at best simply uneducated and untrained. Either way, they are held largely responsible for their own economic plight.

Notice that the focus is on the individual—the argument is that we need to change the individual, to increase her or his motivation, and to increase her or his level of human capital, in order to be competitive for jobs. Little attention is given to features of our social structure such as the growing number of service sector jobs, which generally pay sub-poverty level minimum wage. Yet, what proponents of this perspective fail to ask themselves is, if the bulk of new jobs are being created in the low-paying service sector, can we really train people out of poverty? Won't someone else, then, occupy these roles? Poverty may be transferred to someone else, but it will not be eliminated.

Studies conducted over the past several decades show the persistent popularity of the Individual perspective in this country. Although there are important gender, race, and income variations, generally, individualism is a highly popular explanation of inequality among women and men, African Americans and whites, and the affluent and poor (Feagin, 1975; Hunt, 1996; Kluegel and Smith, 1982; Seccombe, James, and Battle Walters, 1998; Smith and Stone, 1989). One large study conducted in 1969 by sociologist Joe Feagin, with 1,017 randomly selected adults from all regions of the United States, illustrated how deeply rooted this perspective is (1975). More than half of the sample evaluated lack of thrift, laziness and lack of effort, and lack of ability and talent as very important reasons for poverty. Nearly 90 percent said that these were at least somewhat important explanations of poverty. Only 18 percent suggested that poverty was caused by being taken advantage of by rich people (Feagin, 1975, p. 97). Those persons most likely to espouse individualistic explanations were white Protestants and Catholics, residents of the south and north central regions of the United

States, persons older than age 50, middle-income groups, and those with moderate levels of education (p. 98).

In addition, Feagin found little tolerance for welfare recipients, with most respondents indicating a high degree of suspicion and distrust of them. Eighty-four percent of respondents agreed with the statement that "there are too many people receiving welfare who should be working," 71 percent agreed that "many people getting welfare are not honest about their need," and 61 percent felt that "many women getting welfare money are having illegitimate babies to increase the money they get" (p. 103). Opinions about welfare recipients reflect the deeply held beliefs that the poor are largely responsible for their own economic circumstances because of laziness, lack of thrift, or lack of talent.

Welfare recipients are perhaps the most stigmatized subset of the poor. We assume that they should be able to improve their economic circumstances at whim. Yet we are ignoring a critical social fact: The vast majority of welfare recipients are unmarried women with dependent children. Given their daily parental responsibilities, tasks, and time constraints, they do not have the same opportunities to "pull themselves up by their bootstraps" as do other adults who are without children, for example, poor men. To ignore the emotional and time commitments involved in taking care of dependent children, and to fail to recognize the ways in which caretaking can inhibit women's ability for social mobility, is to ignore the reality of many women's existence. Is it fair to assume that unmarried women who stay home to take care of their dependent children are lazy, lacking in thrift, or have little or no talent?

Social Structuralism

A social structural perspective, in contrast, assumes that poverty is a result of economic or social imbalances within our social structure that serve to restrict opportunities for some people. Social structure is defined as the social institutions, organizations, groups, statuses and roles, values, and norms that exist in our culture. Three distinct themes exist under this broad perspective: (1) A concern with capitalism, (2) a focus on a changing economy, and (3) a concern that the welfare system itself exacerbates poverty. Social conservatives seeking to dismantle the welfare system have often invoked this last theme.

Concerning the first theme, some in our society contend that poverty is an inherent feature of capitalism (Marx and Engels, 1968). The subsequent control over other social structures, such as education and the polity, is designed to serve the interests and maintain the dominance of the wealthy class. Karl Marx's early writings draw attention to the exploitive relationships found within capitalistic societies. They feature a greater division of labor, where workers do not work for themselves but sell their labor for wages to capitalists. Marx argued that workers are not paid wages that reflect their true worth (e.g., their output). Instead, capitalists prefer to keep wages low, pocketing the remainder as profit. Producing more goods with fewer workers, especially when they are not paid wages equivalent to their output, ensures higher profits. Capitalism thrives on a reserve labor force—people who are available to work in times of booming economic expansion or union busting. This reserve labor force is expendable, and many are discarded when the boom subsides. Consequently, their poverty is an inevitable feature of capitalism.

Marx paid little attention to the ways in which capitalism affects women directly. More recent socialist feminists have pointed out that doing away with capitalism may not necessarily improve the lives of women appreciably. Until women are liberated from their privatized domestic roles, they are likely to always be exploited. They suggest that a more collectivist approach to carrying out housework and child care, alongside the development of a more socialist economy, is needed to really eliminate poverty and improve women's lives.

Other structuralists, secondly, point to the features of a changing economy, such as the growth in low-paying service sector jobs, the erosion of the minimum wage, or the relocation of jobs from the inner-city (Wilson, W. J., 1987; 1996). For example, dual labor market theory posits that the economy can be divided into at least two sectors, primary and secondary. Workers' location in one or the other sector systematically affects their earnings, bargaining power, and likelihood of fringe benefits such as health insurance—even when workers have similar levels of education, training, tenure on the job, other skills, or human capital. Furthermore, there is little mobility, and workers tend to become trapped in one sector or the other. The characteristics of the job vary dramatically in these two sectors. Jobs in the primary sector tend to offer positions possessing higher wages, better working conditions, more opportunities for advancement, greater employment stability, and generous fringe benefits. The secondary sector, in comparison, offers lower wages, fewer possibilities for promotion, higher turnover rates or seasonal employment, and fewer critical fringe benefits.

Women tend to be concentrated in relatively few occupations, and most of these fall into the secondary sector. The majority of women work in clerical, sales, and service jobs. In addition, gender inequality exists within these sectors. For example, women do not receive the same returns that men do when they are employed in jobs with similar occupational characteristics, occupational prestige, or within identical job classifications (Bose and Rossi, 1983; U.S. Bureau of Labor Statistics, 1992).

The third structural approach suggests that social programs and welfare policies themselves contribute to poverty and exacerbate welfare use by trapping people into poverty and welfare dependency instead of helping them escape. As such, this theory is popular with social conservatives and welfare critics (Anderson, 1978; Murray, 1988, 1984) and is used as argument favoring a dismantling of welfare programs. They claim, as did Alexis de Tocqueville in the late 19th century, that people are inherently lazy, and will lose motivation and incentive if they know that governmental programs are there to take care of them. For example, people will snub work at low-paying jobs and will instead rely on the free money of welfare if given the opportunity. These proponents argue that eliminating or drastically reducing welfare is a critical first step to curbing poverty. However, these discussions are problematic because they assume that welfare is a gender neutral program. It is not. Recipients are predominantly women, and the needs and concerns embedded in women's real life experiences as caretakers of dependent children are not contextualized within their recommendations to reduce or eliminate welfare.

Culture of Poverty

The Culture of Poverty perspective blends features of the two previously mentioned perspectives. It suggests that a subcultural set of values, traits, and expectations have developed as a direct result of the structural constraints associated with living in isolated pockets of poverty. People in poverty are said to live in a subculture with a weak family structure, present-time orientation, and they display a helplessness and resignation toward work (Burton, 1992). The subculture is said to be at odds with the dominant middle-class culture because it downplays the importance of hard work, self-discipline, and deferring gratification. Although there is a wide range of opinion regarding the specific antecedents, features, and consequences of the subculture (Gilder, 1981; Lewis, 1966; Mead, 1992; Moynihan, 1965; Wilson, 1993, 1987), concern is voiced about the transmission of these values from parents to children. The question of whether poverty and welfare-use are intergenerational—that is, are passed on from parents to their children—is an enduring theme in the poverty literature.

Oscar Lewis first introduced this perspective as he studied poor barrios in Latin American communities. The idea of a poverty subcultural phenomenon caught the media by storm. He wrote:

> The culture of poverty is both an adaptation and a reaction of the poor to their marginal position in a class-stratified, highly individuated, capitalistic society. It represents an effort to cope with feelings of hopelessness and despair which develop from the realization of the improbability of achieving success in terms of the values and goals of the larger society. Indeed, many of the traits of the culture of poverty can be viewed as attempts at local solutions for problems not met by existing institutions and agencies because the people are not eligible for them, cannot afford them, or are ignorant or suspicious of them. The culture of poverty, however, is not only an adaptation to a set of objective conditions about the larger society. Once it comes into existence it tends to perpetuate itself from generation to generation because of its effect on the children. By the time slum children are age six or seven they have usually absorbed the basic values and attitudes of their subculture and are not psychologically geared to take full advantage of changing conditions or increased opportunities which may occur in their lifetime. (Lewis, 1966: xliii–xlv)

Unfortunately, Lewis' work has sometimes been misinterpreted as a victim-blaming approach in which deviant values are seen as the causes of poverty itself. This is not a correct interpretation of his work. Harvey and Reed (1996) suggest that Lewis' ideas are firmly grounded in a Marxist critique of capitalism. A subculture was constructed to ease the pain associated with being a part of the reserve and discarded labor force that is an inherent by-product of capitalism. They suggest that the culture of poverty is "a positive social construction—the result of a process by which the poor pragmatically winnow what works from what does not, and pass it on to their children" (1996: 482).

More recently, William Julius Wilson attributed poverty among the African American "underclass" in inner cities (1996, 1987) to their social, economic, and geographic isolation. He argued that class, not race, is the primary factor in explaining their poverty. Wilson suggests that the loss of well-paying manufacturing jobs from urban areas has had disastrous effects on those persons living in the area. Male unemployment and subsequent poverty increased dramatically, and consequently reduced the pool of men eligible for marriage and increased the number of children born out of wedlock and raised in single parent families. Moreover, the middle class migrated out of urban areas, leading to development of ghettos. Their migration out to the suburbs means that those persons who remain in the urban core have few role models of mainstream success.

Wilson's work is notable on several fronts. First, he contends that, although class is more important than race as a cause of intergenerational inequality, his model applies primarily to minorities because few poor whites reside in highly poor neighborhoods. Second, his model focuses on the interaction of structure and culture. He blames labor markets and demographic changes for isolating the inner city minority poor, and it is these structural constraints that thereby affect the organization of family and community life. His concept of social isolation does not imply a self-perpetuating or permanent phenomenon. When job opportunities and appropriate social services for inner-city residents are provided, the subcultural adaptation will eventually disappear.

To make the culture of poverty perspective more relevant to understanding the lives of poor women, it should examine additional aspects of the social structure that inhibit mobility, specifically those features that affect women's lives. For example, it should critique the features of marriage and family life that affect women's ability to transcend economic marginality and may therefore encourage adaptation. These may include such things as fathers' lack of involvement in direct child care, the limited availability of daycare facilities, or insufficient enforcement of child support policies by the government. In the absence of these features, women may develop their own adaptations, such as relying on extended families to care for their children or to pool their financial resources.

Fatalism

Finally, Fatalism attributes the causes of wealth and poverty to quirks of birth, chance, luck, human nature, illness, or other forces over which people have no control. Poverty is not viewed as anyone's fault *per se*, but rather is a potential consequence of unplanned, random, or natural human events. It assumes that poverty is caused by forces outside our control, thereby denying that the behaviors of the rest of the population contribute to poverty and social inequality. Hernstein and Murray (1994), for example suggest that low intelligence is a primary cause of poverty and welfare dependency. Arguing that intelligence is largely genetic, they argue that poor people with low intelligence quotients (IQs) give birth to another cohort with low IQs and thus the children remain in poverty.

In his 1969 survey, Feagin found that people shied away from attributing poverty to simply bad luck (1975). In his survey of 1,017 adults, only eight percent of respondents emphasized that "bad luck" was a very important reason for poverty. More recently, Smith and Stone (1989), in their study of 200 randomly selected respondents in southeast Texas, also found that fatalistic perspectives were unpopular compared to individualistic explanations. For example, only 10 percent of respondents agreed that "bad luck" or being born inferior is a very important explanation. Moreover, only 14 percent attributed low intelligence as a very important explanation for poverty.

It is critical to note that the previously mentioned studies do not distinguish the gender of the impoverished person. These studies are not unusual; we commonly talk about poverty, and discuss the poor as though they are nameless, faceless, genderless, and generic beings. They are not. The poor, especially those who receive welfare, are primarily women and children. When we fail to identify them as such, when we do not specifically refer to the poor as "women," or as "she," most often a male mental image emerges. I suggest that our degree of tolerance for attributing poverty to "bad luck" or "fate" is indeed gendered; that is, it varies between men and women. Men are expected to be independent; they are assumed to be able to actively construct their own lives. In our society, men are not allowed to simply have "bad luck," and fall into poverty and need assistance. Instead, men must have extenuating and serious circumstances in order for us to excuse their poverty. Women, in contrast, have traditionally been socialized to be more dependent on others for their economic and social position. Therefore, they are more vulnerable to fluctuations in these statuses through no fault of their own. AFDC was originally created to protect women who are single mothers from these vulnerabilities that are beyond their control, such as violence, abuse, or desertion. Today, however, we are in a state of flux. We are less understanding, less confident of the type of protection women need, and less enthusiastic about providing it.

These four perspectives offer competing explanations for poverty, welfare use, and social inequality more generally. They are not new; they reflect historic and persisting dilemmas about human nature, the importance of hard work, and the vice of idleness, and they reflect our notions of appropriate roles for men and women. AFDC and TANF were created from these dilemmas. Yet these perspectives fail to acknowledge the ways that gender also influences our explanations and understandings of poverty. Little attention has been given to the ways in which individual achievement, social structure, culture, or fate may operate or be perceived differently for women and men. The goal here has been to expand these explanations so that they are more inclusive of women's lived experience. The in-depth interviews show us the usefulness of these perspectives, and allow us to revise and reanalyze them to better fit the real-world experiences of women on welfare.

3 Stigma and Discrimination

Stereotype

Conjure up in your mind an image of a "welfare mother." What does she look like? How does she sound? Why is she on welfare? How does she feel about being on the system?

For many people, a woman like Dawn would come to mind. She embodies many of the stereotypical traits of a woman on welfare, yet, as shown in Chapter 1, Dawn is anything but typical of women who receive welfare. Nonetheless, she fits the largely negative images that we have of "welfare mothers"—images wielded by the mass media.

Dawn is a large, gregarious woman. She is African American, 31 years old, and has never been married. Her grandmother raised her, although her mother is alive and they have always been close. "Momma didn't live there, but we would always see her. She was always close by," said Dawn. "That's a trend in my family." Dawn's grandmother received welfare for her care. "Granny," as she affectionately called her grandmother, and to whom she referred to several times throughout the interview, recently passed away.

Dawn has four children, fathered by four different men. Her first child was born to her when she was only 13. "Me and my oldest daughter—we were both children growing up," she told me. Dawn had her second child when she was 18 years old, her third one at 20, and her fourth child at age 21. Her mother volunteered to raise her second child for her, a son, and her mother therefore receives welfare for him. Dawn sees her mother and her son regularly. She does not find the living arrangement odd; after all, it mirrors her own childhood. She's appreciative that her mother offered this help.

> I guess my life was going kind of fast, having children. By the time I was 21 I had four kids. And my mom, one day she came to me because by the time my son was one year old I had another baby and was pregnant. So my mom, she felt sorry for me. And so she asked me if she could take one of the kids. At first it was going to be a temporary thing. But she asked me if I wanted her to help out, to at least take one kid. She offered to take him or the other. And he was the one I chose. And that helped me out a lot. So, she raised him since he was about a year, or something like that. But I see him all the time freely. Me and my mom, you know, we're close family.

He doesn't live in the household, but he knows. I wonder if I'll raise my grandchild? I don't want to. But I don't know what will happen.

The children's fathers, in contrast, provide very little help. Only one pays child support to the county welfare office, but he pays only sporadically. When he does pay, Dawn is given an extra fifty dollars in her welfare benefits for that month. "But, he hasn't paid lately," she tells me. "I guess he's in jail or something. But when we don't get those checks, it's a long time until my kids get shoes." Without this added assistance, Dawn receives a $365 cash grant and $345 a month in food stamps for her and her three children who live with her. The rent on her modest but neatly kept single family home is subsidized and she therefore pays only $21 a month, plus approximately $150 a month for utilities. And, like virtually all AFDC recipients, she and her children receive Medicaid.

Unlike Dawn's early years, she told me that she really no longer has an interest in men or romantic relationships. She feels that a father figure for her children, at this point, is relatively unimportant. She didn't have a father, and as she sees it, that did not harm her. Dawn was not the first woman who, after bearing several children, flatly told me that she was not interested in any further relationships. Several women expressed discomfort around men. Some alluded to be being sexually abused. Dawn, however, was more vague.

> I didn't grow up around anyone but my grandmother. I had an uncle who lived in the house for awhile, my grandmother's house, and I just didn't like that man. When he wasn't there, it was good and I loved it. But when he was there, I just didn't like him. I didn't like him at all. So I guess that's a pattern that I had. When there was a man in the house, I don't know. That's why I don't have a husband. I can't. For some reason I have real big problems in that department. So when they aren't there, I just feel kind of content. More comfortable. So I guess I don't want a husband. I wouldn't want him here all the time. Although sometimes I want a boyfriend to help out financially. And then, again, sometimes I say it's not worth it, just forget it and go back to the way it was.

Dawn has been off and on welfare for most of her life. She has also worked at a number of jobs as well, as a cashier, a nurse's aide, and she has washed cars. She works for a few months at a time, then gets "bored" and switches jobs or quits. None of the jobs have been particularly high-paying. Several times when she was employed she withheld her employment and income information from her caseworker, and continued to receive a welfare check in addition to her earnings. She did this, only temporarily, she told me, so that she would be able to pay off her bills at the first of the month. Once when she did it, she was caught, found guilty of committing welfare fraud, and given probation for 18 months. She now has a criminal record.

On first glance, Dawn is an easy target to use in the quest for welfare reform. She corroborates the negative stereotypes we have of women on welfare: She appears to be lazy, unmotivated, and dependent on the system. We assume that she lives in a culture of poverty, where her "deviant" family values and her criminal record for welfare fraud are normative, and perhaps even encouraged. No more information about her life is needed for judgment. Onlookers do not probe deeper. Instead, many people suggest that *she* is the precise reason why we need to reform welfare: We need to eliminate Dawn, and the suspected millions of women like her, from abusing the welfare system.

Dawn is, however, an atypical welfare recipient in most respects. Compared with an average welfare mother, Dawn has more children, she has been on welfare longer, and her racial background represents only a third of welfare recipients nationally. She is an anomaly. Yet, somehow, she fits the image that Americans have of women who receive welfare—an image that is inaccurate. Perhaps the principal way in which Dawn is typical of others who received welfare is that her life is considerably more complex than acknowledged at first blush.

Stereotypes of women who receive welfare are fed to us regularly by multiple forms of media. It is not only the middle and upper classes who are bombarded with these negative images of welfare mothers. Poor women are bombarded as well. Are women on welfare, then, also aware of these stereotypes? If so, how do they justify being on the system, with welfare mothers so widely denigrated? How do they manage, or cope with this stigma? The poor make judgments not only from the same media and cultural influences as do the more affluent, but also from their very own personal experiences with limited employment opportunities, lack of available child care, and other constraints. This chapter addresses these questions. It examines whether recipients attribute welfare use to forces beyond their control, or whether they, instead, share the same stigmatized view found within the general population—that welfare recipients are largely responsible for their own economic plight.

Awareness of Societal Attitudes toward Welfare Recipients

First, let us examine the issue of recipients' firsthand experience with stigma and discrimination. We know that distrust and hostility toward welfare recipients is widespread within the more affluent population. Do women who receive welfare know the extent of the negative sentiment felt towards welfare and welfare recipients? Do they have firsthand experience with stigma and discrimination?

Other studies indicate that many welfare recipients do indeed feel stigmatized for receiving welfare. Goodban (1985), for example, using a sample of 100 African American women on welfare, reported that nearly two-thirds claimed they experienced some sense of shame at various times for being on welfare. Rank (1994), in his study of welfare recipients in Wisconsin, found that the lack of privacy and the stigma associated with welfare, at least in part, fueled recipients' desire to exit from welfare. Another study focusing solely on African American mothers found that women felt stigmatized as nonworkers, single parents, and inner-city dwellers (Jarrett, 1996). Another study based on in-depth interviews with 10 divorced or separated women on welfare did not find stigma to be a constant entity, but found that it varied depending on the social audience, situation, and recipients' life history (Rogers-Dillan, 1995). Her analysis, which was based on food stamp use, a public acknowledgment of welfare receipt, suggests that stigma was not experienced in the same way, in all contexts, by all recipients.

Our interviews also revealed that welfare recipients tend to be well aware of their stigmatized status. When asked if they ever hear negative comments about people on welfare, answers were overwhelmingly "yes," and most claimed that criticism has been directed at them personally. Dawn told me of her experiences:

> Yeah, I have had people look down at me. And it makes me feel bad. I don't want to—oh, I don't know. I'd probably be the same way, I guess. I don't know. I think they should understand though, that if I didn't need them, I would not be embarrassing myself like that. You know what I'm saying? Maybe they don't understand because they've never had to have them. I wish I could feel that way. But, you know. I kind of know how they feel, but then again, if I didn't have this, me and my children wouldn't be able to eat. Then how would you look at it?

Most welfare recipients who were interviewed, African American and white, as well as young and old, reported that they hear considerable personal blame and criticism. For example, when asked what kinds of things they had heard said about welfare recipients, a 28-year-old white woman named Rhonda, who has one son, told me:

> I've heard one girl was going to quit working because all the taxes come to us. Plus, you know, they downgrade us in every kind of way there is. They say we look like slobs, we keep our houses this way and that way. And our children, depending on the way they're dressed, we're like bad parents and all sorts of things like that.

The theme of laziness, an image embodied in the individualist perspective, emerged frequently. Welfare recipients are well aware that mothers on welfare are criticized for being lazy, unmotivated, and for taking advantage of the welfare system. Leah, a 24-year-old African American woman with four children, commented:

> I've had people who didn't know I was receiving assistance and everything was just fine. But when people find out you're receiving assistance, it's like, "Why? Why did you get lazy all of a sudden?" People automatically just put you in this category of people that don't do anything except sit on their butts and do nothing. It's just all out there in the community.

Mandy, another African American woman, who is 20 years old with two young children, told me:

> They say you lazy. They say you lazy and don't want to work. You want people to take care of you. You want to sit home and watch stories all day, which I don't. And they say it's a handout.

Erving Goffman's book *Stigma* (1963) provides an insightful analysis of this phenomenon. He is interested in the gap between the image the individual wishes his or her public identity to be, "virtual social identity," and what the public identity actually is, "actual social identity." A person is stigmatized when there is a discrepancy in these identities. It can be a powerfully negative social label that radically changes a person's self-concept and identity. Goffman divided stigmatized individuals into two groups: Those whose stigma is known or easily perceivable (such as a paraplegic or someone who is disfigured), and those whose stigma is hidden or not easily identified. When it is identified, the stigmatized person can become deeply discredited, labeled as deviant, and deemed to be morally flawed (Gans, 1995). The label associated with stigmatization focuses on only one aspect of the individual's character. This one aspect is elevated to the level of a "master" status—it becomes the primary mechanism through which that person is identified. One suddenly becomes, "the cripple," "the lesbian," the "cross-dresser," "the person with AIDS," "the man in a wheelchair," or "the welfare mother." Other statuses, such as Sunday school teacher, school volunteer, swimmer, friend, and daughter are largely overlooked.

The stigma surrounding welfare is deep and widespread, and research has documented that it may even keep some eligible families from applying for aid (Yaniv, 1997). Because women are well aware of the ways in which welfare is denigrated, they are often embarrassed about being poor and receiving welfare. So are their children. Many women told me of this embarrassment, including Sarah. Sarah is a white, 30-year-old divorced mother who works part-time at a fast food franchise. She also attends college, and is working toward her Associate of Arts (AA) degree. Both she and her daughter are embarrassed at wearing hand-me-down clothing. She described an incident in which her daughter's only coat did not fit her because it was originally purchased for someone else.

> She inherited my mom's winter coat because we couldn't afford one. Her arm was up here, and the sleeve was down here, but hey, she wore it. She stayed warm. You do what you have to do. You try to make it so it's not as embarrassing. But it really is. I mean, the parents made more fun than the kids did.

Dawn, our "stereotypical" welfare recipient, also discussed her embarrassment about receiving welfare:

> First of all, I'm embarrassed about being on welfare. I'm not going to tell you no lie. Maybe I've been on it all my life, but maybe that's why I'm embarrassed about it. But the kids used to go, "Momma, the check is here." And that was so embarrassing. Downstairs, upstairs could hear. I had to stop them from doing that. I had to tell them, "This is not good. Don't be happy because we're getting a welfare check. This is not nothing good."

Most women, like Sarah and Dawn, could not hide their stigma, and were publicly embarrassed by it. In Sarah's case, her family's poverty was on display every day in which the coat or other hand-me-down clothing was worn. In Dawn's case, despite living in a public housing project in which all of her neighbors were on welfare, she was embarrassed when her children loudly announced the arrival of the welfare check. By her children doing this, she lost all pretenses that she was not really receiving welfare.

Racism and Welfare

One of the many reasons that welfare use is stigmatized is that it is associated with use primarily by African Americans. Welfare is put in racial terms because many whites incorrectly assume that the majority of the poor and the majority of welfare recipients are African American. They see welfare as a program primarily serving African American mothers who have never married. Yet, although African Americans are over-represented among the poor and among welfare recipients given their proportion of the population in the United States, a nearly equal proportion of welfare recipients are white, as shown in Chapter 1. Whites and African Americans constitute 37 percent and 36 percent of welfare recipients, respectively. But because of this misperception, racist overtones were evident in the comments made to women on welfare. One woman heard welfare recipients referred to as "white and black niggers sucking off the system." The racist view that welfare is a program primarily for the African American community was epitomized in the comments made by Beth, a 27-year-old white woman with one child:

> Oh they say silly stuff, prejudiced stuff, "The black people are getting it, so we might as well—you might as well go ahead and get it too while you can. They're driving Cadillacs," and this and that. It just shows how ignorant they are—to me.

Several African American women commented that the public unfairly labels welfare as a problem primarily within the African American community, ". . . they want to say that there are more black people on the system than white people." Dee is an African American woman, 24 years of age, with three children aged four and under, and she told us that the most negative comments she has heard come from white males:

> That's mainly who I hear it from. I mean, I hear a couple of things from black guys, but a lot of black guys I know grew up on the system. You know, they are trying to get off that system. So you don't really hear it much from them. They have first hand experience with it. Those who don't have first hand experience have friends who have. So, the majority of them have come into contact with it sometime in their lifetime. As for the white males, a lot of them grew up in the upper middle class, you know,

above the poverty line, so they never run across it, unless they had friends who were on the system. But there are as many white people on it as black people.

As Kluegel and Smith (1982) reveal, many whites see African American's experience as having improved significantly in recent years, and tend to deny that our social structure limits their opportunities. Many white Americans are resentful. They often feel that they themselves are victimized by policies of "reverse discrimination," while African Americans and other minorities reap employment and social welfare benefits. A survey from the National Opinion Research Center reveals that only 17 percent of the adult population in the United States strongly or somewhat agree to the statement "the government is obligated to help blacks," whereas nearly half disagree (National Opinion Research Center, 1993). Moreover, data from the General Social Survey indicates that less than 40 percent of whites support increased social spending to help African Americans (Bobo and Smith, 1994). African Americans are not seen as needing special treatment or privilege, and many whites are resentful that African Americans are receiving these privileges nonetheless.

Our nation tends to deny racial inequalities, and instead claims to embrace the idea that "we are all created equal." Consequently we oppose Affirmative Action programs that demand that we acknowledge the differences among us—the inequalities in earlier life circumstances that affect one's opportunities today. But can we really deny that adults and children are treated differently, and have different experiences and opportunities based on their skin color and position in our class structure? Even public education—supposedly the great equalizer by providing all children with the same quality education and chance for the good life, perpetuates "savage inequalities," according to author Jonathan Kozol (1991). In comparing two high schools, one poor and with a 99.9 percent black student population, and one consisting of mostly white upper-middle-class students, he found dramatic differences in school funding, in their facilities, and in personnel. For example, high school students in poor East Orange can afford few athletic facilities. The track team has no field, and they must do their running in the hallway of the school. Meanwhile, in nearby upper-middle-class Montclair, money is available to buy two recreation fields, four gyms, a dance room, a wrestling room, a weight room with a universal gym, tennis courts, a track, and indoor areas for fencing. Money is also available in Montclair High to hire 13 full-time physical education teachers for their 1,900 students. East Orange High School, by comparison, has four physical education teachers for 2,000 students. Drastic differences such as these not only provide different current experiences and future opportunities, but they also send a clear message about the value of education. It should come as no surprise that graduation rates from high school are race and class correlated. Students with lower family incomes and members of most minority groups in the United States are significantly more likely to drop out of high school than are more affluent whites.

Individual and institutional racism are prevalent in the United States. It is manifested in many ways, including hatred and distrust towards those African Americans most in need. William Julius Wilson suggests that young African American women are actually *more* likely to be blamed for their economic circumstances than are their white counterparts, and they are considered less worthy of government assistance (Wilson, 1996). Many Americans associate the Culture of Poverty perspective with African Americans, and criticize the supposed subcultural adaptations in the African American community as aberrant and antithetical with mainstream American values associated with hard work and family. Women's poverty, African American women's in particular, is blamed on a breakdown in women's moral virtue, which has resulted in declining marriage rates and rising illegitimacy.

These concerns stem, at least in part, from several important demographic factors, both of which can be seen in Dawn's experiences. First, African Americans are indeed less likely to marry than are whites; and second, they are more likely to have a child outside of marriage. National data show that race, ethnicity, and social class do affect marriage patterns in many critical ways. In 1996, 42 percent of African Americans age 18 and older were married, compared with 63 percent of whites and 58 percent of Hispanics (U.S. Bureau of the Census, 1997b, Table 58, p. 55). In addition, a higher proportion of African Americans, as compared to whites and Hispanics, have never been married (39, 21, and 30 percent, respectively). Critics are quick to implicate this as a subcultural adaptation at odds with American values. But here are two primary reasons for this. Both reasons are rational and pragmatic, and have little to do with a culture of poverty *per se*. First, high rates of unemployment and underemployment discourage young adults from marrying. Unemployment among young African American males is more than twice that for whites their age. And, among those males who are employed, their earnings are significantly less than that of whites. Therefore, given high rates of unemployment and underemployment, young men are less eager to take on the responsibility of a family, and young women are less apt to see these men as desirable marriage prospects. The second reason for the lower rate of marriage among African Americans is sheer demographics. The number of eligible African American women for marriage far exceeds the number of available men. The statistics are alarming: one out of every 80 African American males is the victim of a violent death, and a disturbingly high percentage of men are incarcerated. Thus, for African American females, the search for a lifetime marriage partner can be a daunting task. There is a critical shortage of marriageable men. Like many other African American women, Dawn has not found a man to marry. Given her less-than-likely chance of finding a man to support herself and her four children, her reluctance to look for one is therefore not surprising.

Higher rates of nonmarital births among African Americans also influence the belief that a separate subculture exists that is antithetical to mainstream American values. The nonmarital fertility rate for African Americans is about 2.3 times that of white women (84 vs. 36 births per 1,000 women, respectively), and the nonmarital fertility rate among Hispanic women is about 2.6 times that of non-Hispanic whites, at 95 births per 1,000 women (National Center for Health Statistics [NCHS], 1995). Part of these differences can be traced back to income or education levels. Significant racial differences persist, however, even after the effects of socioeconomic status and other individual and family characteristics are accounted for. These nonmarital births are not simply the result of accidental pregnancies. Corresponding with these demographic trends, birth *intentions* also differ among racial and ethnic groups. Using a national sample of 12,686 males and females between the ages of 14 and 21 from the U.S. National Longitudinal Surveys of Labor Market Experience of Youth (NSLY), researchers compared birth intentions of African Americans, Hispanics, and whites. They report that African Americans were twice as likely to expect an adolescent birth as were whites (10.6 vs. 5.5, respectively), and were nearly four times as likely to expect a nonmarital birth (15.2 vs. 4.2, respectively). Hispanics fared somewhere between these two groups (Trent and Crowder, 1997). Dawn's pregnancies were not planned, but, at the same time, they were not particularly surprising to her either. Yet today, the rate of teen pregnancies alarms her. Her values, and those of many other women interviewed, were not at odds with conventional expectations. She did not hold separate subcultural values that encourage or tolerate teen pregnancy. Rather, Dawn is concerned about the high rates of teenage pregnancy that plague young women and severely limit the work and educational opportunities available to them. Consequently, she is actively trying to prevent her own daughters from becoming pregnant. Dawn, and other women, told me that they were trying to ward off teenage sexual activity, among both their daughters and their sons, through repeated warnings, keeping a watchful eye on them after school, and through a series of rewards and punishments. Referring to her oldest daughter, who is now 17 years old, Dawn said:

> I'm real proud of her, because she did not do like I did. She did not have a baby at 13, or 14, or 17. She's doing good. I told her not to. Oh, so many times. All the time, right up until this day. I don't remember how long ago I used to start talking with her. But now I have a 10-year-old daughter, and I see that she's maturing, so I know she must have been about 9 or 10 when I started preaching my little preach. Ten is not too early at all.

These two demographic trends—lower rates of marriage and higher rates of nonmarital births—have become the rallying cry for Individualists and Culture of Poverty enthusiasts. African American women, in particular, are assumed to be the cause of their own poverty. Supposedly, they are poor because of their own immoral and indiscriminant sexual behavior, and their failure to find suitable lifetime mates, or so the story line goes. "It is the moral fabric of individuals, not the social and economic structure of society, that is taken to be the root of the problem" (Wilson, 1996: 164). Poverty and welfare use is racialized by many white Americans because they are increasingly weary of social programs, they believe that racism has declined, and they blame African Americans as failing to expend the effort needed to improve their financial standing.

Contexts in Which Stigma and Discrimination Occur

Recipients commented that they heard criticism most often in public places such as grocery stores. In this context, one cannot hide being on welfare; food stamps are used in full view of anyone who cares to notice. Food stamps are what Goffman has termed "stigma symbols." Using them forces a welfare recipient to publicly acknowledge her devalued status; her use of welfare becomes a highly visible attribute. She becomes, in the eyes of the public, a "welfare mother" with all the negative connotations that title evokes. One African American woman named Lonnie, who has been on and off of welfare several times, and most recently has received welfare for two years, revealed the hostilities she encountered in the grocery store when using food stamps:

> And I've went in the grocery store, and when you get ready to buy your groceries, people have made nasty little remarks about the groceries you're buying. They'll go, "We're paying for that." Once there was some university students and I guess they felt like that. They had a small amount in their buggy, and I had large amounts. He started talking, so his girlfriend kept trying to get him to be quiet. And he kept talking and talking. And then he said, "That's why the president is trying to cut off welfare because of people like that!" I turned to him and I say, I say, "Well, you know something? I have worked in my time too. And I will work again. It's not like I'm asking you for anything. And I hope you don't come and ask me for anything 'cause with me and my five kids I couldn't give you none anyway!" And he stomped out of there when I told him that. But I was being honest with him. I have worked. I felt real bad that day, I really did.

Cashiers and others who are looking for evidence of fraud or abuse closely scrutinize the foods that women purchase. "Welfare mothers who purchase steak with food stamps" is a classic metaphor used by many people to illustrate the supposed fraud and abuse within the food stamp program. One woman in our study described how the fellow students in her class at the community college believed the stereotypes about women on welfare, and criticized them for buying "steaks or shrimp with food stamps." The assumption is made that welfare mothers live "high on the hog" at taxpayer expense and must be closely monitored in order to prevent irresponsible behavior and abuse of the system.

One woman told us about an actual experience purchasing a steak with food stamps. She described the critical responses she received by other shoppers in line who witnessed it. Acknowledging that she was feeding the stereotype, she tried to not let it bother her:

> I did have this instance where I was in the store, and I was buying groceries, and I got a thin three dollar steak, and this lady behind me said, "It must be nice to be able to buy steak. I can't afford to buy steak with my money!" And the lady behind her said, "Well, if you were on food stamps, you could afford to buy two or three steaks!" And I just shook my head. It really didn't bother me, because I was, like, as long as I can feed my kids, I don't care what people say. And if food stamps help me buy my kids a steak every now and then, then so be it . . . I don't look at what somebody else gets and say, "Oh look what they got? A steak or pork chops." That's their business.

Using food stamps or other "stigma symbols" requires women to give up their privacy and their choices. Their lives, their shopping habits, and their food preferences are closely scrutinized. Welfare critics are quick to judge their spending habits as inappropriate and wasteful, and look for examples of this to verify these assumptions. They look for women who buy steak with food stamps, and are vindicated when they find them. Yes, she purchased a steak, but in order to do so, what else did she give up? In what other ways did she scrimp and save during the rest of the month? Purchasing a month's worth of food on the food stamp allotment provided to families takes resourcefulness and ingenuity. At a funding level of approximately 75 cents per person, per meal, wastefulness is unlikely.

The women interviewed responded in a variety of ways to using food stamps. Some were embarrassed about using them, and preferred to shop only in specific stores where they felt welcome. It was generally common knowledge which stores have cashiers who are less sympathetic to food stamps, and women tried to avoid shopping there. Other women were more defensive, saying, "What do they want us to do, starve?"

Interestingly, another common context, other than grocery stores, in which negative comments were routinely heard was the welfare office itself. Rather then being viewed as a place for help, the welfare office is viewed with disdain. It is run by people who are seen as self-serving and who have contempt for their clients. The caseworkers are the gatekeepers to welfare, and many welfare recipients resent this, and believe that caseworkers take their function far too seriously, "They act like it's their own money they're giving away." Women commonly reported ill feelings toward their caseworker. Two women specifically suggested caseworkers should be community volunteers or representatives from churches to insure that caseworkers' first concerns were humanitarian, rather than simply viewing welfare and welfare recipients as a routine and boring job. Welfare recipients felt demeaned by their caseworkers: "They think you ain't much of nothing . . . ," "They try and make you feel bad and say little mean things . . . ," "Some of them talk to you like dirt . . . ," were frequent comments. As one mother, a 41-year-old white woman named Denise, revealed:

> Some of them treat you like you got to take this, "Because I got your case in my hand and I'm the one who decides whether you get these stamps." And some of them talk to you like dirt and some of them are all right. It's like they have no respect for you, but you have to take it because you need it. You need that check, you need that Medicaid. It's like, if you make them mad, you can hang it up, because you ain't going to get it! One lady said, "I have 30 days to approve your case or not." It didn't matter if you had kids or not. I've heard some of the workers talk to the elderly people and some of them talk to the elderly people so bad. And they don't care, it's like, "I got my job."

Amy is a 23-year-old white mother of one child who attends a university full-time and plans to go to graduate school. She will earn her bachelor's degree next year, and plans to get a master's degree in physical therapy. She told me about her experience going into the welfare office to meet with her caseworker:

> It's a very humiliating experience—being on welfare and being involved in the system. You are treated as though you are the scum of the earth. A stupid, lazy, nasty person. How dare you take this money? It's a very unpleasant experience. I'd avoid it at all costs. But unfortunately, I can't avoid it right now.

Recipients felt stigmatized and discriminated against in other ways as well. They felt mistreated by public health clinics, for example. Several women mentioned that they have to sit many hours in the waiting room before being seen, or that doctors and nurses talk "down" to them, as though they are too ignorant to understand basic medical or health terminology. Others talked about the stigma they experience when applying for a job and revealing that they currently receive welfare. They felt that they had been denied job opportunities because they were labeled as "stupid" for being on welfare. Kim, a 29-year-old African American mother of three children, is employed part-time, and told me that she is diligently looking for full-time employment. She talked about her frustration in dealing with people when applying for jobs:

> Yeah, people in employment offices, when you go looking for a job and say you're on AFDC, they automatically look at you and assume you're a dummy, "Here's another drop out." . . . If you put all this stuff down on your application they, like, double question you about the information, like you're lying. And I don't think that's fair. I don't think that you should be judged, just for being on AFDC.

Other contexts in which stigma and discrimination occurred were more personalized. Women told me that their friends, neighbors, boyfriends, or family members were sometimes extremely critical of their use of welfare. Many told me of their anxiety with telling certain people, or of the ways in which they tried to keep it a secret from them.

But perhaps the disapproval from family, friends, or acquaintances hit the children the hardest. They don't understand the societal disapproval heaped on their families. Dawn revealed a story in which her daughter, unsuspecting that food stamps were stigmatized, pulled one out of her backpack on the school bus. She was teased unmercifully by her school mates, "the kids picked on her so bad, she came home crying." Likewise, Sheila's daughter Melanie, who was introduced in Chapter 1, is shy and a loner, and Sheila attributes this to feeling self-conscious among her peers at school about being poor and on welfare. "That's why she, Melanie now, she's a loner too. When she comes in that door, she don't go back outside." Criticism from peers is especially difficult for children and teens; peers are an important reference group. Teens, in particular, spend an inordinate amount of time trying to look, dress, and behave in certain ways that reflect those of the peer group. Criticism from them is a painful and blatant reminder of the stigma attached to welfare.

Managing Stigma

How do women on welfare feel about such sentiment levied at themselves and their families? Many of the women who were interviewed volunteered that derogatory comments were painful to hear, "It makes me feel bad," "It's just discouraging," "It's a humiliating experience," "Some days it kind of hurts your feelings. You think, oh, they really hate us."

How do women cope with or manage the stigma of being on welfare? As Goffman (1963) suggests, for someone with a known stigma, the basic problem is managing the tension produced by the fact that people know of the problem. For someone who is effectively hiding their stigma, the problem is in managing information so that the problem remains unknown to the audience. But it is difficult to completely hide being on welfare. One can hide it in some contexts, such as with friends, family members, and with neighbors unless living in the housing projects. But it is revealed in other contexts, such as in grocery stores when using food stamps or in the welfare office when waiting in line for recertification or to pick up stamps.

During the course of interviewing women, it became apparent that they used one or more of four primary strategies for coping with the stigma attached to using welfare. These four strategies were: (1) denial, (2) distancing themselves from other women who used welfare, (3) blaming external forces and thus denying that using welfare was their fault, and (4) extolling the importance of motherhood. Each of these is discussed in the following sections.

Denial

As is the case with other types of stigmas, some women denied that they had encountered negative sentiment against them. Ten women, including both African Americans and whites, said that neither they nor their children have ever experienced stigma or discrimination because of being on welfare. Denying that it occurred frees women from feeling bad, guilty, or embarrassed. Half of these women, however, followed their denial with statements such as, "and I don't listen to it anyhow," indicating that they had indeed heard such comments, but chose to deny them or dismiss them as irrelevant to themselves. Kim told me how she dismisses and ignores the comments or innuendoes that she receives:

> I'm trying to make it. So whatever opinion you have, just keep it to yourself. I don't, I guess I haven't ran into nobody who really said anything about it because it really don't matter to me. Right now, I know what I got to do, so just leave me alone.

Several women suggested that people had been especially kind to them when they revealed to others that they were on welfare. For example, one woman reported that clerks in stores steered her to special in-store savings or pointed out cheaper brands to buy.

Denial also took another important form. A few women seemed genuinely unaware of the stigma levied at welfare recipients. They were perplexed when they were asked what kinds of things they had heard said about welfare recipients, and didn't quite know what was meant by the question because most or all of their social network of family and friends also received welfare. They didn't feel stigmatized because they rarely interacted with people who weren't receiving welfare. These women likely lived in one of the several large housing projects, they associated primarily with other women who receive welfare, and they shopped at the neighborhood store that is considered "user friendly" to welfare recipients by offering such services as quick check cashing and day-old baked goods at reduced prices. One mother with two children reflected on her homogenous network:

> The majority of the black females that I hang around with are on welfare also. Except for one, and she doesn't have a child. She's my best friend, and her mother used to be on it, so, you know, it's all the same. Everyone is treated equal.

Comments such as these lend some credence to the Culture of Poverty perspectives. For these few women at least, welfare use was normative and ceased being stigmatized. They successfully eschew the stigma associated with welfare by avoiding people or places where stigma is likely to be encountered. It is important to acknowledge that, for a small number of women, welfare use may be viewed as common, rather than the exception. But unfortunately, it is this small group that receives the most media attention, despite their relatively modest number within the welfare population. It gives the general public the exaggerated and false notion, a racialized one, that the majority of welfare recipients live within a separate subculture, with values that are at odds with hardworking Americans.

Distancing Themselves from Other Welfare Recipients

Drawing upon the Individualistic and Culture of Poverty themes, a second strategy for managing the stigma associated with welfare use was distancing themselves from other welfare recipients. Some women made a concerted effort to identify themselves with higher economic classes, such as the middle class. Several women said they do not let other people know they are on welfare, "I tell people I receive aid from the state," leaving the source of the aid vague. One 42-year-old African American woman named Treena, who also received welfare as a child for a brief period when her father was in jail, told me:

> I don't really tell a lot of people that I'm on AFDC. Not that I'm getting anything much. But I don't, you know. Because I dress myself up and I look nice once I'm dressed up. And I carry myself in a professional manner, and I try to be professional and respectful and go about my business.

It makes a lot of difference to other people, especially those that got something. It does. It makes a difference, it really does.

Women talked about buying their children expensive, popular brand athletic shoes so that no one will know they receive welfare. One African American mother in particular commented that dressing as to appear middle class, such as buying name brand clothing and shoes, was very important in keeping her sons away from drug dealers who are known to offer young children these items as a way to entice them to sell drugs for them. Although it takes a sizable chunk out of her monthly budget, it is worth it in order to "pass" as middle class. She and her son lived in the housing projects, and she commented that drugs and drug dealers were commonplace.

Others try to disassociate themselves from women on welfare by criticizing and blaming them for their own economic circumstances. I found that women on welfare sounded much like the more affluent; they blamed other poor women for their own economic circumstances. Drawing upon the Individual perspective, the narratives revealed that they attributed other women's poverty and use of welfare to that person's own: (1) laziness, (2) drug use, (3) lack of human capital, (4) personal choice, or (5) other personal shortcomings or irresponsible behavior.

Janie is a 19-year-old white mother of a two-year-old child who characterizes the Individual perspective. She lives in an apartment that is not subsidized and has a roommate to share expenses. The apartment is in good repair, although her furnishings are modest and sparse. Despite being only 19, Janie has been living virtually on her own for years. She ran away from home as a young teenager, lived on the streets for a period of time, stayed in shelters, and more recently has shared apartments with one or two other people. Janie was gang raped several years ago, and she became pregnant as a result. She decided to keep the baby, and turned to welfare for help. Janie has received welfare since her daughter was born two years ago, but, like others I interviewed, is convinced that welfare is just a temporary step in her otherwise busy, confused, and complicated life. She hopes to be off the system within a year or two, after she pays off her bills and "gets established." But she feels that many others who receive assistance are far less motivated than she is:

> There are some people on welfare who don't need to be on welfare. They can go out and get a job. They have nothing better to do than to live off of welfare and to live off the system. I'm sorry. I have no sympathy. Look at all the signs on the road, "Will work for food." Go down to Day Labor, for crying out loud. They'll pay you more money than you can make in a regular day. It's by choice. Either (1) they don't want to work, (2) they are being supported by others, or (3) they don't give a damn about themselves.

Sheri is a 27-year-old African American with three children who has been on welfare for seven years. She referred back to the idea that people on welfare are lazy. She clearly did not include herself in this category, despite the fact that outsiders may be concerned over her supposed long-term welfare "dependency."

I think a lot of them are on it just to be on it. Lazy. Don't want to do nothing. Lot of them on it 'cause a lot of them are on drugs. Keep having kids to get more money, more food stamps. Now that's abusing the system. And a lot of women are abusing the system.

She, like other woman on welfare, distanced herself from other recipients physically, emotionally, or both. Clear distinctions were drawn between "me" and "them." Many women believed that other women did not deserve to receive welfare, were bad mothers who neglected their children, or in other ways committed fraud or deliberately abused the system. Even Dawn prefers to distance herself from other welfare recipients:

I think some people are lazy. Some people, umm, it's like passed down, and that's how they think. They think that's how it is supposed to be. Some people are lazy. Some people are uneducated, and you can't really get the—yes you can. Yes, you can get a job. I think some people are lazy and they just want some kind of income. Not everybody just sits around. But some people do. I think the people who are just sitting around are lazy, to tell you the truth.

Several women, both African American and white, admitted that they didn't know anyone who committed fraud or abuse personally, but claimed that "there are a lot of people like that out there." They subscribe to the common perception of welfare mothers, even though this perception contradicts their own personal experience, and contradicts the lives of other women they know personally.

Forty-seven-year-old Mary, who is white, expressed concern over the fraud she believes is committed by welfare recipients, African Americans in particular. Mary is separated from her husband and receives welfare for one of her seven children who still resides in the home. She has worked most of her life as a waitress and cashier, but has several health problems that she feels prevent her now from working. She comments that she just "knows" people are being fraudulent, even though she acknowledges that she doesn't personally know anyone who is.

MARY: How can they afford to drive fancy new cars and fancy—excuse me, there's a lot of blacks wearing $100 shoes that I can't even afford to buy my daughter a $10 pair. Now, you tell me what is wrong with that picture.

INTERVIEWER: And you know these cases?

MARY: Not personally. But you can walk down the street, or go to the food stamp office or the welfare office and see who drives up in the fancy cars and the new fancy clothes and stuff. You tell me.

Concern about fraud and abuse of the system transcends racial prejudice and discrimination. Tamara, a 31-year-old African American woman with three children, voiced a similar, albeit less racially charged concern about fraud and abuse.

> TAMARA: A lot of those mothers on AFDC get food stamps and stuff, and take the stamps and sell them. If not, they'll take the money and, you know, buy crack and leave the kids hungry, and they don't have clothes to put on, and shoes to wear. Once they're on drugs, they'll do anything to get them.
>
> INTERVIEWER: Do you know of any cases where people are actually doing this?
>
> TAMARA: I've heard of some people, but, uh . . . . It's happening everywhere.

It appears that women on welfare subscribe to the popular Individual perspective to explain poverty and welfare use—at least to explain why other women use welfare. They assume that other women are poor and on welfare primarily through their own doing, and that they lack incentive and motivation to improve their economic circumstances. The women interviewed want to distance themselves as far as possible from other recipients.

I found that recipients also draw on Cultural of Poverty metaphors to distance themselves from other women who are on welfare. They invoked images of a separate subculture in which these other welfare mothers and their families live. It is a subculture with separate values, norms, and cultural milieu. The themes which emerged from the narratives revolved around such subcultural issues as: (1) women who rely on welfare for the long-term as a "way of life," (2) intergenerational welfare use, (3) unmarried teenagers who have babies and assume that welfare will take care of them, (4) women who have additional children simply to increase the amount of their welfare benefits, and (5) the cultural milieu in the projects. Again, recipients distanced themselves from these cultural contexts, and in doing so voiced that they have little in common with other recipients.

First, Amy characterized the concern that some people see welfare as a way of life. She, like the others, sees her situation as unique and different from the norm, despite the fact that many welfare recipients are in school obtaining further education or vocational training in order to increase their opportunities for social mobility. Our sample was obtained in a region in which an experimental welfare reform program was being implemented. It provided educational opportunities and an extensive array of incentives, such as assistance with transportation and childcare, for the women who were randomly selected, and who agreed to participate in the program. Thus, an unusually high percentage of welfare recipients in the region, including 40 percent of our sample, were in school or vocational training. Yet, this young mother, working towards a college degree in a health field, insisted that her situation was distinctly different from the norm:

> Well, there are people like me who are using it as a means to make ends meet while they are preparing to support themselves. And I think we are a pretty small number. I think that there are those people for whom welfare and AFDC are a way of life. Their parents were on it, their parent's par-

ents were on it, and this is how they live. I think they are not the majority, but I think they exist.

Second, many women, both African American and white, were alarmed by intergenerational welfare use. Some claimed to know families in which the mothers and then the daughters received welfare, referring to it as "a cycle that keeps on going." They suggested that young girls need to be educated about the difficulties of raising children, and that they be told that welfare is likely to be changed in the future and cannot be relied on to help them. In reality, the number of people who are affected by intergenerational welfare use is quite small. As shown in Chapter 1, national data indicate that half of all women on welfare have used it for two years or less, and fewer than one out of five recipients uses welfare for five years or longer, continuously. Although there is considerable movement on and off welfare, it is likely that only a modest number of these women use welfare for decades and within multigenerations. Nonetheless, many welfare recipients, as is the case with the more affluent, exaggerate the frequency of intergenerational welfare use and are concerned that it is widespread.

Third, concern and anger were also expressed over young unmarried teenage girls who have babies and automatically assume that welfare will support them. A Culture of Poverty, of sorts, was alluded to—that young girls haven't been taught that reliance on welfare is not a good thing. Interestingly, older women who also had babies out of wedlock while they were teenagers often voiced this concern. For example, Dawn told me, "I think some girls have a certain amount of babies just to get a check. I'm not sure." Kim, a 29-year-old African American, expressed both disgust and concern over the epidemic of teenage pregnancy and their subsequent reliance on welfare. Yet Kim had her first of three children when she was 17 years of age, a teenager herself. Despite being in similar circumstances, she distanced herself from the behavior of teenagers today. She expressed concern over the fact that many young girls want to get pregnant and rely on welfare. Kim saw herself as different from others: very ambitious and working hard to try to improve her situation for herself and her three children. She had recently finished a community college program, and was trying to secure full-time employment during the day while her children were in school. At the time of the interview she was working at a part-time job with hours during the late afternoon and early evening, a schedule that she felt interfered with her responsibilities as a mother. She commented:

> These girls are having babies younger and younger, and I say it's more to having a baby than just getting a check and some food stamps. A lot of people. I say they shouldn't even give them a check until they graduate. 'Cause a lot of them, that's all they are waiting for . . . and they just steadily having babies. They having babies at 12 and 13. They aren't even at a legal age to get a job.

Kim's concerns are not unfounded, at least in part. Births occurring out of wedlock have increased dramatically during the past few decades, increasing from 22 percent of all births in 1985 to 33 percent of all births in 1994 (U.S. Bureau of the Census, 1997b, Table 96, p. 78). The increase is particularly acute among white women. It is incorrect to attribute this increase solely to teenagers, however, as Kim and others were inclined to do. Although the number of births to unmarried teenage women increased from 272,000 to 393,000 between 1980 and 1994, this rate of increase, at 45 percent, is small compared to the whopping 450 percent increase in unmarried births among women who are older than age 35 (U.S. Bureau of the Census, 1997b, Table 97, p. 79). However, births among unmarried older women are generally seen as less problematic because they are more likely to have completed their education, have work experience, and are less likely to need welfare to support themselves and their children. Still, it's important to note that, in 1992, 42 percent of families on AFDC included children who had been born to a teenage mother. This figure has remained relatively stable since the 1970s despite concerns voiced by Kim and others about the growing number of teens on welfare (General Accounting Office, 1994).

Fourth, a controversial issue, with passionate arguments on both sides, was whether women continue to have children simply to increase the size of their welfare check. This is a prominent component of President Clinton's welfare reform, as it is popularly believed that poor women have additional children so that they will receive increased welfare benefits. Some women argued adamantly that a $50 per month increase in benefit level would not be enough to encourage a person to have additional children. For example, Molly, a white woman with three children, who also attends community college, disagreed with the widely held perception that women have children to increase their welfare check:

> When I was taking my sociology class at [Community College], we had this talk, and it sickened me some of the things people were saying. They were not true. You can't generalize and say that everyone is the same, "She has babies so she can have this extra money to live on!" I don't think I've met anybody who wanted to be on welfare.

Many respondents, however, felt differently, and argued that other women do have additional children to increase the size of "the check," as it is routinely referred to. As a 28-year-old African American mother with four children claimed:

> A lot of people are saying that the only reason that they are having a baby is to get money from the system. And nine times out of ten it's true. Because I know a lot of young girls that are pregnant and having babies. I try to talk to them, and say in the future welfare is going to be cut out, it's going to be cut out for everybody. So why go out, why have a baby and risk getting the AIDS virus? Why risk all that, your life and health and everything just so you can get on welfare? I don't understand that.

A 42-year-old African American mother of two young children, Kate, voiced a similar sentiment:

INTERVIEWER: I think some lawmakers think that women on AFDC have more children just. . . .

KATE: Just to get more AFDC. I believe that too. I really believe that too. But not me. No. Some women are just breeders.

INTERVIEWER: They're just breeders? What does that mean?

KATE: They like to have babies. If they don't go get themselves stopped, they'll just keep having them. If it were me, I wouldn't have no more babies just to get more AFDC. No.

INTERVIEWER: But you do think some people do it?

KATE: Yeah, I do. I really do.

Again, we can see how women on welfare distanced themselves from others who received aid. Kate, and others, distinguishes between "me" and "them." Other welfare recipients are viewed as having deviant values and engaging in negative behaviors that fuel their dependence on welfare.

Finally, the cultural milieu in the housing projects was also of considerable concern. The majority of our respondents lived in housing subsidized by the government. There are several types of federal housing programs: (1) public housing, which generally consists of high rises and "garden apartment" rental units owned and operated by public housing authorities; (2) Section 8 certificates, which allow tenants to rent in the private market, with tenants' paying 30 percent of their income and public housing authorities paying the remainder; and (3) project-based Section 8, which is not administered by the public housing authorities (Barry, 1998). Owners maintain their own waiting lists, and within federal guidelines, decide who gets admitted.

There is a serious shortage of low-income housing for those who need it. Only one-third of those families eligible receives any form of low-income housing. And for the first time in the last two decades, there has been a decline in subsidized housing units. In 1995, Congress cut Housing and Urban Development (HUD) funding by 25 percent. It cut funding for the construction of new family units, and it did not pay to increase the pool of available Section 8 certificates. Congress also reduced funding to restore and refurnish older buildings, thus ensuring that more units will deteriorate, and eventually will be destroyed. Equally important, Congress also eliminated the "one-for-one" replacement rule, which required that a new unit be built for every unit demolished (Barry, 1998).

A few women who participated in this study, such as Dawn, lived in single-family homes, by far the most desirable of the subsidized housing available. Others lived in small apartment complexes, sometimes integrated with other residents who were not on public assistance. This too was considered a desirable alternative to the large housing projects. Generally, there were waiting lists for these types of arrangements. Instead, the most common type of subsidized housing, and the one in which more than one-quarter of our respondents, primarily African Americans, resided at the time of the interview, were the public housing projects. These large, often multilevel structures were home to hundreds of families, all of whom were on welfare. They were characterized by the women who live in them as noisy, lacking in privacy, in disrepair, full of loiterers, and as breeding grounds for drug use and other illegal activities.

Many respondents dreamed about the day they would be in a financial position to leave the project—"I'm saying to my boyfriend, if you love me, get me out of here." They expressed surprise, concern, and contempt that their neighbors often seemed to be satisfied living there. One African American woman, Coreen, who attends community college with the hope of someday becoming a teacher, described the cultural milieu she experienced in the projects. She currently lives in a very large multistory housing project, moving there because her mother's house was too crowded for her and her baby. On the Saturday afternoon that I was there, I noticed a large number of men hanging around in the breezeways and on the porches despite the fact that the housing was for welfare recipients, that is, women and their children. When I knocked on her door, she would not open it until I gave her complete information about who I was. She wasn't being unfriendly, just cautious. As she told me later, crime and drugs are commonplace.

> I live out here, and this place really puts you down. A lot of people don't realize about living in projects, it puts you down. I mean, because you have no one to encourage you to get out. If you try to accomplish or achieve anything, then you must think you are better than them and they won't like you. You have people here in the projects who always compete with you about how your house looks, but they won't compete with you about trying to get out of here. You know what I'm saying? Don't compete with me because of my apartment, compete with me with school, compete with me about trying to get out of here. Let's try to race to get out, you know? Some people just don't want to get out.

Because Coreen felt that she had little in common with the hundreds of other families in her project, she did not socialize with neighbors, usually kept her curtains closed, and generally did not allow her young daughter to play outside. This was a common strategy to cope with problems encountered with the high density living in the projects. Other women told us that they also refused to socialize with neighbors, "they just some jealous-hearted people around here, they evil-hearted, and that's why I stay in my house."

What effects might this living environment have on a family? A team of researchers at Northwestern University found that when poor African American single-parent families were given the opportunity to move out of their crime-ridden urban housing projects and into white suburbs, the children's school performance improved dramatically, and mothers were more likely to become financially self-sufficient (*San Francisco Chronicle*, Feb. 22, 1993). Class position, and its resulting environment, affects one's opportunities, self-esteem, and achievements—both adults and children—in ways that we can only begin to know.

Women distanced themselves from other welfare recipients in a variety of ways, drawing on both Individual and Cultural of Poverty perspectives. Although recognizing in the abstract that there may be a multitude of reasons that bring women to the welfare system, most recipients were also quick to cite individual blame. Other women who receive welfare were often portrayed as lazy, unmotivated, or as cheating the system. They were described as living in a separate subculture with differing values and norms. These images are so strong that the women interviewed subscribed to them even if they did not personally know anyone who fit these profiles.

Blaming External Forces: "It's Not My Fault"

The third way in which women managed the stigma associated with welfare is by disregarding it because they believed that their present status was the result of social factors outside of their control. They generally felt that they were on welfare through no fault of their own, and therefore were not really to blame. They were more likely to invoke Structural or Fatalist perspectives to explain their welfare use. As will be shown in Chapter 4, their concerns with the social structure were based primarily on factors such as a lack of jobs paying a living wage; lack of good quality and affordable day care; lack of father involvement and child support enforcement; inadequate transportation systems; broader problems in our social structure such as racism or sexism; and a welfare system that penalizes women for their initiative by eliminating their welfare benefits. They also told me of needing welfare because of bad luck and unfortunate circumstances, such as a relationship gone awry. Sometimes these relationships turned violent. Overall, women voiced that they simply couldn't help turning to welfare; structural problems were in their way, or they were a victim of unfortunate and unplanned circumstances, and "were between a rock and a hard place," "doing what I have to do" to survive. Some women were very articulate, and told us outright of racial or gender discrimination, for example. Others were more vague, and explained "something is kinda like holding me down."

In only a few cases did respondents fail to distance themselves from other women. In these few cases respondents suggested that the social structure or unfortunate events are the primary reason why most other women also receive welfare. They defended welfare recipients as a collective group when they were being attacked, often referring to welfare recipients as "we."

However, most of the women interviewed distanced themselves from other recipients while simultaneously blaming their own welfare use on forces beyond their control. It appears that using these two coping methods were not mutually exclusive. Overall, women generally felt that they were on welfare through no fault of their own, but other recipients were often responsible for their own economic plight.

Extolling the Importance of Motherhood

A fourth strategy for managing the stigma associated with receiving welfare was extolling the importance of their roles as mothers. This provided a personal validation of the work they do in the home as the sole caretakers of their children. When they were asked to name one of their "strengths" or something that they were particularly good at or proud of, the most common answer was "I'm a good mother." Being a competent mother, which was defined as someone who invested a considerable amount of time in the direct care for children, was a highly valued social identity. Dawn told us about the perplexing problem of how to be a "good mother" while going to school, and then being forced to work at the same time because of welfare reforms:

> If I go to school, and have to work, then what happens to my kids? Every time I'm taking from one, I'm taking from another. And my kids are very important to me. I don't want them to grow up on the system. I don't want them growing up on the streets and acting like little hoodlums, and not knowing that education is important. Even though what I did is differ-ent from what I want for them, I always want them to be a better person than me. So I want to be there for them. I want to be there to make sure they're doing their homework. I want, personally to be there. If I have to work, I'll work at night, I guess. It's not good at all.

The dominant cultural ideology of motherhood is embodied in two common images (Thurer, 1994). One is the full-time domestic mother whose primary job is taking care of her family's needs. She is solely responsible for the social, emotional, and physical care of her children. Others, presumably fathers, will provide for their financial needs. The second image is the employed professional "supermom" who successfully juggles her children's needs with the demands of full-time employment or with her own self-fulfillment. Her image is regularly featured on the covers of magazines—with briefcase in one hand, and baby in the other.

Both images are race and class-biased, despite the fact that, as cultural ideolo-gies, they presume to reflect all women's experience. Both perpetuate the assumption that mothers are the primary adults responsible for child care. And finally, both im-ages portray motherhood as an isolated, individual activity; even competing employ-ment and family demands are handled privately. The United States, as compared to Canada, Western Europe, and many other countries throughout the world, has weak family support policies (Bergmann, 1996). Instead, mothers are encouraged to de-velop individual coping strategies to relieve stress.

It has been argued that a somewhat different ideology surrounding motherhood exists among many African Americans (Collins, 1994, 1990) and other minority groups (Segura, 1994). For example, motherhood among African Americans may be less privatized. "Mother" is a powerful figure; a leader in her community, her church, and among other children as well as her own. Motherhood may not be connected to simply one woman based on a biological tie. Instead, "the boundaries distinguishing biological mothers of children from other women who care for children are often fluid and changing" (Collins, 1994: 168). As we saw in the opening segment of this chapter, Dawn and her mother have a more collectivist orientation to parenting. Dawn's mother was raising one of her biological children, just as her grandmother had raised her. Grandmothers can also "mother."

I witnessed each of these three images among the women interviewed, both Af-rican American and white, although the supermom ideology emerged least often be-tween both groups. Sometimes these images occurred in conjunction with one another. Being a "good mother" involved different things to different women, but the common theme was putting children's needs first. Others report similar conclusions: Like the more affluent, women on welfare adhere to the value placed on the importance of the family. Poor women usually place the highest priority on meeting the financial and emotional needs of their children (Berrick, 1995; Edin and Lein, 1997; Rank, 1994). Several of the women I interviewed bragged about not putting their children in day care or turning them over to baby-sitters, especially those women who had young children who were not yet in school. Although many women simultaneously said that they wanted to work, they also praised the importance of staying home to care for their children. Being a "good mother" was the most important occupation of all. Becky, who is the mother of a four year old, commented about the guilt she felt at leaving her son with baby-sitters when she left the house for various house cleaning jobs:

> He cried when I left him in the morning, and I didn't like that. I felt like I should be home with him. I worked for about a year. It got too stressful—with trying to work and all the problems, and trying to, you know, be a good mother. So I gave up.

Working interfered with her attempts to fit the dominant cultural identity: To be a stay-at-home mother who devotes herself fully to her child's physical, emotional, and physical needs. But in this case, there is no father or husband available to take care of their financial needs. She therefore, turned to the state for aid.

One African American woman interviewed, when asked if she ever had a job, curtly replied, "Yes, I take care of my children." Another told me that she felt no guilt in receiving welfare, "This is my paycheck," her remuneration for raising children. As Jarrett (1996) also found, our recipients believed that their ability to manage the challenges of single parenthood elevated their status. They proudly told me of nurturing and teaching young children, of helping older children with their school work, and of trying to keep their teenagers busy and out of trouble. They were hesitant to leave their children alone for any period of time. Most women and their children lived in sections of town with high crime rates. Drug use and drug dealing were common in the large housing projects, I was told. Women did not trust their neighbors. Thus, being a "good mother" was defined by many as staying home to take care of their children themselves, including watching out the window for them to come home off the school bus safely. Although they said that they also wanted to work, women, particularly those with young children, often saw their role first and foremost as providing direct care for their children. Being the family's breadwinner was secondary in importance.

This priority contradicts the changing norms regarding women's roles, as outlined in Chapter 2. Although programs like AFDC were originally created to allow single mothers the ability to stay home and raise their children, the norms about women's roles are in a state of flux. What does it mean to be a "good mother" in the 21st century? The old image of a stay-at-home mom in the kitchen wearing an apron as she bakes cookies for her family no longer fits the economic realities or personal inclinations of most families today. Most women have to, or want to, work outside the home. Our current ideologies suggest that you can be a "good mother" and also be employed. But, it is more difficult to be both a "good mother" and be employed when you are impoverished and therefore cannot buy the amenities that the more affluent families use in order to cope with dual demands. When you have no money for take-out fast food on the nights you are too tired to cook, when you must go to the laundromat twice a week because you cannot afford your own washer and dryer, when you have to leave young children home alone sometimes because you cannot always afford a baby-sitter or round up someone to watch them for free, and when you and your children must rely on the bus for transportation because you cannot afford a reliable car, the glamour of both a career and motherhood begins to vanish. It is reasonable to suggest that the stresses of being both a "good mother" and a full-time employee are compounded by not only poverty, but by being the sole parent—of having no one else to rely on and share the burden and responsibilities.

Many of the tensions in the welfare debate revolve around our expectations of single mothers: Should their priority be to earn a living, or should it be to provide direct physical and emotional care to their children? Although the more affluent suggest that the former should now be the number one priority—that women who receive welfare should get a job—not all women on welfare see the issue so simply. Recognizing the dangers lurking in their neighborhoods, the stresses on children who have only one parent, and the restricted job opportunities and the subsequent low pay they will likely receive, it was common for women on welfare to, instead, glorify the virtues of motherhood rather than the virtues of full-time employment. This was particularly noted among those mothers with young children.

These four mechanisms for managing the stigma associated with welfare: (1) denial, (2) distancing, (3) blaming external forces, and (4) extolling motherhood, were commonplace. They occurred alone or in combination with each other. Women used these strategies to regain a semblance of dignity and self-respect. They are well aware of the negative connotations associated with welfare use: That they are lazy, unmotivated, bad mothers, and that they have no desire to work or otherwise improve their economic circumstances. To keep from adopting these depictions, women on welfare invent ways to merge their "virtual" and "actual" social identities (Goffman, 1963).

Dawn, our previously introduced "stereotypical welfare mother," was very conscious of the stigma and negative sentiment surrounding women and families who receive welfare benefits. She coped with the stigma of welfare primarily by extolling the virtues of motherhood. She is proud of the fact that she stayed at home while her children were young—nurturing and socializing them. She shared "motherhood"—at least the care of her son—with her own mother. And she is a "good mother" herself. There is no ideological conflict here. Yet Dawn would probably evoke little empathy on first glance. We are quick to blame her for her own predicament and wonder, "Why doesn't she go get a job?" We imply that she is lazy or not sufficiently motivated—she has been spoiled by welfare.

Yet our conversation revealed a depth and richness to her life and to her circumstances that are easily overlooked in the zealous quest to reform welfare. She told me of her determination to one day be self-sufficient. Dawn wants to "make it." Toward this goal she attends school full-time to learn business and computer skills that she hopes will one day help her acquire a job as a secretary or an office manager. She wakes up at 6:30 every day, getting herself and her family organized for school. She has no car of her own, so she makes the significant daily trek to school on the city bus.

> My grandmother, bless her heart. She was religious all her life. She died in subsidized housing. She didn't own nothing. She wasn't very educated, and I don't want to be like that. God knows I don't want to be like that. I want to have something to leave behind.

Dawn is 31 years old, has teenage children, and her youngest child is now 10. They are therefore more independent now, and require less direct care from her. They can participate in cooking, cleaning, and other chores so that Dawn may go to school. She feels that she's been on welfare too long already, but she insists that it has taken this long to get her family ready for her extended absences from home. She has been a "good mother," and is now ready for and eagerly looks forward to a life of employment. She hopes that by getting an education, she will be able to find more satisfying work, a job that she will stick with. She shares the same mainstream values as many other Americans. She believes that education is important and will help to find a good job—but all in all, taking care of one's children is the most important job of all.

> I always say, "I don't want my kids to be like this." I was brought up as an AFDC kid. I feel like I've been on it all my life. I really do, and it's real depressing when you think about it. But I don't know. We might have been even poorer if it wasn't for it. It's not easy, and it's not much. I hear a lot of girls say, "They only give me this amount and I don't have enough to do this." But I don't feel like that. They're not supposed to be taking care of me. This is like a supplement. Appreciate what they give you. They don't owe us, you know? That's just how I feel about AFDC. . . . That's why I'm trying to go to school and do this. I've put my mind to it. I know I've waited a long time. But I feel like I can still do this [get off welfare].

CHAPTER

4

Why Welfare?

Why do women use welfare? Given the stigma that surrounds welfare use and the negative perception of welfare mothers, we might wonder why women would choose to receive welfare. Perhaps they are lazy. Perhaps they lack motivation. Or do they seek welfare out of desperation?

As we saw in Chapter 3, women on welfare often disassociate themselves from other welfare recipients. They were critical of the reasons that other women received aid, and often portrayed other recipients in a despairing light. This chapter explores the reasons that women give for why they need welfare, and seeks to explain the discrepancy between these reasons and those afforded to other women. I found that recipients tend to attribute their own welfare use to circumstances that are largely beyond their control. They need welfare, they told me, because "there are no jobs"; "how can I take care of all my kids and work too?"; "I would be fine if he would just pay child support"; "I was raped"; "I was beaten and abused"; "he deserted us, and I'm trying to get my feet on the ground"; "I'm trying to better myself"; "the welfare system penalizes me if I get a job." In the lives of women, these are not small or trivial reasons.

Rhonda, like most women interviewed, believes that she has little in common with other welfare recipients. She says that she knows many other women who receive welfare for their families whom they raise alone: her friends, her neighbors, and her son's father's family. She perceives that they "enjoy" being on welfare and ". . . getting everything handed to them." But what about herself and her son? Why is she on welfare? Her situation is entirely different, she told me. She elaborated on the circumstances that brought her to welfare. She said that she can't find a permanent job, and told me her son has a chronic medical condition. Exactly how is her situation different? Despite her belief that her circumstances are highly unusual, her story has a familiar ring to it.

Rhonda is a 28-year-old white woman with a five-year-old son named Bobby, who is in kindergarten. She has been off and on welfare for four years since her son was born. Rhonda remains in contact with Bobby's father, who lives out of state; he is a truckdriver and visits his son regularly once each month. During that visit he will take Bobby out, buy him clothes, and take him to dinner at McDonalds. He, however, does not pay child support. Rhonda and Bobby's father remain cordial, and she appreciates the monthly visits, clothing, and dinners for her son. She expects little else from Bobby's father, financially or otherwise, and receives little else.

Rhonda and her son's father never married. They were romantically involved, but the relationship ended shortly before Bobby was born. After the birth of her son, she lived with her mother briefly. But it was difficult having two families under one small roof. Rhonda wanted to be on her own, so she applied for welfare.

When I interviewed Rhonda, she and Bobby had recently moved from a trailer to an apartment within a subsidized housing project. They had lived there for six months, and she detested it. Neither she nor her son socialize with neighbors; they were abusive to her son, she told me. She also believes that most of them are criminals, dependent on the system, and have no interest in "bettering themselves."

The apartment in which Rhonda and Bobby live is cramped, dingy, and run down. There is no carpeting, just dark brown linoleum that is peeling in many places. Two chairs, one end table, and a television are about all that fit in her tiny living room. She stays in the projects because, after losing her job, the $11 monthly rent is all she can afford. A sizeable chunk of her $241 welfare check goes for utilities, which cost approximately $140 a month, because her apartment is poorly insulated. Heat and air conditioning (nearly a requirement in Florida's sweltering six-month summers) escape through the windows and door cracks. After paying for car insurance ($22 a month), cleaning supplies, laundry soap, and other miscellaneous expenses, Rhonda has little money left over. When her budget permits, she buys clothes for her son, who is growing rapidly, often from the Salvation Army or Goodwill. She has no opportunity to save money.

Rhonda does not see herself as dependent on the welfare system. During the four years she has been off and on welfare, she has held a variety of jobs. She has worked in the housekeeping department of a hospital, as a cashier, at a warehouse where she sorted lids for a printing company, and she recently ran a day care center out of her home. She took great pride in her day care center and claimed it was her ideal job, and one that she would like to try again someday. She enjoys young children, although is quick to point out that she does not intend to have any more. Having children around the house taught her son Bobby responsibility, and her job did not take her away from Bobby for eight or nine hours a day. Like other women who were interviewed, and consistent with the views of women with greater financial means, an ideal job was seen as one that interfered as little as possible with her responsibilities as a single parent. Unfortunately, Rhonda was forced to close her day care because many of her clients were considerably delinquent in paying their child care bills. Unable to force them to pay the money they owed her, Rhonda wasn't able to keep up with her own bills, and thus was forced to close her business.

Rhonda told me that she "hates welfare." Then why is she receiving it? She, like so many others before and after her, told of having a very difficult time finding a permanent job that pays well enough for her to take care of her family. She had an easier time securing employment when she lived in Maryland. She moved to Florida to be near her sister and father, but has had a difficult time finding a full-time permanent job in a university town. Moreover, her job options are limited; Rhonda quit school in the 10th grade, eventually earning her GED after Bobby was born. She says she actively looks for work, but usually can only find temporary jobs that expire after a period of several months. Rhonda told me that she desperately wants to work because she sees it as a ticket to a better life for her and Bobby. Because he's now enrolled in school, she will not have to shell out the $200 a month for day care like she used to do. A job, she believes, holds promise for a better life. She enthusiastically told me about a job lead she had from her sister. A nearby factory may be hiring more than 20 new people, and she is hopeful that she will be one of them. She submitted her application last week. She knows that by securing a job, her rent will go up, her welfare check will be eliminated, and her food stamps will likely be significantly reduced. She acknowledges that these are "disadvantages" but she insists that she prefers "to be out working, meeting people, you know. Making it better for me and my son."

Rhonda sees herself as different from others on welfare. She described this difference to me:

> A lot of my friends are on welfare. But see, they enjoy getting the check and I don't. They have a different view of welfare than I do. You know, they've been on it for 8 to 12 years, and I've only been on it for four. They can go without things, and it don't bother them. Every time I go off welfare and go to work, it's like they condemn me for it. It's not easy going off and on. But it's like you got to face the real world. They don't look ahead. They haven't come to terms that they're going to cut welfare.

Rhonda is concerned, however, about losing her medical benefits. As a welfare recipient she receives virtually free medical care for herself and Bobby. Finding a job that would provide medical benefits poses a challenge. But given Bobby's condition, medical benefits are of paramount importance, and she ranks them as her most critical welfare benefit. Bobby suffers from lead-paint poisoning. As a baby he ingested paint peeling off a wall in a house they rented. Lead-paint poisoning is a serious and common problem in old, dilapidated structures that the poor often inhabit. An estimated 3 million poor children may be at risk of impaired physical and mental development related to ingesting lead-based paint flaking off the walls of older homes (Needleman, Schell, Bellinger, Leviton, and Allred, 1990). Low-income preschoolers are three times more likely than children living in moderate income families to have lead levels in their bloodstream of at least 10 micrograms of lead per deciliter of blood, a level at which harmful effects have been noted. Lead exposure damages the brain and central nervous system. Consequently, one study reported that second grade children with high levels of lead in their bloodstream were six times more likely to have a reading disability, had significantly lower IQ rates, and lower scores on vocabulary tests. When researchers followed these children over time, they noted that the children were seven times more likely to drop out of high school (Children's Defense Fund, 1998, 1994). Bobby continues to suffer from the poisoning several years after ingesting it. He endures frequent pain, and during these episodes is lethargic and without an appetite. His flare-ups occur every few months, and physicians closely monitor him. He continues to be in and out of the hospital with regularity.

Despite what Rhonda may think, her situation is fairly typical. She receives no child support from her son's father. She has difficulty finding permanent work with pay sufficient to pull her above the level she would be at if she stayed home and received welfare. Moreover, a job necessitates that she will lose most of her welfare benefits, including Medicaid. Given the health problems in her family, losing medical benefits is a steep price to pay for a minimum wage job. Despite her insistence that she will be off of welfare very shortly, would we be surprised to find that she later returned to the system?

The truth is that Rhonda is on welfare because of structural problems more so than personal shortcomings. She is not lacking in personal drive or initiative. Since having a baby she has earned a GED and has opened her own business—impressive accomplishments for someone who is the sole parent to a young child, a child with a serious illness. She describes one of her personal strengths as being "responsible. I've made accomplishments along the way." Rhonda ingeniously sought to combine work and motherhood so that she could excel at both, and neither would suffer. She struggled as a small business owner, as do many small business owners, until she was forced to close her business because of clients who refused to pay their bills. Rhonda is hardworking and is motivated to improve her circumstances in life. In these ways, she is quite typical of many women I met who receive welfare. Despite her thinking to the contrary, she was not the exceptional case.

Women on welfare, including Rhonda, largely point to two general explanations identified in Chapter 2, to explain their own use of welfare: They cite the problems inherent in our social structure, and they cite fate. Neither perspective focuses on the individual as much as the external forces largely outside of her control. A structural perspective attributes poverty and welfare use to economic or social imbalances that restrict opportunities for some people. Fatalism assumes that poverty and welfare use can be traced to bad luck, unpredictable quirks of human nature, or simply to chance. As we saw in Chapter 3, these explanations generally are not accorded to other welfare recipients. They are, however, used routinely by recipients to elucidate why they themselves receive aid.

The Influence of Social Structure

Women on welfare commonly attributed their reliance on welfare to problems and concerns related to the way our social structure is organized. Their concerns, they told me, primarily revolved around: (1) a lack of jobs paying a living wage; (2) a lack of good quality and affordable daycare; (3) a lack of father involvement and child support enforcement; (4) inadequate transportation systems; (5) broader problems in our social structure, such as racism or sexism; and (6) a welfare system that penalizes women for initiative and eliminates their welfare benefits prematurely. Each of these concerns is discussed in the following sections.

Employment

Many women talked about the difficulty of finding employment, particularly a job that pays a living wage. Although the unemployment rate in the nation is a relatively low 5.2 percent, many women told me of submitting application after application to

no avail. "You can't make someone hire you," they said. The reason for their difficulty becomes more apparent when we recognize that certain segments of the population have extraordinarily high rates of unemployment, particularly young African
Americans and other minority groups without a high school diploma. In 1997, the
unemployment among African American woman age 15–25 who had not completed
high school was 22 percent. Those young women who had a high school diploma
fared only slightly better at 19.7 percent (Bernstein, 1997; Herbert, 1997). With these
high rates of unemployment, it is not surprising that women have difficulty securing
employment. Searching for work and coming up with nothing is a demoralizing experience. Consequently, some women quit looking for a job after many unsuccessful attempts.

One woman, Cassandra, told me of her frustration after applying for job after
job with no luck at landing one. Her responsibilities related to taking care of her
home and her children are not considered legitimate work experience, even for service sector occupations. She described her frustration after applying for a job as a cus-
todian.

> I even applied for custodial work at the university, and I know I'm quali-
> fied to sweep floors. And the lady even told me at the desk that I'd be
> competing with people who already have experience in this area. Now, I
> know I'm qualified to sweep floors. If I'm going to do it at home for free, I
> might as well get paid to do it.

Sarah, a white 30-year-old divorced mother who, after an extended job search,
finally landed a part-time job at a fast food franchise while also attending college in
pursuit of an Associate of Arts (AA) degree. She commented on her difficulty in finding even minimum wage work. She has many years of experience, including as a manager in the fast food industry. She wondered if her difficulty in finding work was
caused by the fact that she has been on Workman's Compensation, and therefore was
viewed as a high risk by potential employers. But too many others voiced similar complaints for her case to be an isolated incident.

> It is very hard to find a job. Because people are picky and some of these
> places, you'll only get a job if you know someone. I spent a year looking
> for a job, and Colonel Sanders was the first place to hire me. I've gone
> places, because when you are on Workman's Comp you have to fill out a
> list every month, and how many jobs you've applied in. I've applied for 20
> to 100 a month. And this was the first place that even contacted me in a
> year. It's not that I'm not qualified. I've had 6 years of management.

Moreover, when women do find work, most are employed in service sector jobs,
such as the fast food industry, which generally pay minimum wage and offer no fringe
benefits. Fast food franchises such as Wendy's, McDonalds, Burger King, Hardees,
and several others offer the most recurrent avenues of employment to women on welfare. They generally do not require a high school diploma or extensive experience.

Yet, despite their possibilities, these jobs do not pay enough to support a family or even pull them above the poverty line. At $5.50 an hour, working 40 hours per week yields approximately $900 per month before taxes. Working 52 weeks a year, an employee would average around $11,800 per year. For even the smallest families who have only one child, living and surviving on minimum wage poses a challenge.

Yet many women were eager to take on this challenge. They told me that they want to work, and enthusiastically told me about leads or tips that they had heard regarding which businesses were hiring, and at how much pay. Although most women did not shun minimum wage jobs, jobs that paid $8 an hour or more were highly sought after. Women felt confident that they could live on the nearly $16,000 a year that such jobs would provide. Several women told me that they heard the postal service might be hiring—the postal service is notorious for paying "good money." Three other women told me about jobs in the nearby jails or prisons that also offer wages substantially higher than minimum wage.

> They are hiring and so I want to submit my application for this corrections job. They pay $5 an hour to start out with the training. Then, when you get past the correctional course, then you go to the prison and you start working. But they don't pay $5 an hour for being a correctional officer. They pay more than that. They pay you about $9 or $10 an hour! Plus benefits. See, I'm looking for where the money is at!

In 1997 there were 3,100 welfare recipients in the region in which the interviews were conducted on the list to move from welfare to work. On year later, in early 1998, the figure had dropped to about 2,000. The welfare rolls had been reduced. Some women found jobs, but, there is no tracking system to find out if those individuals are still working and where they are working, according to Richard Cunningham, Chair of the Work and Gain Economic Self-sufficiency Coalition (WAGES)—Florida's welfare reform law—which is responsible for implementing WAGES in the area (Chandler, January 8, 1998). It is easy to reduce the number of people on welfare; simply make them ineligible for benefits after two or three years, as federal law now mandates. In this sleight of hand, statistics can be pulled out and dangled to the public showing that welfare use, thus poverty itself, has declined. This, however, is incorrect. Explored more fully in Chapter 8, we see that the true extent of poverty will not decline until the poor are paid higher wages for the work that they do, and that working conditions change significantly to provide stable, reliable employment complete with critical fringe benefits.

Child Care

The question of who will care for children is one of the most pressing and perplexing questions of our time. If we expect poor single mothers to be employed, who then, will care for, socialize, nurture, discipline, play with, teach, and love their children? And how much will this cost, both financially and socially? "There is no more important job than raising a child," claimed President Clinton, as he recently insisted that parents should not have to choose between their jobs and their children. In 1998, he proposed a record investment in childcare—$22 billion over five years to make care more affordable, accessible, and safe. The money was requested to help parents and businesses pay for care through tax credits; to improve the quality of care by giving states money to improve safety inspections, conduct research, and provide scholarships to students training to be childcare workers; to expand Head Start programs to low-income youngsters, including doubling to 80,000 the number of infants and toddlers in a new program called Early Head Start; and to increase the availability of after-school care (Enda, January 8, 1998).

Concern over the lack of safe and affordable child care emerged as a common structural reason why women turned to or remained on welfare. They know that children need more than custodial care in large and crowded day care centers in order to thrive. Yet for most poor and working class families, child care is often patched together in a fashion that leaves mothers anxious. Some told me that they did not feel comfortable leaving their children with strangers. They preferred to depend on other family members. National data from the Survey of Income and Program Participation (SIPP) reveal that 53 percent of children whose mothers work and also receive AFDC are taken care of by a relative (usually a grandparent), 17 percent are taken care of by a nonrelative in a family-based care setting, and 20 percent are cared for in formal day care settings (Burns, Ballew, Yi, and Mountford, 1996). A significantly higher number of AFDC mothers who have child care needs rely on relatives than do other low-income single mothers (53 percent versus 37 percent, respectively). Although extended families are the preferred child care provider, women acknowledged that their mothers, sisters, or other relatives could not always be counted on. They have their own family responsibilities and obligations, and cannot always provide day care when needed. But living in high-density and high-crime areas, they worried about the safety of their children in day care centers or with other babysitters that they did not know well. "I'm not going to leave him with someone I don't know until he's old enough to tell me what happened." Thirty-two states do not require teachers in child care centers to have completed any training, and 39 states do not require family child care providers to have completed any training prior to serving children (Children's Defense Fund, 1998). And mothers worried about the psychological effects of inadequate care—crowded, dirty, or impersonal conditions—on their children. These concerns have largely been overlooked in quantitative studies that simply focus on the availability of day care—are there enough day care slots for the children who need them? These in-depth interviews reveal that an important reason that women elect to receive welfare rather than work is because they do not trust the care of their children to strangers. The availability of day care slots is not the primary consideration; rather, it is the quality of day care that is most imperative.

Moreover, mothers worried about the cost of day care. Unless a program within the welfare office subsidized child care, costs for child care within the interview area approximated $300 to $500 a month, depending on the type of care provided. The size of an AFDC grant for a mother and one child in the region is $241 a month, obviously making full-time child care an impossibility, prompting many women to comment, "I had to quit—the money went to the baby-sitter." Child care costs vary dramatically across the country, with costs in many communities in Florida being well below average costs in other communities, yet still beyond the reach of most poor and low-income families. A recent study that compared child care costs in six communities around the nation found that average annual costs for care of a two year old ranged from $3,100 in Birmingham, Alabama, to almost $8,100 in Boulder, Colorado (Clark and Long, 1995). Not surprisingly, then, a study sponsored by Wellesley College found that more than 15 percent of low-income parents reported that their 4- to 7-year-old children regularly spent time all by themselves or in the care of a sibling under the age of 12 (Alter, 1998). Their parents cannot afford the costs of child care.

Moreover, Rhonda, who has a GED, reminded us that jobs in the service sector required evening and weekend hours, when child care might not be available. Her son Bobby is only five years old, far too young to remain at home alone at night while she works.

> My hardest problem is—I can find a job—it's trying to work around my son. On weekends I ain't got nobody on weekends to watch him. Like my sister, she's busy with her own kids. And my dad, he's kind of a senior citizen, you know. And that's the only problem I have. It's like they always want nights and weekends. See I can do days while he's in school, you know. It's hard.

National data reported in the Monthly Labor Review indicate that Rhonda's concerns are well-founded (Presser and Cox, 1997). Women with only high school diplomas or less are disproportionately found working irregular schedules that include night and weekend shifts, and varying hours. Forty-three percent of women with a high school education or less work at least some weekend days or have varying shifts, compared with 36 percent of women who have more than a high school education. Most women do not work these schedules out of personal inclination, but because these are the required working conditions of their jobs, such as cashier, maids, nursing aids, cooks, and waitresses. Moreover, these occupations are likely to grow in the future. Working in these types of jobs has important implications for the availability and costs of formal child care. It also affects the degree to which family, friends, and neighbors are able to provide child care. Sociologists Harriet Presser and Amy Cox reveal:

> To the extent that mothers who receive AFDC do not wish to work during nonstandard times, but find that it is their only job opportunity, many will have to find childcare arrangements that are complex and far from optimal. Reliance on grandmothers and other family members may be an option, but these relatives are often themselves employed, leading to complex split-shift arrangements that may be stressful or temporary only. For mothers who have school-aged children, school cannot function as an alternative to childcare. Furthermore, the little we know about the availability of formal childcare during nonstandard times suggests that it is a rare option. Moreover, formal childcare during nonstandard times is likely to be more expensive than during standard times. In sum, the childcare issue is clearly problematic. (1997, pp. 32–33)

Child care is not simply an issue for mothers of young children. Mothers with older, school-age children also face considerable dilemmas about how to juggle employment and parental responsibilities. Low-income children are less likely to live in neighborhoods that have before and after school programs. Only 33 percent of schools in low-income neighborhoods had these school programs, compared to more than 50 percent of schools in more affluent neighborhoods (Alter, 1998; U.S. Department of Education, 1994). Yet these programs have been shown to help low-income students perform better academically, and they help improve student conduct and study habits (Posner and Vandell, 1994). Unfortunately, the average cost of after school care to parents is $45 a week, or more than $2,000 a year, which is beyond the means of many who need it the most (Alter, 1998).

Some mothers interviewed suggested that parenting is more time consuming and labor intensive as children become teenagers. Peer pressure is strong, including pressure to act out and behave in destructive ways. They feared that their children would get into trouble with the law; that they might use, abuse, or sell drugs; that they may get pregnant or impregnate others; or that they may drop out of school. Mothers here, as well as those responding to nationwide studies, clamored for more organized activities for their school-age children (Center for Research on Women, 1996; Meyers and Kyle, 1996). Moreover, because they are the sole parent to their children, they have no one to share the burden and responsibilities of child care. They do not have a spouse, and generally they cannot rely on the father of their children for assistance or relief from their duties.

Women on welfare juggle their employment and parental responsibilities in a variety of ways, but one aspect was very clear: Their children are more important than any specific job. Their jobs were seen as "work"; they were not careers, with the degree of commitment that careers entail. Although "work" was considered important psychologically and financially, under no circumstances should it interfere significantly with family responsibilities. Their first and foremost responsibility was perceived as being a "good mother" to their children. So, how do women on welfare reconcile being good mothers with working? Many women did not want to work before their children were in preschool. Some women refused work that entailed weekends when their children were out of school. Others preferred to work the night shift so that they could be home in the afternoons to help their children with their homework after school. Some women wanted to work in the afternoons so that they could get their children up and off to school. Others insisted that they could only work part-time so that they could be available to their children in the morning and at night. And finally, other women pursued or dreamed of work that allowed them to stay at home, such as Rhonda's child care center, or several other women's stated desire to be cosmetologists working out of their home. The structure of the desired workday or setting may differ significantly, but the underlying theme is that work should be built around their family schedule and important family events, rather than vice versa. This, however, is not easily accomplished.

One woman, Cassie, revealed a strong preference for working the night shift, leaving her children home alone at night despite the fact that they are only 12, 9, 8, and 6 years of age. Although some people might abhor the thought of leaving children this age alone at night, she saw it as the best possible alternative because it allowed her to spend her days with them. She further explained that her oldest daughter has experience getting the kids up and ready for school. All her children chip in with chores and are very responsible, she elaborated.

> I'd rather work at night. I could be home with my kids when they get home from school. Yeah, I'd have the whole afternoon to be with them. It's from 12 midnight to eight. And at midnight I'd be gone to work, I'd come home at eight and get me some sleep. And when they come home I'll be fresh and ready to go again. . . . My daughter was getting them up when I worked at [fast food franchise], and she was not but nine. Eight or nine. I had to be at work at six o'clock in the morning, so I would call home and she would be up, and everybody would be up and ready to go to school. I taught her to help me, and that's what she's been doing.

Fathers' Involvement

A third structural problem cited was the lack of involvement on the part of the children's fathers. Fathers' participation in the emotional or financial upbringing of their children was noticeably absent in the vast majority of cases I interviewed. Absentee fathers represent a growing and alarming national trend. As described more thoroughly in Chapter 6, since 1988 the government has stepped up its efforts to enforce court-ordered child support with the passage of the Family Support Act (P.L. 100-485). Despite more coordinated efforts, half of fathers who are court ordered to provide child support payments do not pay the full amount regularly (U.S. Bureau of the Census, 1997b, Table 609, p. 389).

In order to receive cash assistance, federal law requires recipients to assign their support rights to the state. They must cooperate with the state in establishing paternity of a child born outside of marriage, and in obtaining child support payments. The women I interviewed were required to report the name and whereabouts of the fathers of their children, if known, when they signed up for welfare. When the children's fathers did pay child support, the money went to the welfare agency, and mothers were given an additional fifty dollars per month in their check. This fifty dollars is disregarded in benefit calculations, and is designed to serve as an incentive to provide information on the children's fathers to the welfare agency, just in case women are reluctant to do so. Yet, despite the mandatory ruling that fathers be identified, the apparent eagerness of women to comply with this ruling, and the welfare agency's supposed vigorous search for the fathers, the majority of the women interviewed continued to receive no or very sporadic child support. Some women resented this. They resented the freedom that their children's fathers' have while they themselves are stigmatized for receiving welfare. A divorced African American mother who received welfare for her two children responded typically to my question as to whether she received child support.

No, I don't. And with my ex-husband, he was court ordered to pay child support. He works. But I don't get child support from him. They have money—they can go out and buy themselves cars and they can save money in the bank, but they're not supporting their kids. And I don't like it. I don't think the government should have to take care of a man's kids, especially if he can take care of his own kids. I don't understand it. They are so hard on us, but where is my child support? My kids deserve that money.

She and many others acknowledged that mothers on welfare are stigmatized for caring for their children, whereas fathers are rarely stigmatized for their failure to support their children. Pearl, likewise, summarized the sentiment of many when she expressed that their fathers' resistance to paying child support has cheated her children. She is a 48-year-old African American woman who is divorced. Pearl has born eight children, three of whom still reside in the home and receive welfare. They live in the housing projects, where she has lived for 25 years. Pearl's life has been hard. She only finished school to the 8th grade, quitting so that she could work as a farm laborer and help support her siblings. She's been married twice, divorced because of her husbands' continual infidelity. She has worked on and off for most of her life—hard jobs, such as farm laborer and housecleaner. Now alone, she dreams about taking her younger children out of the projects to live in the country where she envisions a safer life for them, free from the pressures of drugs and dropping out of school. The likelihood of her dream materializing is extremely slim. She complained of health problems, and has not held a job in many years. The father of her older children is in prison, as are her two oldest sons. The father of the younger children previously contributed to their support, but quit paying child support a few years prior to this interview. He remarried, "He figured he got a new wife and shouldn't have to pay," she told me. Pearl continued:

All my kids' daddies owe child support. I used to talk to their daddies about that. I said, well, if you would have been willing to help take care of your kids, they would have had a living and wouldn't have had to been on welfare.

In Chapter 6, I elaborate on the reasons that child support enforcement policies have met with limited success and have not significantly reduced the number of children in poverty. Until the dismal trends in child support are altered through stricter enforcement, and through changing norms of greater paternal involvement, it will be very difficult for many women to fully support their children on their own without additional assistance.

Transportation

It also became clear in the interviews that transportation was a major structural barrier to women getting or keeping jobs. Past recipients of Job Opportunities and Basic

Skills (JOBS) programs report that the lack of affordable transportation presents a barrier even more serious than the lack of child care to securing employment (Kaplan, 1998). Women on welfare cannot afford to buy reliable automobiles. Those few women who owned newer models likely received them as gifts from family members or boyfriends. Often they did not put the car in their name, hiding it from the welfare office even if they were the sole driver, because it would jeopardize their welfare benefits. The personal asset value of an automobile (value minus debt) must be less than $1,500; otherwise it disqualifies one for welfare. This poses a dilemma for a rational person— how can I find and maintain a respectable job if I am not allowed to have reliable (e.g., more expensive) transportation? Most women who had cars, even those exceeding the maximum asset level, owned older models that were in a constant state of disrepair. One woman explained that her car, although a necessity in many respects, also assisted in keeping her poor, "It's either your tires, or extra gas, or a part tearing up on your car. No, I can never really get caught up." Obviously, women on welfare are not driving Cadillacs.

Public transportation and walking are the primary alternatives to the private automobile. Although public transportation is available in the largest community in the area in which the interviews were conducted, women complained that it was expensive ($1, plus an additional 25¢ per transfer), unreliable, and inconvenient. They reported long waits, and complained that they had to wait even longer to transfer to a second bus in order to get to their destination. Bus service was reduced or eliminated on weekends or at night. Moreover, public transportation, even with all its logistic problems, was completely unavailable in some of the smaller communities within the county.

Bicycling or walking was the primary mode of transportation for some women, or had been in the past. Tamela, a 23-year-old African American woman with two young children, told me how she used to put them in a wagon and walk to the grocery store and to do other errands. But communities built since the 1950s are often spread out, not geared toward pedestrians or public transportation systems, but geared instead toward private automobile ownership. A strong, central, vibrant downtown area for work, shopping, and entertainment are memories of a bygone era in most communities. Instead, numerous "strip malls" are spread throughout the city limits and fringe areas. Sidewalks may not exist, traffic whizzes by at 45 or more miles per hour, and without a central core, walking, bicycling, or relying on public transportation becomes difficult and inconvenient. Although offhand it is easy to say, "you can walk to work," reality may dictate something else. In many communities walking to work can be more than just inconvenient, it can be dangerous or impractical. Walking through high-crime neighborhoods or crossing highways, especially at night, poses special dangers. Walking can add an hour or two to child care bills, and may necessitate being away from one's children for 9, 10, or 11 hours a day instead of the usual 8. Moreover, in inclement weather, such as heavy rains or snow, it is impractical to expect women to walk for miles and still appear freshly groomed and ready for work. Life without a car is difficult in most cities and towns in the United States. Even with the best intentions, it is not surprising that women without cars find it difficult to maintain steady work.

Several women revealed to us elaborate transportation logistics that allowed them to work or go to school, including commutes of an hour to an hour and a half each way. One African American mother, Dee, who is studying to become an accountant, lives five miles from campus and described her transportation ordeal using the city bus:

> I leave here by 6:45 to get to school at 8:00. So that's an hour and fifteen minutes. I leave school at 2:00 to get home by 4:00, so that's two hours. So that's three hours and fifteen minutes I spend. If I had a car I could leave here at 7:30 and be there by 8:00. And then I have three-hour breaks in between so I could be home relaxing or doing something.

Transportation problems prevent many women from seeking work altogether, and they inhibit other women from staying at their job. Several women told me that they quit otherwise "good" jobs because of inadequate transportation schemes. When they worked at night, after the buses stopped running, they were forced to rely on friends, family, or a taxicab service for rides home after work. Friends and family, although well meaning, were sometimes unreliable. Taxis were expensive. Consequently, the risk of job failure increases, often becoming an eventuality. Many might ask, why try?

> I just had a job in September where I worked six days. But I had to quit my job because I had to pay transportation. And transportation was costing me, like $40 a week. Sometimes at night it was difficult because the shift that I was working was 3:00 to 12:00—3:00 in the afternoon to 12:00 at night. And a lot of people don't want to get up and come get you. So, I had to quit the job because of the transportation costs that I had to pay.

In this instance, and several others like it, a recipient sought work despite the obstacles, explored alternative transportation with some optimism, and finally quit because of rational personal economics. People who have always had reliable personal automobiles often overlook the magnitude of this issue for many would-be workers. Growing urban sprawl increases the likelihood of distance to the workplace, and therefore reduces the likelihood of regularly getting to a job without a personal automobile.

Racism and Sexism

Racism and sexism are unpleasant realities in our polarized society. The famous tennis star, Authur Ashe, before dying of AIDS in 1993, disagreed with a reporter who assumed that AIDS must be the heaviest burden he has ever had to bear. "No, it isn't," Ashe told the reporter. "Being black is the greatest burden I've had to bear. Having to live as a minority in America. . . . because of what we as a people have experienced historically in America, and what we as individuals experience each and every day" (Ashe and Rampersad, 1994: 139–141). Likewise the social construction of gender permeates all aspects of life, and people continually distinguish between males and females and evaluate them differently. It is difficult to escape both racism and sexism.

Racism and sexism generally have three components: (1) negative attitudes toward minority group members or toward women; (2) stereotypical beliefs that reinforce, complement, or justify the prejudice; and (3) discrimination—acts that exclude, distance, or segregate minorities or women (Lott, 1994). These components can be blatant or more subtle. Blatant racism and sexism can take the form of not being hired in the first place, being passed over for a job promotion or a pay raise, or being fired prematurely. A few African American women told us directly that racism had hindered their ability to get, or keep, a good paying job. One woman spoke of her neighbor in the housing project who "has a problem with, excuse my language, white people. They did her real bad."

Racism and sexism can also be more subtle, and this form is sometimes referred to as "institutional" racism or sexism. Patterns of inequality may be woven into the fabric of society, so that it becomes institutionalized, or normative. It may be imbedded in our culture or our social policy and often goes unnoticed. When pointed out, sometimes people will fail to grasp its significance. For example, job opportunities for women are limited in ways that men's generally are not, in part because of structural barriers, but also because of the ways women are socialized. Women may not seek training in the higher paying skilled trades, for example, because they have been taught that these are "unfeminine" occupations.

Stephanie, a 26-year-old mother who is in the nursing program at the university, explicitly acknowledged that sexism as well as racism were likely to limit opportunities for social mobility. She is the mother of one young daughter, and is attuned to issues of social inequality. Like many of the women I interviewed, she was married when she had her daughter, and assumed that her marriage would last forever. Instead, after a painful divorce, her husband has never once paid child support or contacted his daughter.

> Why are people on welfare? There have to be at least a thousand reasons why people are on welfare. Like I tell my daughter, life isn't fair. Things happen. And you have to do the best you can. There are lots of socioeconomic groups in this country, races, blacks, Hispanics, women who don't really have the same opportunities that most people consider normal opportunities. I mean, for myself, look who got stuck taking care of the child?

The Welfare System Breeds "Dependence" on the System

Finally, a recurring theme in the narratives was that the welfare system itself is responsible for their reliance on welfare. A few respondents felt that the welfare system can indeed make people get lazy and lose their motivation to work, as some social conservatives have argued. A 29-year-old African American woman with three children who has been on and off the system repeatedly said:

> Sometimes I think people get a little too satisfied with it and stay on it a little longer than they should. Once you start getting this check they way we do, you get a little lazy sometimes.

However, the majority of women who expressed concerns with the welfare system said it wasn't that it made recipients lazy *per se*, but rather that the welfare system had built-in disincentives or penalties for work. Working, especially at minimum wage jobs that usually lack health insurance and other critical benefits, would not achieve their goals of self-sufficiency, and in fact would jeopardize the health and well-being of their children because they would lose critically needed benefits. Moreover, as good mothers, they said, they would never want to jeopardize their children's well-being. From these interviews, it became clear that without continued assistance with (1) health insurance, (2) child care, (3) transportation, (4) food stamps, and (5) subsidized housing, working becomes not only prohibitive, but sometimes was seen as downright dangerous. Many women claimed that they want to work, or that they could find a job, or even that they had a job previously, but felt compelled to quit because working and the automatic reduction in their welfare benefits actually lowered their standard of living or jeopardized their children's health. They expressed frustration that the welfare system, as currently structured, actually discourages them from working by raising their rent, eliminating Medicaid, and cutting them off of needed social services before they had a chance to establish themselves. Jo Lynn, a mother of two young children, claimed:

> I've had a job before, and I know I can get a job. It's just really hard. It's like, I got a job at Hardee's [fast food franchise] and I had a friend take me back and forth. I was paying her $20 a week for gas. I got off the system. I was honest about it and told them I had a job. They took my assistance away, and they raised my rent $200. And they said they weren't going to give me any Medicaid for them either, and I didn't have any health insurance. I had a baby at the time, and she was only a year old. She had to go to the periodic appointments and stuff, and I was like, "Okay, well I'm going to try to do it." And I had to work there six months to a year to get health insurance. I was really scared, like, what am I going to do? But I'm gonna do it. So I started doing it, and then I started realizing that, you know, that after about two months, I was *under* the welfare level. I mean, by making minimum wage I couldn't keep my bills up, and I could never afford to take her to the doctor. It wasn't getting me ahead. I was being penalized for trying to get off the system, and it's happened to all my friends that are on welfare. It's like a trap, and they don't help.

Jo Lynn did what our society expects of welfare mothers—she found a job. But with that job, her financial picture became even more bleak. She told me it caused her to be "under the welfare level." Jo's situation was not an isolated case. Therefore, without considerable change in the welfare system and the structure of low-tier work, what hope is there for her and for other mothers trying to get off welfare?

Concern about losing Medicaid was commonly expressed. Medicaid is a program designed to pay the health care costs of the poor. Not all poor are eligible for Medicaid, however. Like other welfare benefits, Medicaid has specific eligibility requirements, some of which are established at the state level. Today, less than 50 percent of the poor are covered by Medicaid, down from 71 percent in 1975 (Lewin, 1991). Each state is required to extend Medicaid to recipients of Aid to Families with Dependent Children (AFDC), and now Temporary Assistance to Needy Families (TANF), and to recipients of Supplemental Security Income (SSI), which covers the impoverished elderly and the disabled. However, it is up to state discretion whether to cover others who are impoverished, such as the homeless or the working poor. Medicaid benefits are a primary reason why women stayed on welfare as long as they have. If they leave welfare, they risk joining the ranks of the uninsured. More than 37 million Americans, or 18 percent of the population, have no health insurance from any source whatsoever (U.S. Department of Health and Human Services, 1996). Nearly three-quarters of these individuals are employed or are the dependents of an employed adult, usually working at a low-wage, part-time, or temporary position. More than 10 million of the uninsured are children under age 15. Another 25 to 48 million people are "underinsured"—meaning that their insurance is inadequate to meet the needs of their family because of extraordinarily high deductibles or copayments, or because certain procedures are not included, or specific family members are not covered.

It is well documented that persons without health insurance or with inadequate insurance use the health care system less frequently than do others, resulting in a variety of negative health outcomes (Children's Defense Fund, 1998; Cornwell, Berne, Belzberg, Asensio, Velmahos, Murray, and Demetriades, 1996; Seccombe, 1995; U.S. Congress, Office of Technology Assessment, 1992). The uninsured are more likely than both privately and publicly insured individuals to lack a usual source of care; to have fewer episodes of inpatient hospital care and lack preventive services; and to report delays in receiving health care. They are less likely to seek prenatal care, more likely to deliver low-birthweight babies, and their children are less likely to receive needed immunizations. They typically seek care at hospital emergency rooms, which are increasingly turning people away and transferring the most serious cases to public hospitals (Cornwell, Berne, Belzberg, Asensio, Velmahos, Murray, and Demetriades, 1996). Consequently, without health insurance, adults and children are more likely to experience unnecessary pain, suffering, disability, and even death. Women on welfare know this. They fear joining the ranks of the uninsured or underinsured if they were to take a job. Stephanie, in school to become a registered nurse, echoed this concern with losing Medicaid. Her daughter has several specific health problems:

> We gripe and we gripe about the fact that we are paying all this money for people who don't seem to be doing very much for themselves, but if you looked at the system from an insider's point of view, you would see that

there are actually penalties built into the system for a person with initiative, going out to get a job, or doing something to try to better themselves. As soon as you earn a buck, they take it away from you. You are penalized if you have any kind of asset whatsoever. You have to be so damn poor that it's not even funny. . . . Next summer in nursing school there are no classes. Yet I can't work. And I will tell you why. I would like to work as a nurses' aide, and that is something I can do with my training that I have had. But I can't afford to lose my benefits, specifically my medical benefits. Because if I went to work, they would cut me off. Even though I would not be making enough to pay my bills, I would be cut off from Medicaid. And I can't afford that, you know? It's part-time, usually a nurses aide gets $5–6 an hour, which is not that much above minimum wage. And you know, you work 20 or 30 hours a week. No health benefits, no nothing. So I can't work. It's not that I don't want to work. I'd love to work. But I can't.

An African American mother of two, who works part-time as a nurses' aide but continues to receive a partial welfare benefit, explains how her benefits were reduced when she began to work:

The thing that gets me, being a single parent, once my income exceeds a certain amount, I'm in a project, and my rent goes up. It has been close to $300 for this [she laughs and sweeps her arms around the room]. And then I have to end up paying expensive childcare, and the Medicaid stops for me and my children. You know, most jobs the health insurance is so expensive you can't afford it. Then, you pretty much be where you started from. You end up with nothing.

These interviews, which are grounded in the real-world receipt of welfare, suggest that the presumed link between social programs and welfare dependency touted by social conservatives is flawed. Yes, on a cursory glance, the welfare system does appear to "reduce" one's incentive to work, but a more thorough examination from an *insider's perspective* reveals that welfare programs do not encourage laziness or dependency. Both white and African American women talked about desperately wanting to work, but felt that employment reduced their already meager standard of living and often placed their children at risk because it eliminated or reduced their eligibility for critical medical and social services. They repeatedly pleaded that the welfare system be changed so as to not penalize them by cutting them off of critically needed services, at least temporarily, while they "pull themselves up by their bootstraps." Rather than being lazy or dependent on the system, they are making the most rational, intelligent choice they can, given their circumstances. These issues will be revisited in Chapter 8, when I further examine the obstacles involved in getting off of welfare.

In summary, these women frequently cited concerns related to the social structure when explaining their welfare use. Problems with finding inexpensive or reliable child care; a scarcity of jobs, particularly those which pay a livable wage; lack of father involvement with their children and ineffective child support policies; inadequate public transportation systems; racism and sexism; and a welfare system that prematurely reduces income and benefits, were recognized as factors that inhibited their upward social mobility.

Fatalism

Bad luck, unfortunate circumstances, and soured relationships—many women alluded to these when asked to explain why they are on welfare. They felt that they simply couldn't help it; they turned to welfare as a way out of a desperate, unplanned, and unfortunate situation.

Bad Luck

For example, many discussed their bad luck at becoming pregnant. Several, who were unmarried teenage girls when they had their first child, told me that they were surprised at becoming pregnant—they didn't know that sexual activity caused pregnancy, or they didn't know that they could get pregnant the first time that they had sexual intercourse. They were confused and unknowledgeable about sex. Many disclosed that they had intercourse as a way to please a boyfriend, or because of peer pressure from their girlfriends at school or in their neighborhoods. They rarely used birth control. Either they didn't know it was necessary, or their partner complained about wearing a condom and they acquiesced to his wishes. When they discovered they were pregnant, they were surprised. How did this happen? Abortion was rarely a consideration among the women interviewed. Instead, these young girls accepted that they somehow got "caught," and they had their babies.

Terri Lynn, the young mother previously introduced who works at the bowling alley to support herself and her six-year-old son, told me of her surprise at becoming pregnant. She did well in high school, and never suspected that it would "happen" to her.

> Sure, I don't want to be on AFDC, but I don't have a choice. You know, I didn't plan to get pregnant with him, but it just happened. You know? I don't want to be on AFDC. I'm going to get off it as soon as I put him in school.

An African American woman with four children commented on the bad luck that young women have in their encounters with young men. Her attitude indicated that teenage pregnancies are unfortunate, but that not much can be done about it. It's acceptable, or at least unavoidable. Her greater concern is with women who have multiple births out of wedlock, but having one child "just happens":

> I know a first baby is a mistake. You know what I'm saying? It happens. You go out there, you young, you have sex. It's a mistake. I mean, they got

birth control methods, but guys are so persuasive about sex these days. Girls don't think about rubbers or birth control. They just think about impressing him, so they have sex. So they get pregnant. If they keep having babies then they should get a job and help support the rest of those kids, but not the first child.

As both women allude to, peer pressure to have sex is powerful and difficult to avoid. One recent study involving 1,000 girls in Atlanta found that 82 percent said the subject they wanted to learn most about in their sex education class was "How to say no without hurting the other person's feelings" (reported in Besharov, 1993). Furthermore, the 1995 Nation Survey of Family Growth found that the younger the girl is at first intercourse the more likely the experience was coercive. Twenty-two percent of girls who had sex before age 13 describe their first experience as "nonvoluntary" (including girls who said they were raped). An additional 49 percent claimed it was "unwanted" (Children's Defense Fund, 1998).

National data indicate that more than 20 percent of 14 year olds have had sexual intercourse, and this increases to 30 percent by age 15, 42 percent by age 16, and up to 59 percent by age 17. Approximately half of women aged 15 to 19 have had sexual intercourse regardless of race, income, religion, or residential location. Nearly one-quarter of teenage women never use contraceptives. Others use contraceptives sporadically. The United States' rate of premarital pregnancy, at 97 pregnancies per 1,000 women under the age of 19, is more than double that of most of western European nations and Canada, nearly three times that of Scandinavian nations, and nearly 10 times that of Japan. Although nearly half of teen pregnancies in the United States are aborted, our birth rate among teens is among the highest in industrialized nations (Forrest and Singh, 1990; McElroy and Moore, 1997; Sonenstein, Pleck, and Ku, 1989). Although the teen birth rate shows signs of reduction, particularly among African Americans, it is still problematically high at 57 births per 1,000 females aged 15–19, compared to 26 in Canada, 11 in Sweden, 9 in France, and 4 in Japan (McElroy and Moore, 1997).

Poor Health

For other women, health concerns interfered with their ability to look for, or keep a job, and thus they continued to rely on welfare. Nearly one-third of women interviewed complained of health problems, including asthma, depression, high blood pressure, or back pain. These figures compare with other larger statewide or national studies that find that many welfare recipients are in poor health. For example, AFDC recipients are nearly three times as likely as other women to report to have poor or fair health (22 percent versus 8 percent, respectively). Furthermore, between 10 and 11 percent of recipients report that they are unable to work because of a disability or serious medical condition. Many other women, approximately one in four, report that they are limited to some degree in the kind or amount of work that they can do. These limitations also carry over into the home. Approximately 8 to 10 percent reported that they need help with or are unable to perform specific functional tasks of daily living, such as dressing, eating, bathing, using the telephone, or walking up stairs, whereas another 12 percent reported that they have some degree of difficulty performing these tasks (Acs, and Loprest, 1995; Loprest and Acs, 1996; Meyers, Lukemeyer, and Smeeding, 1996).

Many other women told us that their children were sickly or had emotional problems, and consequently they did not feel comfortable leaving their children with baby-sitters. Program and caseload data document the high proportion of welfare families with poor health, special needs, or disabilities. In case records, reviews conducted in Colorado, Iowa, and Utah, 15, 18, and 13 percent of the cases, respectively, included documentation noting a child medical or behavioral problem as a potential or actual barrier to participation in work training programs or actual employment (Pavetti and Duke, 1995). Poor children are more likely to suffer a wide array of ailments, both chronic and acute, than are more affluent children (Children's Defense Fund, 1994). For example they are more than three times as likely to be iron deficient; 1.5 times more likely to have frequent diarrhea or colitis; two times more likely to suffer from severe asthma; and 1.5 times more likely to suffer from partial or complete blindness or deafness. These are caused by a variety of prenatal and postnatal factors. One important culprit is that poor children are more often born with a lower birthweight than are other children because of the mother's poor nutrition, lack of prenatal care, stress, youth, insufficient weight gain, or smoking or other drug use. In addition, poor children are also more likely to die. According to the Children's Defense Fund, "poor children are about three times more likely to die during childhood as their non-poor peers" (1994). Thus, the effects of poverty on the health and well-being of children and adults is not exaggerated. They are significant, long-term, and can cause considerable heartache, consternation, and chaos in the lives of families.

Parents whose children have serious or chronic health problems, disabilities, or behavioral problems must attend to a variety of needs, such as multiple doctor appointments, or meeting with school officials. Mothers expressed worry that, should they go off to work, their children would not get the attention, physically and emotionally, that they might need because of their ailments. Jasmine, for example, has a history of working full-time, often at several different jobs in order to make ends meet. She is divorced, and has a 10-year-old daughter who lives with her ex-husband's sister, and a 5-year-old daughter and an infant to care for. Doctor's appointments are routine for Jasmine and her two young children, but they are stressful nonetheless. Both of her children have severe cases of asthma. She's been on welfare for four years, because of "the sickness of the children," she told me. She gives them breathing treatments on and off, as needed. For Jasmine, as was the case with many other women we interviewed, being a "good mother" means being there physically to care for her sick or needy children. Women routinely told us that they did not feel comfortable leaving their sick children in day care, with a baby-sitter, or even with family members for extended hours. They know that they may have to take time off from work to attend to their children. Thirty-two percent of AFDC families report making at least one trip to the emergency room per year, and the figure is 55 percent in families with a severely disabled child (Meyers, Lukemeyer, and Smeeding, 1996). They see, first and foremost, that their job is to provide the direct care that they believe their child needs.

Among the more affluent, these "family values" of placing children's needs before employment would be applauded. Returning to more traditional "family values" is a popular theme espoused by Democrats as well as conservative Republicans. However, among poor women who receive welfare, such values are not applauded; instead, they are suspect.

The Termination of Relationships

A primary reason that women turned to welfare was that a relationship ended and they could not solely support their family. When married or living together, a spouse or partner may have provided an important source of income for the family. When a relationship ends, that income is abruptly halted. Some women find that they are unable to secure a job providing wages above the poverty line. Or they may have no experience working, and do not know how to go about finding a job to support the family. The termination of a relationship was a primary reason that women turned to welfare. Patrice, an African American with two young sons, explained to me the difficulty she experienced when relationships with her children's father ended:

> I prefer to be in a stable family environment. You know, have a husband, and with my children, feel like a family. Because, I have always been pretty much alone after it ended with my children's fathers. One guy I was with for five years. When I got pregnant, he left. It was kind of a shock, and I knew he was financially able for a child because he had been in the military for like 11 years, so it hurt. And I was kind of depressed, moping over that, and, before I knew it, got in another relationship. The other guy just took up with me while I was pregnant and was kind of there for me while I was still depressed about my first relationship. And then, before I knew it I was pregnant again. It just happened so fast. At first he was there for me until I got real big, you know in my pregnancy. Then it seemed like when I started having problems in my pregnancy he wasn't anywhere to be found and I was stuck there by myself. And from that point on, I'm like, if he couldn't be there for me in time of need, he sure didn't need to be there for me once I got on my feet. So I got rid of him, and just stayed by myself for a year before I tried dating again. Tried to make sure that I wasn't vulnerable and that I had recuperated, you know, so I wouldn't be another target. And from that point on it has just been me and my boys ever since.

A 35-year-old divorced African American woman felt that her use of welfare was directly related to her divorce. She told me,

> What made me get on was, I guess, my broken marriage. Because when I was married, I wasn't on AFDC. My husband was employed, and I was working.

The United States has the highest rate of divorce of any country in the world. Our divorce rate rose dramatically in the 1970s and 1980s, and has since declined slightly to 19.8 divorces per 1,000 married women older than age 15 (U.S. Bureau of the Census, 1997b, Table 145, p. 105). Divorce is more prevalent among lower socio-economic classes, despite the economic hardships it creates. One national study of men and women between the ages of 25 and 34 found that people who had only high school diplomas were significantly more likely to divorce than were people who had bachelor's degrees (Glick, 1984). This is caused by a variety of reasons, including younger age at marriage; greater likelihood of premarital pregnancy and childbirth; as well as greater stress, crises, and disruptions in their lives related to economic vulnerability. When people marry young, for example, they are less prepared for marital responsibilities. They are more unhappy about their partners in terms of love, affection, sex, wage earning, companionship, and faithfulness. They also are more likely than their older counterparts to complain that their spouses are moody, jealous, spend money foolishly, or get in trouble with the law (Booth and Edwards, 1985; Teti, Lamb, and Elster, 1987).

African Americans are more likely to divorce than are whites. In 1996, approximately 12 percent of African Americans aged 18 and older were divorced, compared to 9 percent of whites and 8 percent of Hispanics (U.S. Bureau of the Census, 1997b. Table 58, p. 55). The higher divorce rate is caused by many factors, including the fact that African Americans are disproportionately poor or have low incomes, and therefore face many poverty-related stresses. Moreover, they are more likely to marry earlier, have a premarital pregnancy, and have a child born out of wedlock. These factors increase their odds of divorce.

Women and men face different odds of remarriage after a divorce. Men are more likely to remarry, and they remarry more quickly than do women. Lillian Rubin, in her book *Families on the Fault Line* (1994), reinterviewed 32 working-class families 20 years after their original interviews and found that 56 percent of them had divorced sometime during this period. All but one of the men had remarried, and the lone exception was already in a serious relationship after being separated for only a few months. In contrast, Rubin found that divorced women fared differently. They remained single for a longer period of time after a divorce, and more than half needed either welfare or food stamps during this financially difficult period. More than one-third of the women had not remarried. For most of these women, life continued to be a series of economic struggles.

Although both men and women go through financial adjustments after divorce, women's income declines more dramatically than does men's. Although the decline may be less than originally proposed by Lenore Weitzman in her well-publicized book *The Divorce Revolution* (1985), a re-analysis of these data by others confirms her hypothesis that divorce tends to be more financially disruptive to women than men (Peterson, 1996). Women's standard of living declines more than 20 percent after a divorce, whereas men's actually increases, on average. Most women have little experience being the "primary" breadwinner in relationships. When they are forced to do so, while taking care of the children as well, it can be overwhelming. Many women reported that receiving welfare was perceived as a method of regaining control over their lives. It allowed them the opportunity to take stock of their situation, to regroup, to assess their options, or to attend school or find a job. Some women reported that they were deserted by their partners, and left alone to care for their children. One such case was Dee, an African American woman with three small children under the age of five. Dee served five years in the Army, a career that she enjoyed. But her husband pressured her to quit, saying that her job was too hard on the family. She quit and became a housewife at her ex-husband's insistence. Then, when she was dependent on him for financial support, he left her without warning.

> My husband left us with no food. The rent was due. You know, when he left he just split. It was like he was never there, no clothes, nothing.

Stephanie, the nursing student at the university, spoke about the shock of having to raise her child alone. Since the divorce, her husband has never once paid child support, nor visited or contacted their daughter. She, like all women, thought that their marriage would last forever, and that he would support both her and their child. She made a wrong choice, but she had no way of knowing it was wrong at the time. It was a choice that any woman could make. She never imagined that she would be on welfare.

> I gave birth thinking—he begged me to keep the child when I found out I was pregnant—thinking that we would be a couple, that we would always be together, and he would always want her. And now, it's four years later, and I am by myself, and I am doing this by myself. Even the best-laid plans sometimes go down the drain.

Both Dee and Stephanie, and many others that we interviewed, saw welfare as a critical but temporary form of assistance that enabled them to take care of their children immediately after a husband or partner disappeared, or when the marriage or relationship ended. Welfare made it possible for them to pursue further training so that they could be the sole support of a family, or it provided some base level of financial support while they reassessed their life options. They did not see themselves as being irresponsible. Instead, the temporary receipt of welfare was viewed more positively. It allowed them to take control of their lives and provide a better home environment for their children until they could provide it themselves.

Violence

Some detrimental relationships involved violence and abuse. Violence, or its threat, is a part of every woman's reality. No woman is really exempt. A rape, for example, is reported in the United States every five minutes (U.S. Federal Bureau of Investigation, 1995), and most rapes remain unreported. Two women interviewed revealed that they bore children as a result of rapes. They credit welfare with giving them the opportunity to bear and raise their children, rather than forcing them to have abortions or give up the child for adoption.

Although no direct question about violence was asked, many other women volunteered that they were fleeing abusive relationships or had left an abusive relationship in the past. Violence in the home has reached staggering levels. It is a critical social problem affecting the lives of millions, poor or rich. The true rate of domestic violence can perhaps never be known, as it often occurs "behind closed doors," where a "man's home is his castle." Groundbreaking research by Straus and Gelles (1986), referred to as the National Family Violence Surveys, was conducted in 1975 and 1985 with a nationwide sample of 8,145 husbands, wives, and cohabiting couples. They define violence as "an act carried out with the intention, or perceived intention, of causing physical pain to another person," synonymous with the legal definition of assault. The respondents of these surveys were asked about their involvement in violent acts such as: throwing something at the other person; pushing; grabbing; shoving; slapping; kicking; biting; hitting with fists; hitting with an object; beatings; burning, scalding, or choking; threatening with a knife or gun; and using a knife or gun. Together, the two surveys found that in 16 percent of the couples, at least one of the partners had engaged in a violent act against the other during the previous year. In other words, these data reveal that every year in the United States approximately one out of every six couples have at least one act of violence in their relationship. Moreover, Straus and Gelles found that, over the course of the entire marriage, 28 percent of the relationships, or nearly one out of three couples, contained violence (Straus and Gelles, 1986, 1988). The true rate may be even higher (Straus, 1991).

Other data from the National Crime Survey by the United States Justice Department estimates that more than 600,000 cases of violence between intimate partners occurs each year—murders, rapes, or assaults committed by spouses, ex-spouses, boyfriends, girlfriends, or former lovers. This represents more than 13 percent of violent crimes committed within these categories each year (U.S. Department of Justice, 1994). As many as 3,000 women are killed by their husbands or boyfriends each year.

Although domestic violence occurs in all social classes, the preponderance of data indicate an inverse relationship between social class and likelihood of violence. That is, women who have lower incomes and lower levels of education are more likely to be victimized than are more affluent or well-educated women. Some of this difference may be because of social class differences in the likelihood of reporting violence. Nonetheless, a Justice Department report, for example, stated that women living in households with annual incomes below $10,000 are four times more likely to be violently attacked than are other women, usually by their intimate partners. When income and educational levels are taken into account, white, African American, and Hispanic women have equivalent rates of domestic violence committed against them.

One battered woman who fled violence, Molly, turned to welfare for support after escaping while her husband was asleep. She has three young sons, the oldest of whom was four at the time she fled. They lived in a rural, mountainous area, 30 miles from the nearest town. Her husband deliberately kept her isolated from family and friends, and put a block on the telephone. He was abusive to both her and the children:

I left my husband when he was asleep. I stayed in a shelter. I grabbed some clothes for the kids and left. My mom came up and got us. I had no car, no nothing. No furniture. Zero. That was August of '92. So I had to start completely over from scratch. I got a few of my things back, but basically I lost everything that I had.

Molly has been on welfare for three years, continuously, since leaving her husband. During that time she had nearly completed an Associate of Arts (AA) degree at a community college, and intends to transfer to a university to work on her bachelor's degree. At the same time, she cares for her three young children, the oldest of whom is now seven years of age. Two of her children have been diagnosed with attention deficit disorder (ADD), a disruptive and challenging learning disability. They had difficulty in school until they were correctly diagnosed and began to take appropriate medication. Working through these issues by herself, she cannot imagine what her life would be like without the help she received from welfare. She receives no child support, and doubts that her ex-husband will ever pay the tens of thousands of dollars that he currently owes.

Jessie, a 42-year-old African American woman, reflected on the common problem of physical abuse:

> I would say that most women who are on the system, it's due to abuse, either from their spouse or something that happened in the past, like a sexual abuse, and they have low self-esteem about themselves. And that's why they are on the system. Because they just don't have the willpower to go out there and fight to try to struggle or get a job. They just feel lonely, you know. Not highly of themselves.

The belief that poverty and welfare use are something that is not one's fault and are beyond one's control, something that was forced on them, was commonly used to explain their own use of welfare. Because of bad luck with relationships, or being raped or victimized in abusive relationships, many women felt that they had no other choice but to turn to welfare to help them out of an unplanned but potentially desperate situation. Many women implied that turning to welfare was the responsible and rational thing to do for their children and for themselves. They indicated that they were not to blame, and in fact, for many, welfare was a source of empowerment. It allowed them to be independent of an abusive spouse, retain custody of their children, or to take care of their family when a husband or lover deserted them. These are laudable goals, ones that our society would support, at least in theory. Who would really suggest that a woman remain in an abusive situation, lose custody of her children simply because of money, or move her family to a homeless shelter? The women interviewed were likely to see welfare as a short-term phenomenon, a temporary helping hand while they planned the next step in their lives. Each woman interviewed, with few exceptions, was confident that she would be off of welfare within five years. Yet, as we witnessed in Chapter 3, women were less optimistic about the lives of other women who receive assistance, and were quick to denigrate them as stereotypical welfare mothers, immersed in a subculture that tolerates indolence.

Why the Inconsistency Between Explanations of Their Own and Others' Use of Welfare?

These interviews revealed an important contradiction: Women perceived that their own use of welfare was caused by structural factors, or fate, or to the idiosyncrasies of the welfare system itself; but welfare use by other women, in contrast, was often attributed to laziness, personal shortcomings, or other inadequacies. This was the case for both the African American and the white women interviewed. They perceived the economic hierarchy in the United States as essentially fair, and that one's placement in the hierarchy tends to reflect work effort and motivation. They generally believed the popular constructions of the "welfare mother," but evaluated their own situation as distinctly different from the norm. When asked directly how their situation was different from other women, only a few women reported similarities. Instead, the majority claimed that they were different because: (1) they want to make something of themselves; (2) they don't abuse the system like other women do; (3) they make a concerted effort to live within their means; (4) they have health problems or some other serious difficulty that prohibits them from working; and (5) unlike other women, they are on welfare solely for their children and not for themselves. They tended to segregate themselves from other recipients, and saw structural constraints as applying uniquely to themselves "I'm sure people look at me and say the same thing, but I really do have a legitimate excuse"; or "my situation is different because I injured my back," they told me.

Rhonda, who opened this chapter, distanced herself from other welfare recipients as she told me:

> They have all these children. You know, they take it for granted. I mean, just like people in public housing take it for granted. That's why the neighborhoods are the way they are.

Mary, a 47-year-old white woman who has seven children, receives welfare for her one child who still lives at home. Mary has received welfare sporadically for two years since she and her husband separated. She disassociated herself from other women on welfare:

> I may be on welfare, but I don't live in poverty. I think I got a pretty little home here. Anybody that's on welfare can do the same thing. They shouldn't be on welfare though if they can help it. You know, like me. If it wasn't for my back, I'd be waiting tables.

Janie, who has been on welfare since being ganged raped and giving birth to her daughter two years ago, denied being on welfare altogether:

> I'm not on welfare. I don't even know exactly what welfare is. I'm just receiving AFDC, and that might be considered welfare, I'm not sure. As it stands, most of them get on it because they don't want to work, they don't want to take care of their kids. I've seen more people on welfare lose their

kids because of it, rather than to take care of themselves. Why they do that is beyond me.

Given the strong negative messages about welfare and welfare recipients, perhaps it is not surprising that both white and African American women who receive welfare also subscribe to Individual or Cultural of Poverty blaming perspectives. An enduring theme in the social sciences has been to explain the persistence of social inequality. Sociologists, political scientists, and others regard legitimation—defined here as justifications that are widely believed and taken for granted—as one of several important mechanisms through which inequality is maintained (e.g., Bourdieu, 1977; Dahrendorf, 1959; Della Fave, 1980; Habermas, 1973; Marx and Engles, 1959). Critical theorists, such as Michel Foucault (1980), suggest that our social structures produce cultural ideologies of truth and knowledge that are disadvantageous to the less powerful. These cultural ideologies camouflage the self-serving interests of the powerful by making them appear as though they are natural, normal, and serving the interests of everyone. Likewise, Antonio Gramsci's (1971) notion of "ideological hegemony" refers to the process by which consensus is obtained between dominant and subordinate groups, such as the rich and the poor. Social arrangements, which are in the best interest of the dominant group, are presented as being in everyone's best interests. Subordinates come to accept these interests as their own, and the contradictions inherent in the interests of the dominant and subordinate groups are ignored. Thus, the ideology becomes "common sense" and normative, and cohesion is created where there would otherwise be conflict. The ideologies reflect the interests and perspectives of the elite, but the poor, who fail to see the shared political nature of their problems, also internalize them. Instead, poverty and welfare use are relegated to the realm of a personal problem, rather than a social problem (Mills, 1956). Consequently, like others who are more affluent, women on welfare essentially deem that the popular construction of the "welfare mother" is just. They accept the dominant ideology that stigmatizes welfare recipients.

However, it is important to note that these women infused Structural and Fatalistic perspectives in their worldviews as well, constructed out of their own experiences. They suggested, at least insofar as their own experiences were concerned, that their needs for welfare were caused by circumstances over which they had little control.

This research is not alone in these findings. A classic study by Briar (1966), using a sample from 92 African American, white, and Mexican American families receiving AFDC, also found that the respondents almost never referred to welfare recipients as "we" but instead used the word "they." The tendency to view oneself as an atypical recipient, disassociating oneself from other recipients, was identified as a coping mechanism for dealing with stigma. More recently, interviewing 16 women in focus groups, Davis and Hagen (1996) also found that welfare recipients had the tendency to view themselves as atypical recipients. For example, while they were quick to condemn others for being welfare frauds, they did not see their own actions as fraudulent. Instead, they were merely "beating the system" by working to get extra money to pay for necessary items that their checks could not pay for.

What, then, may explain why many women do not see the commonalties of their experience? One explanation may be found in attribution theory, which proposes that people have a tendency to overestimate the degree to which other people's behavior is caused by individual traits or dispositions, and to underestimate the degree to which it is caused by structural factors. And, in contrast, although we tend to attribute other people's actions to their own personal traits or dispositions, we are more likely to attribute our own behaviors to the social structure or situational factors over which we have little control (Jones and Nisbett, 1972).

Consistent with attribution theory, our respondents assigned individual traits or dispositions to other women to explain their use of welfare, ones that are well touted in the media and within the larger cultural milieu. Recipients were accused of laziness, of lacking sufficient motivation to improve their condition, of having deficiencies in human capital such as low education or few job skills, of having little desire to "better themselves," and of living in cultural surroundings that encourage welfare use. It appears that welfare recipients, just like the more affluent, overestimate the degree to which individualistic notions of very negative personality traits or dispositions shape welfare use behavior. Yet when it comes to explaining the causes of their own welfare use behavior, also consistent with attribution theory, they tend to blame it on structural or situational causes that are beyond their control. They assess little personal blame; it is simply not their fault. "There are no jobs"; "How can I take care of all my kids and work too?"; "I would be fine if he would just pay child support"; "I was raped"; "I was beaten and abused"; "He deserted us, and I'm trying to get my feet on the ground"; "I'm trying to better myself"; "the welfare system penalizes me if I get a job," were frequently voiced. Although all of these factors may be justifiable reasons why a woman would turn to welfare, they are reasons that can apply to all women, and indeed, they did apply to the majority of women interviewed. Women assumed they were exceptions to general trends; however, these "exceptions" were common and widespread. They were grounded in their experiences as women in a patriarchal society. Few women were nonchalant about welfare. Instead, most were embarrassed, pained, appreciative, or resigned, and applied for welfare as a last resort. As Rhonda bluntly told me,

> It's not what I want for me and my son. It's just that there are a lot of disadvantages to it. I just don't want to be on it. I'd rather be out working, meeting people. Making it better for me and my son.

5 Day-to-Day Living and Decision Making

"Officials May Gain Welfare Insight" declared a recent headline in a local newspaper (*Gainesville Sun*, September 2, 1997). A group of Florida legislators and state policymakers have voluntarily signed up to be paired with a welfare recipient for one month "to walk a mile in the shoes of a welfare recipient." For 30 days policymakers will talk on the telephone with their welfare "match" at least once a week, and they will do something with her related to her life, such as shopping with food stamps, visiting the welfare office, participating in training programs, or visiting a food bank. Perhaps most importantly, during this month, they pledge to feed themselves and their families on a food stamp budget, although they will use cash rather than food stamps to purchase their food. Those legislators who have volunteered for this experiment have been applauded for their interest and sensitivity towards welfare recipients. It is considered a noble experiment.

Although this is an important step toward understanding the day-to-day experience of welfare recipients, it should not be confused with the actual realities of welfare existence. How is it different? The legislators' "welfare experience" is of short duration, takes place weekly at largely their convenience, and has a fixed beginning and ending point. They do not have to use "stigma symbols" such as food stamps during this period. Furthermore, they know that, at the end of 30 days, they may resume their upper-middle-class lifestyle, replete with expensive clothes, late-model cars, and dinners in lavish restaurants. Who can't "rough it" for 30 days? Finally, because the experiment is only temporary, there are no real decisions that need to be made to cope with the monotony, struggles, or stresses associated with poverty.

For welfare recipients in Florida, living with a child on a monthly income of $241 in cash and $212 in food stamps is not an experiment. In addition, many recipients would argue that it is not truly voluntary and that they are on welfare because they are "between a rock and a hard place, doing what I've got to do." Moreover, for most recipients, their stay on welfare is considerably longer than 30 days, and they do not have the security of returning to an upper-middle-class lifestyle afterwards. Women on welfare do not simply "rough it." Instead, they actually must learn how to live and survive on meager amounts, knowing full well that their financial circumstances may never improve considerably. Their clothes come from the thrift shops and garage sales, their cars are old and in disrepair, and dinners out are likely to be once a month excursions to a fast food restaurant. Their stays on welfare are not an experiment. Unlike state legislators, women on welfare are not considered noble for enduring poverty of this magnitude.

This chapter considers what life is like, then, on a day-to-day basis, for someone who is poor. It examines the kinds of decisions and struggles that ensue, and asks if these are different from those faced by persons who are more affluent. Do the poor simply live a less-affluent version of the middle class dream and family ideal? Or have their lives been significantly reconfigured in order to survive on a day-to-day basis?

Jana's life is a far cry from that of any state legislator's. She is a 28-year-old African American woman with four children. Her oldest child, a 10-year-old son, resides in a center for emotionally disturbed children, located more than 120 miles away. Because Jana has no car, she relies on the county welfare office to take her to see him, but unfortunately, these visits are restricted to once a week. In between visits she calls him on the telephone. "I miss him terribly," she told me.

Jana's other children are aged 7, 4, and 18 months, all of whom live at home with her. She has voluntarily been sterilized so that she will have no more children. Their home is a dilapidated house in one of the poorest sections of town. The small two-bedroom structure sits on a small dirt lot without grass or other shrubbery. Walking up to the front door requires one to hop a series of makeshift stepping stones in order to prevent falling into large and deep holes in her yard. Several of these deep holes are adjacent to her front porch, a potentially dangerous situation for herself, her children, and visitors. From the front of the house, a broken living room window is visible. No apparent attempt has been made to fix it. Thus, her house would be an easy target to burglarize, if only she had something to steal.

The brightly painted but chipping lime green exterior of the house sharply contrasted with the brown, dark, interior. The living room where we sat was very small and crowded. It was hot and stuffy, despite having the door wide open on a sunny 70-degree day in the middle of Florida's winter. The dirty, dark carpet and the faded and well-worn furniture added to the dankness of the living room. A soiled blanket tacked up in the doorway partitioned off other rooms. Jana's home costs her $160 per month to rent, a sizable component of the $364 she receives in welfare aid for her three children who live at home, and the $50 she receives some months in child support. Utilities average another $70 per month. The rent for her house is not subsidized, and she has no roommate. Thus, she pays approximately $230, or more than half of her welfare grant and sporadic child support, on living quarters that, by most standards, would be deemed unfit and unsafe. Her alternative, she tells me, is the housing projects, which she believes are even more stifling and dangerous for her children. So instead, they live month after month in their decaying house. Jana and her children will be there long after the Florida legislators have completed their noble month-long experiment and have gone back to their comfortable homes.

Jana has no telephone and no car. She cannot afford them, she tells me. Unlike many welfare recipients I met, she does not have an extended family network to help her out. She moved to Florida 10 years ago to distance herself from an unhappy home life, "trying to make a change for myself." She chose Florida because an aunt lived there, but her aunt has since died. Jana is on her own, raising her children with only minimal help from the children's fathers. She has cultivated a strong friendship network to help out when needed, not surprising given her outgoing and gregarious personality. For the most part, however, if she cannot provide something for her children, they do without.

Her day-to-day living reflects both the tedium and struggle of being poor. It is tedious because it is predictable, month after month. There is little money for frivolous expenditures that add sparkle and interest to our lives. Jana takes no vacations, no shopping trips to the mall, and rarely goes to a movie or out to dinner. She stays home day after day, and takes care of her children. She is up at 5:00 A.M. daily, awakened by her toddler who shares her bed; "He gets up at 5 o'clock every morning. I mean *every* morning. And when he gets up, he gets out of bed and walks all the way around the house," she tells me sourly. There are no breaks. She has no husband or partner whom she can turn to and say; "It's your turn. I'm tired and need a break." Instead her day is spent getting her seven year old daughter off to school, taking care of her four year old and her toddler, cleaning the house, helping her daughter with homework when she returns from school, fixing dinner, and getting her family ready for bed. There is no money to vary the routine. She cannot hire a baby-sitter so that she can spend an evening out without her children. The tedium is stressful. "Sometimes I just go in my room and close the door and lay down on the bed. That's about all I can do. I just try to relax myself the best way I can because I get so stressed out sometime that my head hurts. My head really hurts," she recounts.

Jana's life is also a constant struggle. It is not easy to pay the bills on time, to put food on the table, to pay for child care, to nurse sick children, to find a job, and to locate donations and charities to help benefits stretch throughout the month. A task as simple and common as grocery shopping poses its set of challenges. Without a car and without a direct public transportation line near her home, how does she get to the grocery store? With only $367 in food stamps, how can she buy enough food to feed her family for a month? Because food stamps cannot be used for nonfood items, how does she afford necessities like toilet paper, diapers for her baby, laundry detergent, cleaning supplies, and other toiletries and feminine hygiene products? "I use rags for just about everything, if you know what I mean," she winked.

For the more affluent, grocery shopping is a minor errand, conducted without a tremendous degree of thought. For Jana, like other women on welfare, grocery shopping is a major ordeal, and one that has to be dealt with every month. She does not like to rely on others for transportation, and then owe them something, so she often walks to the grocery store, more than a mile each way, taking her four year old and her baby with her. She "borrows" a shopping cart to tote them and haul her groceries in. Unfortunately, there are no sidewalks in her neighborhood, and she therefore must take her montage out on the open roadway. Because of the logistic hassles, and to prevent herself from spending beyond her budget, Jana shops for groceries only once a month, a procedure I found to be relatively common.

Meals at the end of the month are "creative" she tells me, usually involving a dab of whatever she has left in the house. Peanut butter sandwiches made on day-old bread for several days in a row are not uncommon. "I try to make them with different kinds of jelly," she told me. Jana tries to avoid spending her welfare grant on food, but usually finds that she runs short of food stamps, and thereby must spend $30 or $40 of her cash grant at the end of the month on food. When this is coupled with the additional $50 she spends on nonfood necessities such as cleaning supplies, diapers, and toiletries, her meager welfare grant is virtually depleted for the month. When she first gets her check, she tries to squeeze out a family meal at a nearby fast-food restaurant that they can walk to, as a special monthly treat. Afterwards, there is little if anything left for a telephone, a car, or many other conveniences of modern living.

As we all know, unexpected costs or emergencies often impose on even the best made budgets. Buying a simple pair of children's shoes can wreak havoc in her budget for the remainder of the month. What does Jana do when these unanticipated needs arise? Like other women on welfare, Jana lives month to month in a precarious juggling of bills. Paying her rent is her first priority, but on a couple of occasions, the utility bill has gone unpaid and her electricity has been turned off. She vows to never let this happen again, as the turn-on charge is more than she can muster. She sometimes turns to the children's fathers, and they, on occasion, will buy food or clothing. She is also well versed in the location of charities, particularly those that will donate food. "See, I can get food. Food is no problem because they have the Catholic Charities and they will give you food when you need it. In addition, there is the Salvation Army and the Community Ministries. There are different places that you can go to and get help for food," she informs me. So she doesn't really feel that she or her children have ever gone to bed hungry. But without a telephone, and without transportation, even getting free help poses a difficulty. Therefore she usually ends up spending a portion of her cash grant on food. Jana's day-to-day living, as is the case for the other women interviewed, is a shocking attempt at obtaining a standard of living that falls well below what most people in the United States simply take for granted.

Like many other poor women on welfare, Jana and her family live in substandard housing, which poses a potential threat to their health and safety. According to data from the U.S. Census Bureau and the U.S. Department of Housing and Urban Development American Housing Survey, poor children are 3.4 times more likely to live in substandard housing than are the nonpoor. Poor children are also 3.6 times more likely to have signs of rats or mice in their homes during the past three months, are 3.4 times more likely to have family members sharing bedrooms, are 2.7 times more likely to have spent time in a house that was considered by a parent or other survey respondent as "too cold," and are more than 3 times as likely to suffer from lead paint poisoning (Children's Defense Fund, 1998, 1994). Exposure to rodents, crowding, and cold can wreak havoc on a family's health and well-being. For example, manifestations of rats and mice, in addition to the more obvious concern associated with bites, can contribute to asthma and other respiratory problems by filling the air with rodent urinary proteins (Swanson, Agarwhal, and Reed, 1985). A study that summarized 100 anecdotes and articles in a medical journal from doctors, nurses, and social workers estimates that nearly 18,000 children are hospitalized each year because of asthma complications from cockroaches, rats, and mold. Another 1,400 are hospitalized from exposed radiators. Where children live can have a tremendous effect on their health, the authors conclude (*Gainesville Sun*, Feb. 10, 1998). Moreover, poor housing influences families to move frequently, causing school disruptions for children and poorer educational outcomes (Children's Defense Fund, 1998).

Living in poverty is more than simply an economic issue. Although legislators in their month-long voluntary poverty experiment may encounter some of the routine financial experiences that women on welfare face, they are able to gracefully sidestep many other important ones. They do not have to deal with the monotony of poverty, the stigma attached to it, and the hopelessness and despair that can accompany people who feel trapped in dire circumstances. Florida's legislators, in all likelihood, will not grapple with finding adequate child care. They will not face the dilemma of finding a way to care for a sick child while at the same time looking for a job. They will not need to search for small kernels of gratification to energize their spirits and keep their sanity, such as buying a steak or other such treats with their food stamps, only to then have even less money for the remainder of the month. The legislators may miss the fact that there is more to being poor than simply not having enough money to live on. Decisions must be made daily, weekly, monthly, on how to keep your family's spirit alive.

Day-to-Day Activities: Wild Living, or Depressing Routine?

It is difficult to understand the day-to-day struggles of women on welfare without considering the difficulties associated with single motherhood more generally. The interviews I conducted reconfirmed that many single mothers face difficult economic and personal situations that they cannot single-handedly resolve quickly. Having no husband or partner forces them to be both mother and father to their children. They, alone, must be the provider, disciplinarian, nurturer, tutor, housekeeper, cook, nurse, and chauffeur despite having their own semblance of problems or difficulties to work through. Most women interviewed felt that being a good mother was their number one priority. Being a good mother meant, at a minimum, keeping their children safe and out of danger. They wanted their children to say in school, and to stay off drugs. They wanted them to stay out of gangs, and to stay off the streets. They wanted their teenage daughters to not get pregnant. For their sons they said, "I just hope they do the right thing and not end up in jail." Their day-to-day expressions reflect these goals for their children.

For most women on welfare, day-to-day living is a continuous and depressing battle to keep the worst of poverty at bay. On one level, it appears that recipients lead largely uneventful lives: The drug use, alcohol abuse, and child neglect that is suspected by the more affluent is exaggerated. Certainly, drugs and alcohol are not unknown to welfare recipients. For example, one study found that 12 percent of women on Aid to Families with Dependent Children (AFDC) consumed five or more drinks in one sitting at least two times in the past month, defined as binge drinking, compared to six percent of adult women who were not on AFDC. Moreover, this same study reported that 23 percent of welfare recipients used an illicit drug in the past year, compared to 12 percent of non-AFDC women (Center on Addiction and Substance Abuse, Columbia University, 1994). To put these figures in perspective, however, data from the 1990–1992 Consumer Expenditure Survey indicate that a larger percentage of nonpoor households purchased alcohol (or tobacco) than did poor households. Moreover, with respect to binge drinking, it should be noted that the binge alcohol use among college students, at 44 percent, is considerably higher than among welfare recipients, according to a Harvard survey of 18,000 undergraduates (Schlein, 1997). Another study reported that binge drinking is twice as likely to occur in a fraternity as it is on the rest of the campus. This drinking is problematic—an insurance brokerage reviewed 1,200 claims filed against fraternities from 1987 to 1995 and found that alcohol was involved in 90 percent of the claims (Schlein, 1997). It is, however, likely that college students and welfare recipients drink for different reasons. Whereas students may drink because peer pressure, several women told us that they used these substances as a coping strategy for their depression. Thus, while we may conclude that women on welfare are significantly more likely be binge drinkers or use drugs than are other women, it is incorrect to assume that the majority of women on welfare do so, or that problems with alcohol and drugs are restricted to the poor. Nonetheless, some states intend to impose drug testing on welfare recipients. Opponents suggest that drug testing violates privacy rights. Florida House of Representative member Joe Arnell disagrees, "There is no invasion of privacy. Is it their right to abuse their family and their children by abusing drugs? Is it their right to abuse tax dollars?" (Associated Press, April 1, 1998). No mention was made of testing for drugs among college students, who are also recipients of tax dollars.

Instead, the majority of woman interviewed were simply trying their best to be "good mothers," caring for their children the best way they knew how. Heavy drug or alcohol use would conflict with this, and were avoided. Their daily activities largely consist of getting up early to get their children off for school; taking care of preschool-age children; housecleaning; cooking; socializing with extended family members, friends, or neighbors; helping their children with homework; and getting children ready for bed, "really, just being a mother. No spectacular anything, just taking care of my children, running a couple of errands, and then coming back and being a full-time mom." These are routine activities familiar to all stay at home mothers, regardless of income level. Yet they rarely make the headlines. Those women who worked outside the home also had familiar lives; they held paying jobs while having sole parental responsibilities. Patrice, who works part-time for a nearby hospital but continues to receive a partial welfare check because of her low earnings, told me how she spends her day. She has two young sons; one is four years of age, and one is almost three. Her routine sounds hauntingly familiar to single working mothers everywhere:

> Well, usually my days start around 6:30 when my youngest child gets up. Then I'll start getting up, assisting him with brushing his teeth and washing his face and showering. Then I take my bath. Then I fix him something for breakfast. Then my second child usually wakes up round about 7:30, so I assist him with brushing his teeth and taking his morning bath. I used to fix him breakfast, but this past Monday he started school, and gets breakfast there, so all I have to do is just get up, get him ready, and usually around by 8:00 we're out the door. I drop him off at school. Then usually

I drop my second child off around quarter to nine. Then I come back home, clean up a little bit, and then I report to work around 9:30. My mom has to pick up my oldest child at the end of the school day because I'm not off of work. Then usually when I get off from work I have to immediately pick up my second child. Then I start my routines of getting them settled, and start cooking. Then I feed them, clean up, start giving them their baths, and we'll spend maybe an hour together. Then it's usually time to go to bed.

Making Ends Meet with "The Check"

Despite the seemingly routine nature of their daily lives, making ends meet on the income provided by welfare requires ingenuity and creativity. Welfare does not provide enough money to live on, I was told repeatedly. I asked a young mother, Amy, who was a student at a university with hopes of being a physical therapist, if welfare provided enough money for her and her daughter to live on. Her eyes widened as she burst out:

> "NO! In Florida? NO! See, I was on it in New York, and in New York, it's enough money to live on. It's enough money to have a really low-rent apartment, maybe a shack somewhere, and pay these meager little bills. And you can survive, maybe by just a hair. But not down here. It's not enough to even subsist on at all. And I'd like to know everyone's story about how they are getting by. I have financial aid, but what about all the other people who don't? How on earth do they make it, without lying? Every semester I get about five thousand dollars. And I'm pretty frugal. I don't buy things. I don't go out and buy CDs. I don't go out and buy clothes. I spend my money on dishwashing detergent, soap, laundry detergent, and car brake lights and things like that. I don't have money for anything else.

She raises the important question: How are other women getting by on welfare? I tackled this issue in a series of questions to respondents, and like other researchers before me, found that welfare recipients usually run out of money well before the end of the month (Edin and Lein, 1997; Mayer and Jencks, 1989). I talked with women about their budgeting and spending. As Jana told me "sometimes it comes out right, and sometimes it doesn't."

Eliza, an African American mother with four children, was typical in many respects. She is completely out of money before the end of the month, and has to scrape by to provide food and material goods to her family.

> **INTERVIEWER:** Let's say that this is the day you get your check. What do you spend your money on first?

ELIZA: My rent. My light bill. My phone. And then, whatever I have left
I go and buy my kids what they need, like clothes. Then there's household goods, washing powder, bleach, and going to the laundromat.
That's what I usually do with the extra money. Once I get through, I
won't have nothing. Paying bills, buying for them and buying stuff for
the house—soap, toilet paper, and all that kind of stuff, and going to
the laundromat to wash clothes, all of that.

INTERVIEWER: Do you ever run out of money?

ELIZA: I ain't got none now. That's why I need a job. A good paying job.

Eliza's consumption patterns were not exorbitant. They are at the low end of widely
shared consumption norms. She, as was the case for most other women interviewed,
rarely bought clothes for herself, or spent very much on entertainment. Most women
knew precisely what their monthly expenditures were. They spent the greater part of
their check on basic necessities such as shelter, electricity, cleaning supplies, and
clothing for their children, with very little, if any, disposable income left. Data from
the 1990–1992 Consumer Expenditure Survey found that poor households spend approximately 78 percent of their income on three items: housing, food, and transportation (Lino, 1996). This figure may be even higher for families on welfare, as food
stamps alone constitute nearly 50 percent of their monthly income, particularly in
low-grant states such as Florida. Even when presented with the fantasy of having an
extra $50 this month, few mothers told me that they would spend it on themselves.
Most commonly I was told, "I would save it for a rainy day because something always
comes up"; "It would go to pay bills"; "I'd buy my children clothes that they need."
No woman had any significant savings stashed away for emergencies. "Savings? This
is a joke, right?" Few women had a credit card on which they could charge items,
thereby allowing them to amortize their costs over the course of several months.
They are largely removed from the credit-card spurred spending sprees and accompa-
nied debt that many Americans find themselves in.

    In order to make ends meet, women on welfare must do without basic amenities
that many people take for granted. "Being on AFDC, you can't have a lot of luxury,"
was certainly an understatement. Most commonly, they were without cars, telephones, washing machines, and clothes dryers, things most Americans now see as
routine household appliances. According to a survey by the Federal Highway Administration, one-fourth of low-income households do not have a car, compared to just
four percent of other households. Americans may make a billion daily trips to the
store, school, work, and other destinations, but for many low-income persons, particularly those who live on welfare, they make these trips by walking, taking public
transportation, or by depending on the generosity of others (*USA Today*, Sept. 16,
1997). They do not have a private automobile at their disposal.

    Similarly, I also noted that many women do not have a telephone. The fluctuat-
ing nature of a telephone bill caught many women off guard. They, or perhaps their
teenage children, made long-distance calls that they could not afford to pay when the
bill arrived. Consequently, it was not uncommon for telephones to be disconnected

within months after having them hooked up. It may take many more months to get it reinstated, if it is reinstated at all. According to data from the U.S. Census Bureau, one-third of children who live in households who receive AFDC are without telephones, as compared to only four percent nationally (Children's Defense Fund, 1994). Yet telephones are an important resource and can improve the lives of poor families in many ways. They provide greater access to routine and emergency services. They can also help mothers form a social network with other relatives, neighbors, and friends. Keisha, a 33-year-old African American woman with two children, who also works part-time to supplement her welfare check, still feels that she cannot afford a telephone. She uses a common strategy of relying on a neighbor to deliver important messages.

> A phone? No. That's an extra bill I can't afford right now. I had one, and that was a bill I had to let go. My parents, especially my mom, say, "Why don't you get a phone?" Well, Mom, I can't afford a phone right now. "You need a phone! You need a phone! What if something happens to those children in the middle of the night?" she asks me. "You've got to go across the street and use the phone and wake the neighbors up." Well, Mom, let's just pray that doesn't happen.

Washing clothes, a routine task, also posed a major obstacle for the women interviewed. Because most women and their children had very small wardrobes, they washed clothes at least weekly. First, there is the cost associated with washing and drying clothes at a public laundromat, as most women did not own their own washing machines. The approximately $10 spent on laundry per week, or approximately $40 a month, depending on family size, constituted a sizable component of their income after their other bills were paid. Second, there is the difficulty of getting to a laundromat, particularly among women without their own cars. Women who lived in the housing projects or large apartment complexes were likely to have laundry facilities in their building, but other women did not. For these women without in-house facilities, getting to the laundromat and doing their laundry was an all-day chore. Third, some women were nervous of the kind of people who hung out at laundromats, and they did not find them safe or respectable places to take their children. Yet most needed to take their children with them anyway because of having no child care. After witnessing, along with her children, a fight between two men, Lynda decided that finding a way to purchase a washing machine was one of her highest priorities. Even though she set her sights on a used machine, buying one was not easy:

> My washing machine causes me a lot of tears. Buying it. There were a lot of sacrifices I just had to make. I have no clothes. It's so sad, but I have no clothes. There were lots of things I had to sacrifice to get something as basic as a washing machine. And I sacrificed with my kids' school clothes. I have to go through the months when it's warm, and save money out of my check then, just to get my kids their school clothes. It was really hard when I had to try to get school clothes for all of them. My grant was a

little more than what I get now. I think, with four kids and myself, I was only getting $426 in cash for a family of five.

Because money is so tight, even small fluctuations in monthly bills or monthly income, which would be trivial to the more affluent, can be disastrous to those who are trying to survive on a welfare budget. Every dollar is budgeted or set aside for something, so that when the unforeseen arises, or when the expected $50 in child support from the welfare office doesn't come, it is difficult or impossible to cover expenses. There is no money left over to fix the car, repair the washing machine, or purchase shoes for their children. As Alexandra, who lives in a subsidized apartment, continues to tell us, "They just raised my rent $15, and I'm like, 'Fifteen dollars? That was my gas money!' I had everything so figured out, and then something changes." As she reveals, even small fluctuations in monthly income or expenditures can upset even the best made budgets. Her daughter often comes home from school with notices in her backpack about upcoming school or community events that cost money. "If I see things in her backpack that need money, I'll just take it out of her backpack and throw them away. I won't even say anything to her. I mean, if she sees it, she's going to want it."

Holidays, such as Christmas or birthdays, posed tremendous obstacles. Poor children are not isolated from the consumerism that surrounds holidays. They are bombarded with commercials on television for expensive toys; they see their peers wearing high-priced clothing and shoes at school; and they are frustrated by opportunities that are seemingly unavailable to them. How do families on welfare confront Christmas and other holidays? Several women dealt with such holidays by making gifts themselves, justifying their homemade gifts as more meaningful than store-bought ones. Others comb the second-hand stores for clothing and other items that their children need. What their children "want," such as toys, are immaterial, I was told. Pearl, a 48-year-old African American woman, told me that her teenage sons smirk when they receive a used shirt from the second-hand store for Christmas or birthday gifts, but "I don't care; they'll wear them," she proudly told me. Another woman, Sarah, saved part of her food stamps each month, and bought her children food for Christmas. "I can't really afford anything else."

A common strategy among recipients is to try to begin saving for Christmas several months in advance. Beginning in October, after the back-to-school clothes have been purchased, recipients reported trying to save $10 or $20 a month for Christmas. This savings goal, while admirable, still did not provide much money with which to purchase gifts. And, more often than not, they were not even able to set aside even this modest amount each month. Something unexpected came up, and they had to spend it. Many women reported using the layaway program at discount stores, such as K-mart or Wal-Mart. They used layaway programs as a form of interest-free credit: they would pay a little each month, and then when the entire sum was paid, they received the item. Although discount stores are popular among the poor, some specific stores were criticized for their punitive layaway policies—at one store, you lose your entire deposit if the item is not purchased by a particular date. Your money will not be returned.

Living and Surviving on Food Stamps

In addition to running out of money before the end of the month, the majority of women interviewed also did not receive enough food stamps. The food stamp program was created to increase the food purchasing power of low-income households so that they are better able to afford a nutritionally adequate low-cost diet. Approximately 26.6 million persons in the United States, or roughly 10 percent of the population, received food stamps in 1995, representing a slight decline over the previous several years (Committee on Ways and Means, 1996, Table 16-8). The food stamp program has various tests for eligibility, with income being a primary criterion. For example, cash income could not exceed $836 (net) for a family of two in the 48 states, the District of Columbia, and U.S. Territories, in 1996 (Committee on Ways and Means, 1996, Table 16-5). AFDC and Temporary Assistance to Needy Families (TANF) recipients are generally automatically eligible for food stamps in every state, yet only 87 percent actually receive them (Committee on Ways and Means, 1996, Table 16-3).

Stephanie, enrolled in nursing school, is better off financially than most women on welfare because she receives financial aid. Her grants and loans provide some extra money in addition to paying her tuition and books. However, she receives the same amount of food stamps for herself and child as other recipients: $212. When I asked her, as I asked others, if she received enough food stamps every month, she answered emphatically:

No! I eat out very rarely, so I find that food stamps rarely last the month for me. I eat very little meat. But I try to eat a lot of fresh fruits and vegetables. I try to be very healthful in my diet. I eat a low fat diet. And unfortunately, those foods are expensive. When it comes to the end of the month, I sometimes have to pay $20 or $30 until the next time I can get food stamps. Some months are four weeks, and some are five. Like, right now, it's tight. I only have one gallon of milk in the fridge, a half a loaf of bread, and some orange juice. I have to be real creative about what I make to eat. There haven't been any fruits or veggies this past week.

As Stephanie reveals, eating healthy can be more costly than filling up on junk food. The food stamp benefit level is derived from the U.S. Department of Agriculture's lowest cost food plan, named the "Thrifty Food Plan." Its precise amount is varied for household size, and is adjusted annually for inflation. It allowed for $57 a week in March, 1997, for a family of two under the age of 50. Yet this modest amount is only a little more than half of that provided under the more generous $110 food budget constructed by the United States Department of Agriculture (USDA) that is more in line with spending habits of middle-class America (Family Economics and Nutrition Review, 1997).

Poor households are expected to be able to devote 30 percent of their monthly income to food purchases. Food stamps, then, make up the difference between what the household can contribute and the amount judged to be sufficient to purchase the Thrifty Food Plan.

The plan as a basis for food stamps can be criticized on several grounds. First, it was designed to be a temporary budget, "for temporary or emergency use when funds are low" (Peterkin, 1964), not a threshold at which families are to survive indefinitely. Later, the USDA stressed that "the cost of this plan is not a reasonable measure of basic money needs for a good diet," and suggested it be increased by approximately 25 percent (Peterkin and Kerr, 1982).

Second, the Thrifty Food Plan is based on the poor's spending patterns several decades ago adjusted for inflation (Ruggles, 1990). But it does not provide for changing spending habits. For example, it still assumes that families will bake daily, cook foods from scratch, and that they will not buy prepared convenience foods. The plan fails to take into account important changes in cooking styles, family tastes, and women's lifestyles since its creation.

Despite its claim of enabling poor households to buy nutritionally adequate diets, many recipients argued that this plan does not allow sufficient funds to buy nutritious foods. Therefore, it comes as no surprise that the lowest income households consumed 27 percent less fresh fruits than the national average, while the highest income level consumed about 40 percent more than the national average (Lutz, Blaylock, and Smallwood, 1993).

Because purchasing the necessary food to feed their families realistically costs more than their food stamp allocation, women on welfare are required to dip into their small cash benefit to make ends meet.

How do women keep from having to use too much of their own money? Alexandra, a 29-year-old divorced white woman with one child revealed to me a common strategy:

ALEXANDRA: They never last. I get $212. But when you go to the store, you spend at least $50 easily on food a week. So usually, the last week of every month I have no more food stamps. It gets pretty bad.

INTERVIEWER: So, then what do you do?

ALEXANDRA: Rent money. I spend money from the rent that's coming up. I'll buy something like peanut butter and jelly. She'll eat peanut butter and jelly for a week. Breakfast, lunch, and dinner. But it's food. It works. If she complains I say, "Hey, you can have grape or strawberry jelly. It's a choice today."

INTERVIEWER: Would some people say that you should just figure out how to budget better?

ALEXANDRA: I basically buy things that last a long time. Lots of spaghetti. You can make massive amounts for 63 cents. Lots of spaghetti, peanut butter and jelly. I like those frozen pot pies. At least there's a whole day's nutrition in just that. Five for a dollar.

Another commonly used strategy for making food stamps last throughout the month was grocery shopping only once. Many women claimed that they made all food purchases at the beginning of the month after receiving their stamps. They purchased foods designed to last the month—particularly pastas and canned goods. They bragged that they shopped the sales, and shied away from name-brand goods. If, as the weeks progressed, they were running low on food, they cooked "creatively" and sparsely, they spent portions of their cash grant, they visited food banks or charities, or they ate meals with friends or relatives. Beth, a 27-year-old white woman who frankly told of her various jobs that go unreported to the welfare office so that she can make ends meet, also has an extensive social support network:

I usually spend all my food stamps at the first of the month, so if it doesn't last me all month, I don't have any more. So usually I'll go to my mom's and get some few groceries, or my church and get a few groceries.

Other women, particularly those without reliable transportation, shopped for many of their food items in convenience stores. These small neighborhood stores generally carry significantly higher prices for food than do the large chain grocery stores, but they are used nonetheless because they are located closer to home. It is ironic that those who have the least money often pay the most for their food because of where they shop (Rank, 1994).

Juggling Bills

The women interviewed here revealed elaborate schemes in order to live on insufficient welfare checks. There is little financial leeway, so when the unexpected occurs, which it does often, it sets forth in motion a series of decisions that touch every aspect of women's lives. Unexpected events included broken appliances, unexpected medical or pharmaceutical bills, car repairs, and even outgrown clothing. How can I cover these expenses, women wondered? A common method used was juggling these bills because they could not all be paid at one time. Almost every woman interviewed nodded "yes" when asked if she ever juggled bills. For some, it was a common occurrence. For others, it was rare, something done in emergencies only. Whereas virtually all claimed to juggle their bills, they recognized that this was not an efficient way to stay afloat. Dee, a 24-year-old African American mother, in school with plans of becoming an accountant, told me:

Oh, my electricity has been turned off, many times. That's because my bill has been so much higher than what I can pay after my other bills. I pay the rent, and then I pay the utility. Whatever is unpaid goes on the next bill. But then the next bill is higher than it should be. And now I'm just waiting for it to go off again. But they will usually turn it on within a week. I stay at my girlfriend's or I stay at my sister's house. Or sometimes I stay here and just take my kids over there to give them a bath, feed them, and then bring them back over here. At night there isn't anything to look at anyway, so I just put them to bed. So, it works out, kind of.

When deciding which bill to pay and which to let go in a particular month, few claimed that they would juggle something as important as rent. "Having a roof over my children's head is the most important thing," I was told. One woman admitted to living in a homeless shelter at an earlier period in life, and she shuddered when discussing it. Many others had doubled up with family members such as mothers, sisters, and cousins, or had shared housing with friends in order to make ends meet. They know, from first-hand experience, the anxiety of having little privacy, sharing beds, and living in cramped quarters not meant for their children. Coreen, despite detesting her home within public housing project, is at least thankful to no longer have to sleep in a bed with both her mother and her two-year-old daughter. She moved out to the housing projects, where the rent on her small one bedroom apartment is only $26 a month, so that she and her daughter could share their own bedroom, rather than also sharing it with Coreen's mother. The security of having a roof over their head was deemed all-important, and the women interviewed did not want to jeopardize this security. Thus, when asked what bill they pay first, I was repeatedly told, "My rent, absolutely." Kim, a 29-year-old African American woman with three children answered my query as to what she spends her money on first after she gets her check:

Okay, first I have to get a money order to pay my rent—it's due on the fifth. I wait on my light bill, but basically I know about how much all my bills are going to be. So I know how much I'm going to spend and how much I have left over. Like a budget. I don't never go over my budget. Well, this month I bought my kids some clothes with the telephone money. You do what you have to do.

Utility and telephone bills are those bills that are most likely to go unpaid. Like many of the women interviewed, 35-year-old Lynda has had her utilities cut off several times. Utilities are a critical component to everyday living, unlike a telephone, which some people might consider a luxury. Yet, utility companies do not hesitate to turn electricity or gas off, after what they consider sufficient notice. Women routinely complained that utility companies were not willing to "work with me" by accepting a partial payment, or by allowing a month's payment to lapse. Consequently, most women interviewed had at least one experience of having her utilities turned off, leaving their families without basic services. Yet, when turned off, women must find a way to muster not only the remainder of the bill, but also the money it costs to have them turned back on:

I hate for my gas service to get disconnected because when they cut it off it's $15. And when they come back to turn it on it's another $15. So that's an extra $30 right there, which is not a lot of money to a lot of people, but $30 is a lot of money to me. Three hundred and three dollars is not even covering my bills every month.

Coping with the Stress

Legislators, in their month-long experiment, will not have to face these issues. They can bypass the myriad of decisions that welfare recipients have to make for their families on a daily, weekly, or monthly basis. How will I pay the bills? What do I need to juggle this month? Do we have enough food in the house? Who will care for my children while I look for work? Can I afford the costs of public transportation, if I am lucky enough to find a job? If I get a job, will the wage cover my corresponding increase in rent, the decrease in food stamps, and will it provide health insurance for my children? How can I entice my children to do well in school, when they are being tempted to do otherwise by influential peers? Can I fight a well-established drug culture that preys off young, poor teenage boys? How can I get my daughter to understand that having a baby will not fulfill her needs for love, affection, and independence, which she so desperately craves from a man? How can I find the strength to motivate my family, when all around them, they see images of consumption that we can never afford?

Irene, for example, knows the dangers and temptations facing poor children and poor teenagers. Compounding her financial difficulties are the innumerable struggles she encounters trying to keep her five children safe and out of trouble. She knows the potential dangers they face; she worked for a period of time as a school bus driver, and made it a point to get to know the children on her bus route; children who lived in some of the poorest neighborhoods in town. Poor children face multiple difficulties that are less likely to plague the more affluent, she believes. As one example, she describes witnessing elementary school-age children selling drugs:

> Little children in fourth, fifth, and sixth grade, you know what I'm saying? So I know it's out there. These grown men give it to the children to sell it because when police drive in an area, they'll never look at the child. And if the children do get caught, they ain't going to get no time. They'll probably just get community hours and that's that. So, that's what I'm scared of. I'm scared that, if I don't buy my kids the things that they want, somebody out there is gonna say to them, "You want them $100 pair of Nikes? I know where you can make some easy money." I'm scared they're going to influence them that way. So that's why I struggle and try to buy them those seventy dollar shoes.

Irene also elaborates on her other fears for her children, and how she deals with them. For example, she is trying to share her religious-based values about sexuality with her teenage son—explaining that sex is appropriate only in the confines of a committed relationship, preferably marriage. She wants him to consider the benefits of abstinence, but recognizes her uphill battle:

> I just talk to my children about sex, drugs, everything. I don't hide nothing from them because I rather for them to hear it from me than out there. Like sex. My oldest son was going through puberty, and the school was teaching him about rubbers. You know, condoms and stuff. And I thought that was bad. He had some, and was going to keep them, but then his conscience started bothering him because I'd read stretches from the Bible about how God don't want us to have sex until we're married. So we talked about it, and he still got some pressure on him. Because when his friends find out you ain't having sex—when you turn 15 and 16, if you don't done be having sex by then, people will pick at you. They think you odd. So he's trying to deal with it, but I know it's getting to him. I'm going to try to hang in there with him.

Irene also works hard to prevent her children from using the drugs that are commonly passed around the housing project in which she lives:

> The neighbor kids would wait until I go to bed, then they—we didn't have no screens on the window—they would slip cigarettes and reefers through the window to my kids. So I confronted them, and I went to confront the parents. She kept telling me no, that her child wouldn't do this, and so on. And I went and talked to some officer that I knew personally, right? And they told me that if I caught them again I could have them arrested. If you try to nip something in the bud, you have a better chance of stopping it than if you wait for it to go down. I think I got it under control. I don't want them smoking cigarettes and smoking reefers.

Given these many concerns, it is not surprising that welfare recipients are more likely to be depressed and suffer from more psychological distress than do others. In a recent evaluation of the experiences of 790 participants in the Job Opportunities and Basic Skills (JOBS) program, 42 percent of the sample met the formal criteria for clinical depression. This is more than twice the proportion experienced within the general population (Moore, Zaslow, Coiro, Miller, and Magenheim, 1995). Another study followed 833 African American mothers over time, some of whom were on welfare, and some of whom were not. The research found that women on welfare reported more psychological distress and anxious moods at the first time they were interviewed, and again 10 years later, than did the other women who were not on welfare (Ensminger, 1995). Part of the explanation appears to be recipients' poorer health status, including higher rates of chronic conditions, and their lower levels of education, both of which have a significant impact their chances of finding employment.

Adolescent mothers are particularly at risk for stress, depression, and psychological distress. The teenage years are difficult as it is without the added responsibility of motherhood. It is a period of time when children are making the transition from childhood to adulthood, and it is usually fraught with emotion, tension, and quests for independence and then recoiling back into dependence. Consequently, many young mothers are poorly equipped to handle parenthood, because they are still learning how to be adults themselves. Not surprisingly, then, adolescent mothers are more likely to report depressive symptoms, low self-efficacy, and low self-esteem than are older women or those without children. In a longitudinal study of 2,079 teenage mothers on welfare, more than half were at risk of clinical depression at the beginning of the study, and 43 percent remained at risk at the 42 month follow-up (Quint, Bos, and Polit, 1997). High levels of psychological distress can affect the risk of rapid repeat pregnancy and is associated with inadequate parenting (Leadbeater and Bishop, 1994).

Women, much like Irene and Jana, introduced in the beginning of this chapter, deal with these financial and social pressures in multiple ways. Some vent their frustration alone. How do you cope with these pressures, I asked? "I lay on my bed and have a good cry," I was told repeatedly. Other women reported physical ailments from the stress: headaches, insomnia, nervousness, exhaustion, and depression. A couple of women told me that they were seeing a counselor to help deal with their stress. Amy, a college student with a young daughter, told me:

> I get real bad stress, where I get to the point where I don't sleep at all. Or I sleep for two hours and wake up exhausted. I'll go to bed exhausted, but not be able to sleep and stare at the ceiling for six hours. When I wake up I'll have nail prints in my palms, from clenching my fists in my sleep. I've actually had some spine problems in my neck because of muscle spasms. It actually throws my spinal column out of whack. I never feel like I get a reprieve. I never really get a school vacation. As soon as I don't have school stuff to worry about, I have everything else.

Prayer and a belief in God helped many women cope with the stresses of being poor, raising children alone, and being on welfare. The statement "I know the Lord is going to look out for me," symbolizes many women's beliefs. Recognizing that they have little control over their lives, they willingly turn over the control to someone else. "He ain't going to put no more on your shoulders than you can handle," one woman said. Religion gives meaning to life, and provides guidance for seemingly unanswerable questions (Durkheim, 1947). Concerns about social injustice and inequality are often addressed by religion, and a belief in God and in an afterlife make injustices easier to endure (McGuire, 1992). "I pray until I get an answer or something changes" characterizes the coping strategies used by many women.

Finally, a prominent strategy for coping with poverty and welfare use is holding steadfast to the position that this stay on welfare is only temporary, and that things will soon improve. Coreen is a young African American woman who lives in the housing projects with her two-year-old daughter. She works part-time at a fast food restaurant to supplement her welfare check, and does not report her earnings to her caseworker. She is trying to save her money in order to move out of the projects and eventually get her own house.

> I hold on by knowing that I'm going to have something better someday. You know, my hopes are my dreams. It keeps me holding on, knowing what I can do, what I can accomplish. Knowing that this is going to be temporary for me.

Women were nearly unanimous in voicing their certainty that welfare was not going to be their permanent form of financial support. Each woman held on to a goal—from wanting a house, to wanting a high paying job, to wanting to marry a man who would help take care of her. Coreen continued:

> I used to have a boyfriend, and he was abusive. And I used to say, if you love me so much, then why do you let me live in [name of housing project]? If you love me, then get me out of here. I want to have my own home. I'm going to have a house, with or without having a husband. You know, I'm going to work that hard for me and my baby.

Affording Life's "Luxuries"

From these interviews, it became apparent that many women made expenditures that some people would consider as unnecessary luxuries for their families. Quite commonly, women on welfare owned large television sets, VCRs, and paid extra money each month for cable television to supplement the three channels received in the viewing area in which the interviews were conducted. Some people might consider these purchases extravagant. Welfare critics may be tempted to cite these purchases as evidence of fraud, or waste within the welfare system. Other women spent part of their check on cigarettes, or alcohol. Still, other women added fuel to the stereotypes about women on welfare by going into grocery stores to purchase relatively expensive foods with their food stamps, such as steak or seafood. This causes many people to wonder why, and how, do poor women make such extravagant purchases? Are welfare benefits too generous, in that recipients can afford luxuries that many middle-class families struggle to afford?

A more accurate explanation may simply be that poverty is depressing. Affording some luxury helps ward off feelings of hopelessness, despair, and depression. The poor experience a cultural dissonance. They are painfully aware of the American dream, which is heavily laden with consumerism and fueled by cash or credit. However, they are disconnected from it. They see the same advertisements as the more affluent, bellowing at us to eat this, to shop here, to buy that, and to wear this. Despite being bombarded with these cultural images, they cannot consume like average Americans. They are, in many ways, removed from the cultural loop. Thus, in an attempt to allow themselves some sanctity of relative comfort, they may purchase something that makes them feel connected to mainstream America but that welfare critics may argue is an unnecessary luxury: cable television, a VCR, expensive running shoes for their teenage son, a new dress for their daughter, a manicure or set of nails for themselves, or dinner out to a fast food restaurant.

Are these luxuries? Certainly, they are not necessities, in that they are not mandatory for survival. Children and adults need food, shelter, and clothing for survival. In our modern society, we might add health care and education to the list. So, one could argue, that in the strictest sense of the term, all else is really a luxury. Purchases designed to enhance self-esteem, such as clothing or cosmetics, or those designed to keep children busy and off the streets, such as cable television or a VCR, could be designated as "frills"—nonessential items. But are they, really? The vast majority of Americans, from rich to poor have their self-image and self-esteem tied up in material possessions: cars, clothes, stereos, jewelry, and the like. Can we expect welfare recipients and their children to feel differently? How important is it to enhance poor adults and children's self-esteem, or to keep children busy and off the streets? I suggest that many of these purchases are paramount to providing the psychological tools that enable both adults and children to help themselves. For example, teens that feel good about themselves are less likely to experiment with drugs, to get pregnant, or to impregnate others. They are more likely to stay in school and graduate. Adults who have a positive self-image are more likely to have a plan about their future, and are less likely to be emotionally crippled when it comes to implementing that plan. Thus, we should be encouraging self-esteem among welfare recipients and their families, not crippling its development.

Most splurges did not cost excessive amounts, and were a means of building and uniting a family. Meals out were usually to a fast food restaurant or to buffets where children eat free. Women told me of taking their children to the "dollar movie" theaters, where prices for children under 12 were only 50¢. Or they splurged and rented a movie from the local video store and saved even more money. Irene's comments were typical:

> Me and my children used to go to the Dollar Movie on Tuesday. I mean, it was fifty cents for them. We would eat a lot of food before we go, because then I can afford it. We'll eat real good, and then we'll go there, and if there's two or three movies we'll watch them all. But then, they done raised the price, and now we can't afford it. On the weekend, instead, we'll rent movies and pop popcorn. Sometimes we'll set up like we be camping out. We get real comfy.

Molly, a white mother of three young boys agreed:

> I try to treat my kids at least once a month. We go to Shoney's where the kids eat free. Or to Ryan's. That's a big deal for them. I told myself, try to treat them at least once a month. And I would try to take them to a movie at the Dollar Theater. I would use my food stamps and go get whatever we wanted to eat and hide it in my purse. That's kind of sneaky, but that's the

only way we could afford to go to the movies, you know? And they love to go to the movies—that's a big deal.

Likewise, the mother who buys expensive shoes for her teenage son may not necessarily be spending money foolishly. She may be trying to keep him out of the hands of drug dealers, who like to flaunt expensive clothing and name-brand shoes to young boys as a way to entice them into the trade, as I was told on several occasions. Likewise, purchasing a large television set may also be a rational act, if your goal is to keep children satisfied staying indoors. Many mothers, particularly those in the housing projects, did not want their children to go outside unsupervised. They worried about the crime, the drugs, and the peer group that would tempt their children. They did not want their daughters to have boyfriends. Therefore, after school, many children came directly home, and were not allowed outside again. Reports from the Children's Defense Fund (1994, 1997a) suggest that our respondents are not unlike other poor women. A 1998 *Newsweek* magazine poll found that the number of Americans who worry "a lot" that their children will get involved with drugs, alcohol, or with troublemakers increased by a third since 1990 (Alter, 1998).

Some teenagers even fear their own neighborhoods. Bowen and Chapman (1996) surveyed 207 middle and high school students in communities within Florida and North Carolina. They found that low-income youth were significantly more likely to report such neighborhood dangers as gunshots, murders, gang-related fights, or selling illegal drugs during the past 30 days than were their more affluent peers. Although these were not frequent occurrences among either group, it remains that low-income youth did not feel as safe in their neighborhoods as did others. Their fears are not unfounded. An average of 14 children die each day from gunfire, approximately one every 100 minutes. Children are finding guns easier to obtain and are increasingly likely to carry them for "protection." Consequently, the number of gun murders by children has quadrupled since 1985, from approximately 500 to more than 2,000 per year (Children's Defense Fund, 1998). It is heartening to note, however, that data released in 1997 by the Office of Juvenile Justice and Delinquency Prevention (OJJDP) show that arrest rates of young people for violent crimes fell in 1996 for a second year in a row, and homicide rates declined for three straight years. Declines were most dramatic among African American youth (Children's Defense Fund, 1998).

The peak time for juvenile crime is after school, between 3:00 and 7:00. Low-income neighborhoods are less likely to offer after-school programs for children and teens and are less likely to have parks or recreational facilities within them. Moreover, poor families are less able to afford the costs associated with extracurricular activities, such as uniforms or dues. Results from the National Childcare Survey found that organized activities, like sports teams and art or music lessons, accounted for a substantial portion of out-of-school time for middle and upper income children. In contrast, fewer than six percent of children in the three low-income communities studied were enrolled in these formal activities. Poor families cannot afford them, and are instead forced to find ways to entice their children to stay at home and stay out of trouble. Yet police chiefs around the country hail these programs as a vital way to keep teens occupied and off the streets. After-school programs can promote an improved self-image, and provide important alternatives to children who feel cut off and disenfranchised (Alter, 1998; Children's Defense Fund, 1998).

Marissa, a 28-year-old African American mother is concerned about her neighborhood, and she is typical in the way she likes to keep her children occupied. She has four children, the oldest of whom is 12 years old. They all have chores around the house every day after school and on weekends. Her goal is to keep them busy and out of trouble:

> There is nothing out in the streets but trouble. I talk to my children a lot, and I say, "Look, you see how people hang out in the street? It's not good for you." Because there are so many young kids hanging out on the streets. You walk down this main road, and that's all you see is young kids. Hanging out in the streets, I can't handle that. My daughter has a 14-year-old girl going to her school right now and she's pregnant. And it's like, man, I'm not risking that.

Purchasing a television, cable programming, and a VCR were ways to keep their children occupied. Without these items, home could seem confining, boring, and repressive. Therefore, purchases such as expensive athletic shoes or VCRs are, arguably, not irrational acts that waste taxpayers' money. On the contrary, they exemplify the kind of rational decision-making that women on welfare must routinely face in order to keep their children safe and out of danger—decision making that is absent from the month-long welfare experiment conducted by members of the state legislature. Buying $75 shoes for one family member, or a VCR, or steak for dinner is not without its sacrifices. It means that there is that much less in the family budget for something else. It may mean not paying a utility bill in full this month, thus risking the family's well-being in other ways. It may take several months of sacrifice, using the lay-away system available in many stores. Or it may mean that the family will have to scrimp and save on food purchases made for the remainder of the month. And often it means that mothers must find some other way to augment their incomes. They do it, however, to add a glimmer of sparkle and hope to their lives, and especially to the lives of their children.

Supplementing Welfare

A perplexing discrepancy has been documented by other researchers between welfare recipient's self-reported income and their expenditures, a discrepancy that was also noted in these interviews. That is, welfare recipients report that their expenditures on food, housing, medical supplies, household supplies, and other incidentals far exceeded their entire income (Berrick, 1995; Edin and Lein, 1997; Mayer and Jencks, 1989). Edin and Lein (1997) found, for example, through detailed budgeting records, that welfare recipients covered only about three-fifths of their expenditures with their welfare benefits. Their interviews with 214 welfare recipients reveal an average monthly expenditure of $876 for housing; food; necessities such as medical care, clothing, transportation, childcare, toiletries, and cleaning supplies; and other nonessentials such as entertainment, cable television, and cigarettes and alcohol. With an average family size of three people, respondents spent, on average $213 a month on housing, $262 on food, $336 on other necessary expenses, and $64 on those nonessential items that some may label "luxuries."

Meanwhile, the welfare benefits given to poor women in every state do not come anywhere near these expenses. Not surprisingly then, their budgets revealed a constant shortfall of money. In the four cities in which Edin and Lein (1997) conducted their interviews—Charleston, South Carolina; San Antonio, Texas; Chicago, Illinois; and Boston, Massachusetts—the average AFDC benefit was $307, the average food stamp allocation was $222, and the average SSI grant was $36, for a total monthly income of $565. Those who lived in subsidized housing came closest to meeting their monthly expenses with their welfare benefits, but still generally fell short by $200 to $300 a month. Only one mother in eight came within $50 of covering her expenses using her welfare benefit alone.

Consequently, the women Edin and Lein interviewed had to generate additional money or in-kind benefits in order to make ends meet. With the exception of one mother, no welfare recipient interviewed lived on welfare alone. The single exception was a mother who was in danger of losing custody of her child because she failed to provide adequate food and clothing on a regular basis. Edin and Lein conclude that welfare benefits, including food stamps, subsidized housing and other benefits, do not provide an adequate financial floor.

Jana, introduced in the opening of this chapter, is one of many women on welfare whose expenditures exceed her income. Unfortunately, in addition to ingenuity and creativity, making ends meet on a welfare check may also require one to manipulate the system substantially, otherwise known as fraud.

In a follow-up study of the "Walk a Mile" program, 172 legislators, city and county commissioners, and agency heads around the state have signed up for the program to be paired up with a welfare recipient for one month. One such legislator, State Representative Cynthia Chestnut, who represents the area in which the interviews were conducted, feels that she has gained valuable experience from the match. Yet she could not abide by perhaps the most crucial component of the program— living on a food stamp budget for a month. "One part of the Walk a Mile project that many policy makers, including Chestnut, found it difficult to stick to was the agreement to live on a food stamp budget for the month of November," the news article states. It features a picture of Representative Chestnut presiding over an elaborate and expensive traditional Thanksgiving meal, complete with all the trimmings. Meanwhile, her welfare "match" went without Thanksgiving festivities this year (Chandler, Nov. 28, 1997).

It is ironic that while state legislators are feeling noble from their month-long experiment, welfare recipients must be fraudulent in order to be able to provide for, and thus keep, their children. A headline in the New York Times blared, "Welfare Fraud is Nothing New" (Sexton, March 19, 1997), drawing attention to the problem of widespread fraud, manipulation of the system, and underreporting of income. In an attempt to combat fraud in New York City, welfare recipients are required to submit to fingerprinting, among other measures. However, a catchy headline such as this, and the policy measures employed in New York City and other cities around the country, ignores the reasons why such behaviors may indeed be commonplace. Recipients are not given enough money on which to live and raise their families. In Chapter 6, I examine the formal and informal support systems that recipients draw on to augment their welfare benefits for themselves and their children. How do women and their families supplement their welfare benefits in order to make ends meet?

Much like others before me, such as Robin Jarrett (1996, 1994) in her study of 82 poor and never-married African American mothers, and Rosier and Corsaro (1993), in their study of poor mothers whose children were in the Head Start program, I found that women on welfare share conventional, mainstream aspirations. Their goals, for the most part, parallel those of the middle class. Yet, at the same time, harsh economic realities impinge on their abilities to meet these conventional goals. Consequently, women on welfare develop strategies that make sense to them and their families, given their economic constraints. They are not merely passive victims of adverse circumstances, but rather are active agents striving to better the lives of their families through negotiation and exchange. They evaluate each situation as it arises, rationally assess their options, and make decisions that provide some semblance of self-respect. Living and surviving welfare touches all aspects of one's personal life, not simply the economic realm. Some of the daily decisions and coping strategies may be alien or difficult to comprehend to those who are more affluent and thereby find themselves in different circumstances. Poor women make these decisions and develop these strategies because they help to mediate the deleterious effects of poverty on the human spirit.

6 Living and Surviving Welfare

The Importance of Family, Friends, and Formal Support

Women who receive welfare must often find additional sources of assistance in order to take care of their families because they cannot survive on welfare alone. This is a well-guarded secret kept from caseworkers, but it is a well-known fact of life among recipients. It is also a deep suspicion on the part of the American taxpayer and elected policy makers.

Women's accounts of their welfare experience indicate widespread manipulation of the rules and regulations. Only a few, however, label their actions as fraudulent. Instead, most women on welfare have come to see their reliance on family members, friends, neighbors, boyfriends, their children's fathers, charities, and hidden jobs as normative. Without such aid, they could not feed, clothe, shelter, or enliven the spirits of their children. Yet, as I show, not all women have access to the entire spectrum of assistance listed. Some have loving and devoted family close by who are able to help them out financially, offer babysitting, purchase clothing for their children, or provide the family with a large-ticket item such as a car. But other women do not have these family resources. Some women have friends and neighbors whom they have come to rely on for transportation or babysitting. Other do not trust or socialize with their neighbors, perhaps feeling rejected or let down by them too many times. Other women work part-time and keep the money hidden from their caseworkers. Yet others are unable or unwilling to work outside the bounds of welfare. This chapter examines, in their own words, the sources of support that women draw on in order to meet their financial and social obligations.

Assembling a system of social support is part luck, part skill, and part deception. *Lucky* are those women with family and friends who have the inclination and ability to help them out. Yet even good fortune can be temporary and unreliable. A grandmother who can baby-sit today may be unavailable next week. Second, it takes *skill* to seek out the needed services in a fragmented social welfare system. Yet not everyone has the same level of tenacity or resources with which to develop those skills. And third, it takes some *deception* to finesse and manipulate a system, sometimes illegally, to amass the resources needed to provide for one's children. Ambitious women—women with hope—may see that hiding resources from their caseworker is a rational, reasonable, and responsible way to care for their family given the circumstances. Yet, not everyone feels comfortable amassing pay from part-time work, or money from a boyfriend, and not reporting it when the law demands that you do so.

The system of aid and social support that a woman orchestrates, legal or otherwise, not only helps her live and survive on welfare, it is also crucial in helping her exit the system. Success in making the transition off welfare is due in large part to the formal and informal support recipients can muster. This support helps to build assets, relieve stress, provide transportation, render babysitting, and in a multiplicity of ways provides the necessary boost that allows women to leave the welfare system, sometimes temporarily, often permanently.

If assistance of this nature is so crucial to women's success at leaving welfare, why do we leave it up to luck, skill, or deception—in other words, up to chance? In order for women to survive on welfare and in order for them to leave the welfare system successfully, all women need access to a multitude of supportive services. I suggest that these must be institutionalized so that services (1) are available to all women, (2) are reliable, and (3) do not encourage women to become fraudulent in order to receive them.

Kate receives welfare for herself and her two young children, but she could not "make it" without augmenting her check with the generous help of family, friends, and charities. She knows this, and sees it as a fact of life. Welfare is "Okay," she said, but she gently asked that the president of the United States be reminded that it's not enough to live on, "to cover what we really need." She was quick to add that she doesn't want to complain. The last thing Kate wants to be identified as is someone who complains about the size of her welfare check. Rather, she is very appreciative of her small grant, even though it falls short of providing the basic necessities for her family. Like many other women, Kate pieces together her own package of economic aid. This aid comes, in part, from the government, but must be heavily subsidized by her siblings, her grown children, and her friends and neighbors. She receives aid from charities, and she augments her welfare check with the money she earns from working in the informal sector babysitting for her neighbor's children.

Kate is a 42-year-old African American woman with five children ranging in age from 6 to 25 years. Her three grown children have their own apartments, although she sees them regularly. She also has two young school aged children, a boy seven years of age, named Kenny, and a girl six years of age, nicknamed Pru, for whom she collects welfare. She has been on the system for two years this time, since leaving an abusive boyfriend—Kenny's father—whom she lived with in a nearby rural area. After one of their frequent arguments, he tried to kill her and her young children by setting their house on fire when they were inside asleep. In a fit of rage he doused the perimeter of the house with kerosene and lit a match to it. Luckily for Kate, Kenny, and Pru, the grass and leaves surrounding the house were wet, and therefore the fire smoldered slowly and they were able to escape unharmed. Her siblings came to her rescue, and she moved to the city in which the interviews with her were conducted in order to be closer to them and to her adult children. Meanwhile, Kenny's father went to jail

[handwritten note at top: felony defense→charge]

for his crime, although he had been released and was living in a city about 75 miles away from Kate when the interview took place. She has a restraining order against him to ensure that he does not bother her again.

   This is not Kate's first bout with an abusive boyfriend. The father of her oldest son was also physically abusive to her. The abuse was frequent and severe. One day, approximately 25 years ago, in an attempt to defend herself, she fought back, "I had to get him off of me, and I hurt him." He was seriously injured and required hospitalization. He pressed charges against her, and she, at age 17, was charged with a felony assault. Kate doesn't understand the charges, and isn't even exactly sure what the specific charges were. She blames her vagueness on the time that has lapsed between then and now. But I'm not convinced that she ever quite understood why she was charged with a felony crime in the first place and he was not. Her confusion seems to stem, in part, from her inability to articulate the injustice of what happened, and the sexism in the courtroom 25 years ago that treated battered women punitively. Her boyfriend had a history of assaulting her; "It was a weekend thing of him always beating me up." She said that she had called the police before. The court, however, did not forgive her for hurting a man who had repeatedly hurt her. There was little discussion in the court of self-defense, and no discussion of "battered women's syndrome." Twenty-five years ago our society spoke very little of domestic violence. Kate spent 30 days in jail, "But the jury told me I should have gotten 30 years." Her felony record has followed her over the years and has interfered with her ability to procure and especially to keep a job. This is why, she tells me, that she has been off and on welfare since her first child was born. She has a strong work ethic, and not surprisingly has held many jobs. She has worked in the fast food industry, as a maid in a hotel, as a cook for the Head Start program, in the kitchen of a hospital, and as a cook in the coffee shop of a chain discount store. She particularly likes cooking and working with food, and emphasized how much she would like to have a job of this nature. To upgrade her cooking skills she contemplated taking a course at the local community college. Transportation barriers, however, prevented her from pursuing the course. She does not have her own car, and the city bus quits running before the class gets out for the evening, and therefore she would have no way home. The seven mile distance is too far to walk, and she has no bicycle.

   Kate would love to have a job, she informed me, and is resentful of others on welfare who she perceives as not wanting to work. She volunteers regularly at her children's school to pass the time. Despite her experience and her willingness to work, she tells story after story of being dismissed on the job, or having her application ignored because of her criminal record. "I put it on the application. Any job I work on, they do a background check, and it always comes up. And then, that's the end of that," she told me. It's happened so often that she feels defeated. When asked about her plans to get off of welfare she commented that she no longer had any, "because any decent job I could get they'll do a background check on me. I'll probably end up baby-sitting when my kids turn eighteen. I'll do something." An act of self-defense against an abusive boyfriend has cost Kate dearly.

   Kate's inner strength and sense of fortitude primarily comes from the large extended family and social networks that surround her. She, along with her six brothers

[handwritten margin note: factors stopping her from furthering education]

and sisters, were raised in the countryside by an aunt after her mother, and then a year later her father, died. With the help of her aunt, she was able to finish high school and graduate, even though she had her first baby during her senior year. Alongside her aunt, Kate helped raise her younger brothers and sisters. She was the oldest girl and her role as caretaker within the family was important and highly valued.

> I had two sisters. One sister died, so now I have one sister and four brothers. There were seven of us, only six of us now. But we're still a close family. We all lived in the big house together, my momma, her sister, and my granddaddy, and us kids, all lived in the same house. And after my momma died, my aunt was there. So she took care of us. And I helped take care of the younger ones. It was a big family house, but later the wiring went out in it, and the taxes went up, so we had to tear the house down. So, my brother now has a trailer on the land where we grew up. I was living in the trailer for awhile. And that's when my youngest boy's daddy started acting crazy.

Kate remained very close to her siblings as each one grew up and had families of their own. Together they also remained in close contact with their aunt. Kate credits her aunt as being the "father" to her three oldest children in their early years. They lived together in her aunt's home while her children were young, and they shared a warm and happy home life. When her children were in middle school, they, without Kate, moved in to live with Kate's sister. This arrangement was considered by Kate and her family to be a natural extension of a warm and loving extended family. Kate had a full-time job as a cook with Head Start, and her sister could more easily care for the children. This sister always wanted children, but never had any of her own, so she welcomed them into her home. It was a living situation that worked out best for everyone, Kate says, nonchalantly. She seemed unaware that other people may find this arrangement unusual. From her perspective, an extended family is a blessing, and is not indicative of any dysfunction. She told me:

> I know where they were, and I didn't have to worry about them. About three or four years ago, before I moved to Gainesville, they were still staying with her. She didn't want them to go. She bought a doublewide trailer so she'd have room for them. So it's like they have two moms.

This close extended family relationship continues today. Although her aunt is no longer alive, Kate continues to see her siblings, their children, and her own three grown children regularly. One brother and his family live across the street from her and she sees them almost every day. Many of her relatives hold middle- or working-class jobs. One is a teacher in a nearby community. They provide her with a wide variety of financial assistance and informal social support. Because Kate has no car, they drive her to do many of her errands, and they baby-sit for her when the need arises. Her extended family will buy her children the clothing they need when her finances are low, and they will supplement the meager number of Christmas presents that she can afford to buy and have sitting under the tree. They assist her in both the

Successful due to family [handwritten]

routine and irregular aspects of living on welfare. She returns these favors when she can, usually by baby-sitting for them.

The stresses in Kate's life are mediated considerably by knowing that her family is available to take care of her should an emergency arise. She tries not to call on them for help too often, but she knows that she can if need be. They not only have the resources to respond, but they are also very willing to do so. Taking care of her two young children on a welfare level budget is a difficult task, but Kate is successful because she knows that she can, and she does, call on her extended family with regularity.

Although Kate has lived in town only a few years since fleeing the abuse from Kenny's father, she has also developed a small but crucial social support network within the housing project in which she lives. Not one to complain, Kate told of her dream of having a house for her children—a house where she could garden and grow some of her own food, as she did years ago out in the countryside. She holds on to her fantasy, but she also has her feet firmly planted in the real-life day-to-day struggles of trying to live and survive on welfare. Toward that end, she has cultivated several important friendships with neighbors who live near her in the housing project, and these friendships help sustain her. For example, because Kate cannot afford a telephone, a neighbor has generously allowed Kate to use hers whenever the need arises. In fact, Kate gives out this phone number as "hers," when a number is requested. Another neighbor graciously shares her car with Kate, and offers to take her to the store or run other errands when needed. "She's a real nice lady, " Kate informed me.

The two people who do not assist Kate in making ends meet are the fathers of her children. Neither pays child support nor visits their children with any degree of regularity. She has no knowledge of Pru's father's whereabouts. Although she would prefer to have no contact with Kenny's father, given the abuse and his attempt to set the house on fire, she said she would not try to stand in the way of visits between father and son. Kenny's father went to court to demand visitation rights, which Kate feels was in retaliation for being jailed on the arson charge, and for being identified to the welfare office as Kenny's father and thus pursued for child support payments. After going to court and being given visitation rights, Kate says that he has only come by to see his son Kenny twice during the past year. In addition, he only sporadically pays child support. When he does pay, the money goes to the welfare office, and Kate receives only $50 from them. But, she tells me, because he pays only sporadically, she is frustrated by her inability to plan on whether the $50 is actually coming each month. Her rent was increased by nearly $20 in response to the expectation that he will pay child support. Yet according to Kate, he hasn't paid in five months. In a strange twist, her bills have increased, but she rarely gets the corresponding child support to pay those bills. She is worse off than she would be if he never paid child support at all. *bills increase because he should be paying child support* [handwritten]

Kate's assortment of formal and informal support is highly representative of other women I interviewed. They cannot makes ends meet on their welfare grant alone. They live month to month, piecing an existence together in an attempt to stay afloat; to put food on the table for their children; to ward off eviction from their landlords; to obtain furniture on which to sit and sleep; and to find the transportation necessary to get to doctor's appointments and to look for work.

Kate, like the other women interviewed, had no savings account, no checking account, no assets of any real value, no credit cards, no individual retirement account, no life insurance, and no stocks or bonds. She has nothing of her own to fall back on to cushion the blow when unexpected financial problems arise. How does she make it from month to month? Like all women that were interviewed, Kate relies on an assortment of people, community groups, side jobs, and other strategies to pay the bills each month. Most commonly, women depended on their own mothers, sisters, or other family members to provide a wide array of financial help or important goods and services, such as providing them with an automobile, transportation, or free baby-sitting. Some women rely on their children's fathers to slip them money occasionally, or to purchase their children's school clothes, Christmas presents, or a new winter coat. Others rely on the generosity of their current boyfriends to help support children that are not theirs. And still, many women took advantage of the offerings of private charities or churches to get help with food, clothing, or to get a subsidy for their utility bill.

Even with this type of assistance, many women also worked on the side. They baby-sat for neighbors, provided rides to the store for others without a car, fixed other women's hair or nails, raked leaves, or worked in the fields. The work was generally sporadic, and not particularly well paying. Usually it was not reported to their caseworker out of fear that their overall benefits would be reduced, and would therefore be in a worse position than when they started. Other women took side jobs in the more formal sector, most often working in fast food industries or as nurses aides. Sometimes these jobs and their earnings were reported to their caseworker; other times they were not. These interviews support the growing body of research that indicates that having both informal support from family and friends and formal support from agencies and outside employment is crucial to being able to live and survive on welfare. More importantly, however, these support networks are also crucial to getting off welfare. They provide the needed boost that makes it possible to work, collect some minor assets, and leave the welfare system.

The patchwork of help that women draw on is not static. Instead, women continuously expend their energies piecing together a survival strategy. When that strategy no longer works for one reason or another, they piece together a new one. They substitute buying goods from the day-old bakery when they have worn out their welcome borrowing something from a neighbor. They pay for taxicab rides when their brother can no longer pick them up from work late at night. They leave their children home alone when they can no longer pay the fee charged by the baby-sitter. They offer to rake leaves for neighbors when they cannot get their utility bill paid for by a local charity. They have sexual relations in exchange for clothing for their children when their grant runs low. As one woman told me, "Everybody has a scheme, so let me tell you mine." Laura, a 29-year-old white woman with two young children, told me that some caseworkers are more flexible than are others toward recipients' attempts at supplementing their welfare checks so that they can have enough to live on.

The way AFDC is, if you follow all the rules, then you don't get enough to live on. It's just scraping by, and it seems like some caseworkers are more aware of that than are others. The first time that I ever applied for it I didn't know what answers to give or not, and the caseworker's not allowed to coach you or anything. But she did kind of say, if you did have this other situation I would be able to award you more. Oh, you mean, so if I went and got this other form filled out, I could get more. . . . But she couldn't directly tell me that.

Women who have a dependable source of social support generally fare much better than those who do not, on a wide variety of mental health indices. This support is so important because it can mediate the effects of the stresses associated with poverty. Stress can manifest itself in a variety of ways. Unfortunately, it sometimes influences, negatively, the way in which parents interact with their children. For example, poor families have been criticized for having a variety of maladies, including higher rates of violence toward and mistreatment of children, less nurturing of children, and more inconsistent discipline practices (Conger, Conger, Elder, Lorenz, Simons, and Whitbeck, 1992; Hashima and Amato, 1994). Further, Gelles and Straus (1979) found that parents with incomes below the poverty line had the highest rates of violence toward their children, whereas upper-income families had the lowest. They did not, however, examine the role that social support from family, friends, and formal agencies may play in buffering the stresses that lead to greater frequency of abuse.

Sociologists Hashima and Amato (1994), in their study of parental behaviors, examined whether social support can help to minimize the mistreatment of children. They used data from a representative sample of 1,035 families in the United States, from a large data collection effort called the National Survey of Families and Households. They found that, in general, low-income parents were more likely to report behaving in a punitive and unsupportive manner toward their children. However, receiving some type of support significantly reduced the likelihood of these behaviors. Poor parents who reported a greater number of people who they could rely on in times of crisis or when they were having problems were less likely to report that they frequently yelled at or slapped their children, as compared to those parents who had fewer sources of support. Family, friends, neighbors, children's fathers, other individuals, and even social service agencies can be important resources to help alleviate, or at least minimize, the numerous day-to-day tensions and unforeseen disasters that are commonplace when one lives in poverty.

Informal Support: Help from Families, Friends and Neighbors, and Children's Fathers

Assistance from Families

Most women interviewed expressed clear preferences as to where they turn to for help. They often relied on other women in their immediate family for help: mothers, sisters, cousins, or adult daughters. This help was commonplace, although it was not always easily given. Poor women sometimes come from poor families themselves, and therefore family members had little to offer. Other women had families who were in better financial circumstances and were therefore able to offer greater amounts of assistance. But whether the amount received was large or small, I was struck by how frequently it was given. Even family members with meager resources of their own were willing to share what they had with their relatives.

Kim is a 29-year-old African American woman who works part-time in the afternoons while also taking care of three children, aged 12, 9, and 7. Kim is very ambitious and is looking for a full-time job since completing a certificate program at a nearby community college. She spoke of the nice things she wants in life for herself and her children. She has been on and off welfare for 10 years, and looks forward to making a permanent exit as soon as she secures a full-time job. Although ideally she would like to work with computers as an office assistant, the area for which she was trained, out of desperation she has extended her search into a variety of different fields, including the fast food industry and custodial work. "Surely I can get a job doing this, I figured. Believe me, I have lots of experience mopping and cleaning for my family," she winced. Nonetheless, she has not been able to find a full-time job, custodial or otherwise. Her combined income, for her family of four, with her welfare check and her earnings, is approximately $600 a month, significantly more than other women who receive welfare alone. She receives an additional $323 in food stamps. Yet, for all practical purposes, this is not a lot of money with which to support a family of four. How does she make it? Kim's relationship with her family sustains her and her children:

> I have my mother and sisters. I had my first child at 17, so my mother has always been there. Thank God for her. My other sister I see a lot because she picks me up from work because my car is broken. We do a lot together, like we go to the movies with the kids. We are close. Between my mom or sisters, someone is always there.

Kim continues to tell me how she relies on her mother:

> My mother bought me my dining room table. She's always there. She lends me money or sometimes I wash my clothes at her house. Me and my sister drag our laundry over there, but you know, she basically takes me anywhere I want to go. My kids are the first grandchildren, you know . . . My mother helped me to make sure I did finish school. If you don't have that support, that's why a lot of girls don't finish school.

Kim's sister also provides innumerable types of aid:

> Most of the time my sister gives me money. She doesn't have any kids, and works at the university as a custodian. We are tight! She's there no matter what. If I needed money I would go to my sister first. Most of the time I don't like asking other people. I might have a problem with that. I'm one of those who tries to be independent. She has bought me outfits. She

might say, "You want something, Kim?" because she knows most of the time I don't have the money. But, like when she picks me up, I pay her $10 a week. And she eats at my house, because she can't cook [laughter]. She always comes here because I'm always cooking. So whatever she wants, she can have.

Kim's discussion of her relationships with her family is significant on several accounts. There are a number of themes here that are found in many other interviews.

First, it was common for respondents to feel most comfortable borrowing or relying on their family members for help, rather than friends or neighbors. Help from relatives was generally a first resort, not the last, because it is deemed more socially acceptable. Borrowing items, cooking, cleaning, running errands for family, or receiving this type of help from them, is often normative and routine. Yet, at the same time, the borrowing or favors needed by would-be friends or neighbors were seen as troublesome or meddling. "She's always borrowing this or that, but not me, no," said one woman proudly, referring to her neighbor's borrowing habits. But when it comes to blood relatives, the rules change drastically.

Second, family members often also serve in the role of friends. Siblings, cousins, even mothers and daughters frequently reported spending their free time together, socializing with one another. I was, in fact, often told about preferring to avoid nonfamily members. "They ain't nothing but trouble," I was told repeatedly. Neighbors, an obvious potential source for friendships, were often viewed with distrust, particularly in the housing projects. Most often, women preferred the company of family, if they were available.

Third, although money is sometimes exchanged, the assistance that welfare recipients receive is often in goods and services. Kim, as did other women, relied on family members for transportation or for a place to do laundry. These goods and services are important to the women that I interviewed for several reasons. If purchased privately, they would consume a significant portion of women's cash grants; they are logistically difficult to orchestrate; they translate into money saved for other items; and finally, as goods and services, they are not reported to their caseworker.

Fourth, Kim maintains an illusion of trying to be independent. This was not uncommon. Few women acknowledged how much they rely on family members for help. Although they acknowledged how indispensable this exchange is to them for sheer survival, many women did not view it as "assistance" or "help" per se, because of the strong norms associated with sharing among members of the extended family. Even Kim continued a facade of reciprocity by declaring to pay her sister $10 a week for gas. This reciprocity allows Kim, and others, to feel independent and thus maintain their dignity and self-respect. I was told in numerous interviews that they received little or no "help" from family members, but on further elaboration, women would reveal receiving either cars, free rent, baby-sitting, clothing for their children, or numerous Christmas presents. For example, Jo Lynn, a white woman with two children, reported that she received no financial support at all from her family. Yet, I noticed a relatively expensive late model car parked in her driveway. I probed further. She replied:

Financially they don't help me out. No. Well, they do, like on certain holidays. They always get the kids presents and stuff that I could never afford. They buy clothes. My mom always comes with a piece of clothing every time she walks in the door. Another thing my mom does for me is that she will come over here and bring me a present for my grandmother for her birthday and write my name on the card, and then I give it to her. And my dad gave me a car. If I didn't have it I would be in a lot of problems just like everyone else around here. But he did give me that car. I didn't pay a dime for it.

These gifts, goods, and services from family members can tip the balance of the scale from the most dire to one of hopeful survival. I did not talk with anyone who's family support genuinely lifted them from poverty. Rather, many women, knowing they cannot survive on their welfare alone, turned to their families in order to have and to maintain a decent although minimal standard of living for themselves and their children.

These four themes indicate the primacy of the extended family in the lives of many poor women on welfare. Extended families have been shown to provide critical resources for the poor (Oliker, 1995; Stack, 1974). They are important throughout the life course, but may play a particularly critical role for adolescent mothers (Nitz, Ketterlinus, and Brandt, 1995; Panzarine, Slater, and Sharps, 1995). Although teen mothers are at significant risk for psychological distress, extended families, especially warm relationships with their own mothers, can buffer the stresses associated with teen parenting. Certainly, not all adolescents have good relationships with their own mothers, even if they are residing with them. One study based on 75 African American adolescent mothers found that one-third of them cited their mother as a source of conflict. But positive and supportive family relationships have been linked to higher levels of self-esteem, fewer depressive symptoms, a greater likelihood of remaining in school, and avoiding repeat pregnancy and premature marriage, according to data in national samples, and in smaller samples comprised of young African American mothers (Colletta and Lee, 1983; McLanahan and Sandefur, 1994; Panzarine, Slater and Sharps, 1995). Kate and Kim, who were both seventeen when their first child was born, indicate that their female relatives were instrumental in providing the conditions so that they could finish high school while also raising their babies.

Extended families are more prevalent among certain racial and ethnic minority groups. African Americans, for example, are three times more likely to live in extended families than are whites. Moreover, this is not simply a survival strategy among the poor; significant race and ethnic differences in the likelihood of living in an extended family exist at all income levels. Hatchett and Jackson (1993), in their review of the literature, note six features of the African American extended family system: (1) a high degree of geographic closeness; (2) a strong sense of family and familial obligation; (3) fluidity of household boundaries, with a greater willingness to take in relatives, both children and adults, if the need arises; (4) frequent interaction with relatives; (5) frequent extended family get-togethers for special occasions and holidays; and (6) a system of mutual aid.

Yet despite the apparent benefits that an extended family can offer, the dominant ideology in the United States suggests that the extended family is a dysfunctional family (Bernades, 1985; Gubrium and Holstein, 1990). Sharing assistance or residing with family is thought to reflect that something is "wrong," rather than reflecting a normal, and even desirable, family exchange. For example, single mothers who allow other relatives to raise their children, as Kate and Dawn have done, violate the conventional image of the "normal" American family. Extended families are associated with the Culture of Poverty—that they are an example of the ways in which African Americans, in particular, impart a deviant set of cultural values to their children.

These images reflect dominant cultural ideology by glorifying as normative the family that has a husband who is the primary breadwinner and a wife who is devoted primarily to the care of her biological children, whether or not she is employed. Popular television shows such as *Father Knows Best, Ozzie and Harriet,* and, more recently, the *Cosby Show,* serve as powerful reminders of what constitutes the ideal family, and govern how family members are supposed to behave toward other members. Other family structures or values are viewed as nonnormative at best, or deviant and pathological at worst. Recently, however, scholars have noted the dangers associated with the idealized "normal" American family (Baca Zinn, 1994; Bernades, 1985; Gubrium and Holstein, 1990; Smith, 1993). They have accused this ideal of being classist, sexist, and racist. It denigrates racial and ethnic minority families, poor families, single-parent families, and gay and lesbian families. By idealizing only one model of family life, it ignores the strengths and resiliency offered within a multitude of family structures and dynamics. Is it, afterall, dysfunctional for children to have the warmth and love of two women—in essence, as Kate said, to have "two moms"?

Some readers might be tempted to argue that, if aid from family is so commonplace, then we can cut the amount of welfare cash grants accordingly. Can we expect family members to make up the difference between the amount of money needed to live on, and some smaller amount provided by the government? Just as social security benefits were not created to fund retirees in full, can we extend this same logic to welfare? I argue that we cannot. Based on these interviews, some women received a tremendous amount support from their families whereas others received none. Perhaps they were estranged from family members, and others had family who had little or nothing to give. Some women reportedly had very small families, or none at all in the immediate area. Whites, in particular, were less likely to have a close-knit extended family from whom to draw. Unlike retirement, for which people have years to plan, the need for welfare is often surprising and swift. A violent husband, an unplanned pregnancy, health problems that prevent work, a partner who deserts without warning, or a default on court-ordered child support are all reasons that women turn to welfare—reasons that decry planning. We therefore should not expect or mandate that poor families rely on their relatives for aid.

Assistance from Friends and Neighbors

Although family members were apt to be the preferred source of assistance for most women interviewed, some turned to friends and neighbors, rather than, or in addition to, asking their families for help. Some women had no immediate family nearby. Several of these women told of fleeing abusive childhoods, and that they were beginning anew. Others had moved from their hometowns to the area where the interviews were conducted because of promised job prospects, to attend college, or to pursue a relationship that had now ended. Other women had family nearby, but preferred to turn to friends and neighbors for assistance because they felt that they were embarrassing their parents by being on welfare. One woman, who was raised in a middle-class household, refused to tell her parents that she was on welfare, fearing that she would be criticized. Instead, she relied on friends and neighbors to help fill in the significant gap between income and needs.

Stephanie, divorced and with one daughter seven years of age, moved away from her family to attend nursing school at a university. Now in her third year of the program, she struggles to combine motherhood and being a full-time student. Her classes often last all day, and she is up at 3:00 or 4:00 A.M. most mornings to begin her studies or complete her household chores before her daughter wakes. She has no family nearby, and has not seen her ex-husband since their divorce four years ago. Stephanie is, so far, able to "make it" because of student financial aid that supplements her welfare check by several thousand dollars a year, and by relying on her network of other single mothers who live in the university-owned student family housing complex for a variety of goods and services. Together they share baby-sitting, carpooling the children to school, clothing, and offers of help and assistance in a multitude of other ways on a regular basis. "We share. We have to," Stephanie revealed.

> I don't have any family here. But I do have—I've spent the last three years building up a network of friends that I could leave my daughter with in case of an emergency. I have a "made family." I don't think it would happen as easily if I wasn't in family housing. We are all in the same situation. We are either married and have children, or are single who have kids. I could name a half dozen single mothers around here right off the top of my head.

Women who live in the public housing projects also appear to have a wide assortment of potential neighbors whom they could turn to for help. They, like Stephanie, are not isolated in single family homes. However, women in housing projects often would rather not associate with neighbors. Most struck up only a few, if any, friendships. Instead, they complained that their neighbors were jealous, nosy, suspicious, loud and inconsiderate, or were bad mothers. Some women cultivated one or two friends that they could turn to for emergencies, or to share telephones or transportation. As shown in the opening section of this chapter, Kate, for example, relied on her two friends for a wide variety of services to supplement those provided by her large extended family. She routinely used one neighbor's telephone, and relied on another woman to take her to the store when her family was not available. Yet many other women in the housing projects remained inside their apartments; a self-made prison, as they tried to avoid their neighbors and carve out some privacy in an otherwise crowded world. They trusted few people; "I don't borrow from nobody. I just don't. . . ." Many women proudly told me.

Only a few women indicated that they cultivated a wide circle of friends in the housing projects. They created a wide network in which to borrow, to lend, to support, and to be supported. My hour-and-a-half interview with Janie, a 19-year-old mother of a young daughter, was interrupted four times as friends and neighbors called on the telephone or came by her house to visit, borrow an item, or to see if she needed them to pick up anything from the grocery store. Referring to her friends, Janie told me that she and her daughter are not alone: "We have an extended family of sorts."

Many women rely on their boyfriends to help pay the bills that welfare alone does not cover. These were men to whom they were not legally married and who were not the biological fathers of their children. Some of these men were, however, *social* fathers to the respondents' children. They provided additional financial support to augment welfare, although usually only sporadically—$25 towards food last month, nothing this month, and then a high-priced household item, like a VCR, next month. These "gifts" were an important resource to women and their families. Although not usually a steady and reliable source of income, they provided the unexpected "treats" that make the monotony of poverty easier to endure. Patrice is an African American woman with two children who works part-time for a nearby hospital. She explains how her boyfriend contributes financially to her family by buying her a car, although his contributions go unreported to the welfare office:

> Sure, my fiancé helps me out. He helps me because I try to maintain a good level. My boys need things, and we need a place to stay, and my money goes. I don't make very much, so therefore I run short. And that's how I got the car. He put the down payment on it, because when you get any kind of welfare assistance they don't like you to have anything valuable. So I can't have no accounts like a savings account. They want to know all that. So, I don't have access to money. My trade-in was almost ten years old, and kind of run down, so I didn't get much for it. So I had to go to him for my down payment. And usually my monthly payments too. He pretty much helps me with those.

Boyfriends also sometimes provided emotional support to the entire family. Although their level of involvement with children varied, some of the women claimed that their children called their boyfriends "Daddy," indicative of the active role boyfriends played within the families. However, it did not appear that coresidence was common. Instead, boyfriends usually lived elsewhere and were free to come and go as they chose. Coreen, an African American mother with one young daughter, told me the housing projects generally had rules against boyfriends coresiding—these units were reserved for welfare recipients and their children. Yet I noticed many men lingering in the breezeways or parking lots. When I asked Coreen about this, she responded that, "They don't listen. These apartments are for women and their children, but they don't listen," intimating that boyfriends, although barred from living in the projects formally, are often invited guests of the residents and spend a substantial portion of their time there. Yet boyfriends generally do not stay for free. Despite the popular media image that women on welfare support freeloading boyfriends, these interviews suggest that boyfriends are allowed considerable freedom to come and go at their own discretion because of the cash and in-kind contributions that they make to the household. As Edin and Lein note also (1997), women have an informal "no pay, no stay" arrangement. Mothers were unwilling to sustain freeloading boyfriends in their homes for long. Moreover, they found as I did in these interviews that the exchange relationships sometimes made it difficult to distinguish between their serial boyfriends and prostitution. Several women expressed trading sex, or "being his woman," for money, food, or for clothing for their children. "Yeah, I'll be his woman. Hell, why not, he pays my rent." What distinguished them from outright prostitutes in their minds, however, was that they had ongoing relationships with "my man," or "my friend." Prostitutes were those who engaged in one-night stands for money or in-kind goods. I was told that some welfare recipients engage in prostitution, although none of the women I interviewed admitted to doing so. One woman told me that a friend suggested that she should "turn tricks" as an easy way to make money, but she proudly told me, "No, I don't want that. I'm being good, I'm doing my best, you know?"

Not all of the relationships with boyfriends were a positive influence, however. Some boyfriends were emotionally or physically abusive to the women interviewed or to their children, or attempted to use the women for their own financial or personal gain. Tamela was involved with one such man, and shared her story in an interview filled with emotion and pain. She is an African American woman, with two children, six and seven years in age. Although she looks younger than her 23 years, she has the experiences of someone far older. She grew up with a drug- and alcohol-addicted mother, and spent most of her life on welfare and living in the housing projects. As the oldest of four children, she was forced into the role of raising her siblings because of her mother's addictions and inept parenting. She has been on her own and collecting welfare since age 16, when she gave birth to her son. Because her mother has since been deemed an unfit parent, Tamela also has custody of her two teenage brothers. She is often thrust in the difficult role of family caretaker for an extended family that is fraught with personal, emotional, and financial problems: aunts, cousins, brothers, and mother demand Tamela's attention. They continually ask for her help and support, but offer little in return. They cannot distract her from her ultimate goal, however—to be a nurse. She is in a student-nursing program at the nearby community college, but was taking a semester's reprieve from classes at the time of the interview. The tension caused by a demanding extended family, caring for teenage brothers, being a single parent of two young children on a welfare budget, and successfully attending college, is small compared to the stresses and anxiety induced by her ex-boyfriend. He was aggressive, controlling, and abusive. When she wanted to end the relationship, he beat her. When she threatened to call the police on him he lied and told her the housing project would evict her, her brothers, and her children. She was frightened and believed him. She acknowledges now that she was young and naïve, and was easily manipulated. When she mustered the courage to get a restraining order against him, he broke all the windows in her car. He threatened to call the welfare office and tell them that they had been living together while she collected welfare—a charge that is a serious crime—and one that she vehemently denies. When she called the police one final time to have him removed from her home, he was arrested and taken to jail. On being released the next day, he sought revenge. He immediately went to the welfare office and reported that they had been living together and that she had fraudulently collected welfare.

> There was a two-year investigation, where all his friends said, yeah he was living with me. It wasn't true. It was stressful because here I am trying to do what's right: go to school, wanting to get off the system. Not wanting to abuse the system, but just to use it to my advantage. I had him removed from my house because he wouldn't go. I called the police and asked them to remove him, so he blames me for going to jail that night. So, when released, he walks from the jailhouse to the welfare office, and tells them that he was living with me. I felt in the beginning that the system was siding with him the whole time. No one listened to me; they just took sides with what he had to say. I tried to tell them what type of person he was, that he was lying, how he slit his wrist, he had to be in crisis stabilization twice, and how he was so abusive, and I just had enough. But nobody would listen to me. But he would call me up all the time and say, "How's the welfare office? I'll tell them I just made everything up because I was just upset for you putting me in jail, if you take me back." But I just said no, I'd rather . . . because I'm finally free of him.

Tamela refused to continue their relationship, and he therefore refused to alter his story, she told me. She was assigned an attorney and attempted to fight the charge of welfare fraud. After a drawn-out court proceeding, and further action from the State Attorney's Office, the end result is that Tamela was required to pay back the state nearly $8,000. To Tamela, the sum might as well be $8 million. Her attorney suggested that she could have another hearing, but acknowledged that her case is weak: It is his word against hers. She feels lost in the maze and confusion, and is worn down by her ex-boyfriend's lies and manipulations. Meanwhile, the welfare office has reduced her already small welfare grant as a means to repay the thousands that they deemed she collected fraudulently. Living on the reduced grant is difficult, yet she feels a sense of relief; "I'm finally free of him. I've learned an expensive lesson."

Assistance from Children's Fathers

Since 1988, the government has made greater effort to secure child support from the absent fathers' of children with passage of the Family Support Act (Garfinkel, McLanahan, and Robins, 1994). It requires states to increase the percentage of child support collection from those fathers of children supported by welfare who could be identified. Intended to be accomplished by a variety of means, the act includes withholding child support from fathers' wages; requiring states to adopt uniform standards for setting child support awards; and implementing computerized systems for locating delinquent parents. Some states take several further steps: They intercept tax returns, withdraw funds from bank accounts, suspend drivers' licenses, and, as a last resort, put fathers in jail if they fail to pay child support. Mothers are also affected. In order to qualify for welfare, mothers must provide the name and whereabouts of their children's fathers, if known, and they are asked to provide a recent picture, if available. In return, if a child support payment is made directly to the welfare office, the recipient receives an additional $50 each month in her cash grant. Refusal to provide this information is grounds for denial of assistance.

Unfortunately, despite these efforts, there has not been overwhelming improvement in the collection of child support. A recently published study, using national data from nonresidential parents (generally fathers) from the Panel Study of Income Dynamics, indicates that only 52 percent report to pay child support (Smock and Manning, 1997). This figure corresponds with the number of residential parents (mostly mothers) who claim to receive child support—55 percent. The enactment of these policies has not put a substantial dent in the numbers of impoverished children. Data from the National Survey of Families and Households and the Survey of Income and Program Participation indicate that nonresident fathers pay $2,739, and $2,312, respectively, in child support payments annually, in 1996 dollars. This amounts to approximately eight percent of their pre-tax personal income. Why has the collection of child support, and its effect on child poverty, not improved more dramatically?

One reason is that many poor women had children with men who are also impoverished. These men are unlikely to be able to offer significant sums of money to the mothers of their children. They may be unskilled workers earning near minimum wage, or they may be cyclically or chronically unemployed. Unskilled workers generally have unemployment rates double the national average, and their situation has not improved in recent decades. Drawing on U.S. Census data, the Annie C. Casey Foundation determined that the percentage of men aged 25 to 34 earning less than the amount needed to lift a family above the poverty line had increased from 14 percent in 1969 to 32 percent in 1993, more than doubling in that time (*New York Times*, 1995). Other absent fathers whose children are impoverished may be in jail or are dead, and are therefore unable to contribute any support. Leah, a 24-year-old African American mother with four children, was one of several women who told me that their children's fathers were, as far as they knew, in jail.

> No, I don't socialize with my oldest child's father. He's in prison now. He walked out on us, and that was it. I didn't hear anything else from him.

A second reason that child enforcement policies have not put a significant dent into the numbers of impoverished children is that many of the fathers simply disappear, and government does not fund the massive effort that it may take to retrieve these men. Women spoke of being owed thousands, even tens of thousands of dollars in overdue child support payments. Many women were very angry about what they perceived as the lack of child support enforcement. As one woman asked, "Why does he get to be out riding his motorcycle, while I'm being treated like a criminal?" Yet most knew that the chances of retrieving any of the owed support was small or was virtually nonexistent. Many women are disgruntled with the welfare system's low success rate of securing support. Marissa, a 28-year-old African American woman's story was routine. Despite providing the necessary information to the welfare office, she still receives only sporadic child support from one of her children's fathers. She receives nothing from the other fathers.

> Where are the daddies? They need to kick in. I don't get child support. What I get is AFDC and try to live off that. We're trying to work on my son's dad, but I'm tired of going to court, and I'm tired of this bull crap. I have to go to court again on December 1. He missed three months. I think he only paid, like, two months. And I only get $50 a month. When it's supposed to come to you, and then it's not there no more, it messes up your budget.

A third reason that child support policies have only met with minimum success is because some women adamantly do not want child support from their children's fathers. Two of the women interviewed bore children as a result of rapes. They want nothing to do with their attackers. Others were physically, emotionally, or sexually abused by their children's fathers and also do not want any further contact. They worry that, if forced to pay child support, these men will also demand visitation. Although most women complied with the welfare office's policy of identifying fathers, three women told me that they lied to their caseworker outright and claimed that they didn't know who fathered their child. One example is Laura, a 29-year-old white woman with two children. She has a toddler named Jackie and an infant named Sam. She moved more than 1,000 miles to get away from her abusive boyfriend—Sam's father. Her relationship with him is still very tense. Although her relationship with Jackie's father is less strained, it also involves virtually no interaction, and no child support payment.

> Jackie's father—he and I get along just fine. We don't speak. And I like it that way. We're both comfortable with that. I wanted to have a baby, and I guess he didn't. Sam's father is more difficult. He wants to be more involved, and I don't want him to because I don't trust him. We had a very difficult time. We lived together for a very brief period in Chicago and I got pregnant. Then I moved down here. It was too stressful to be there, and . . . I don't like this story. Hopefully we won't have too much to do with him. He is still in Chicago. I don't want him to send me any child support. I told the AFDC office that I don't know who the father is. Jackie's father doesn't pay child support either. I would be more flexible in dealing with him. But Sam's father? No. It doesn't feel right to me to take child support because it has strings attached to it and I don't want to invite him in our life. I'd rather sever the ties completely.

Jasmine, a 35-year-old African American woman now divorced from her husband, believes that he sexually abused their daughter, and she therefore also wanted nothing to do with him. This includes forgoing the $50 child support check she would receive from the welfare office if he were to pay child support. Fifty dollars is not a large enough incentive to overcome the hatred and distrust she has of him.

> If he ever comes around, and we have to go to counseling again, the counselor will see the angry side of me because I'll tell her right then and there that I can't stand to be in the same room as that person. I wish he would admit to a particular incident that he did. That's all, and just let me have my daughter.

Women on welfare may also be willing to forgo child support payments altogether out of fear that the pursuit of support may lead to physical violence against them. A study at the University of Michigan indicates that many abused women reported arguments about such issues as child support (30%); visitation (23%); and child custody (15%) (Raphael and Tolman, 1997). Another study conducted in Massachusetts also found that approximately 30 percent of abuses involved recent problems or arguments about child support (Allard, Albelda, Colton, and Cosenza, 1997).

The extent of violence among women on welfare is not precisely known, but estimates by the NOW Legal Defense Fund and other research suggest that the percentage of women in welfare-to-work programs who were victims of domestic violence could be as high as 80 percent (cited in Institute for Women's Policy Research, 1996). A study conducted by the Institute for Research on Poverty and the Joint Center for Poverty Research in Chicago report that 55 percent of women on AFDC reported having experienced physical aggression (Lloyd, 1997).

Thus, it appears that a large number of welfare recipients are using welfare as a means of fleeing an abusive home situation, such as Kate, who was profiled in the beginning of this chapter. They do not seek child support because they are trying to sever their relationship with their attacker. For many battered women, welfare is a critical alternative source of income to being dependent on the man who abuses them. It can give them the opportunity and incentive to free themselves from their abuser—financially, physically, and psychologically.

Because the relationship between welfare use and domestic violence appears so strong and so clear, victims of violence may be exempt from several Temporary Assistance to Needy Families (TANF) requirements, such as work requirements, time limits, or the requirements of establishing paternity so that child support can be obtained (Center for Law and Social Policy, 1997). These requirements may be waived by individual states in those cases in which the requirements would make it more difficult for women to escape domestic violence, or would unfairly penalize them, or would put them at risk for further violence and retaliation. Senators Wellstone and Murray presented a Senate amendment that frees states from limiting the amount of waivers that can be given under the Family Violence Option, thereby reducing a woman's risk of further abuse related to child support enforcement requirement (Kaplan, 1997a, b).

Finally, a fourth reason that child support policies have not had a large impact is because some women appeared to be relatively indifferent to receiving child support. The number of women who didn't expect fathers' to be responsible financially for their children surprised me. Content with things the way they were, they were appreciative if their children's father occasionally gave them small gifts. The reasons for this indifference are not altogether clear. Some women may have few expectations because of their own lack of self-esteem. Perhaps they did not feel confident "rocking the boat" with their children's fathers. Other women that I interviewed did not have fathers who supported them as children, and may therefore see this behavior as normative.

Rhonda, who, along with her young son Bobby was profiled in Chapter 4, is an example of a woman who does not expect a regular financial commitment from her child's father. She receives no regular child support from Bobby's father, despite the fact that he works as a long-distance truckdriver and has a steady income. She did not express resentment. Rather, she was complimentary, and focused on the gifts he brings when he stops by to see their son approximately once each month. "He takes him to dinner and buys him shoes, and stuff like that," Rhonda told me, with a tone that indicated that she holds no ill will toward him for failing to provide financially for Bobby on a regular basis. Likewise, Dee, a 24-year-old African American mother, in school working towards a degree in accounting, referred to her ex-husband as "sweet" because he will buy his daughter items such as shoes or clothing when he is asked to do so.

These women complied with the welfare office's request for data on the children's father, but were not particularly indignant when money failed to arrive. Instead, they seemed to be more concerned with the lack of emotional involvement on the part of their children's father, rather than the lack of financial support. Kim was typical in her response to my query about her expectations of her children's father:

> All I expect is, even if they don't give them any money or buy them anything, just spend some time with them. Because my daddy never did anything for me and my oldest sister. But he took care of two other boys from somebody else. He and my mother couldn't get along, and he took it out on us. And I don't want to do that. My first kid's daddy, he used to go with this girl in the other building, but he used to walk right past us. He would never even stop and say, "Hey, how you doing," or whatever. Even if he had problems with me, don't take it out on the kids, you know? They didn't ask to come here.

Twenty-year-old Mandy concurs:

> I really don't expect nothing from them. But they can help out in many different ways: Money-wise and clothing, or sometimes baby-sitting. There might be something I want to do, or something that comes up for me and I'm not supposed to bring a child along, or whatever. I don't go out that much, regardless. But I might have some luck and get a job one day. You know, things like that.

These four reasons suggest that, although pursuing fathers' support is a laudable and worthwhile goal and should be vigorously enforced, it is only one of many problems faced in reversing the plight of poor children and their mothers. Many poor families need additional help as they struggle to improve their economic plight.

Formal Support: Help from Charities and Social Services

It was not unusual for women to turn to private or public charities and social service agencies to augment their welfare check. These agencies provided important and valuable resources, at least occasionally, for the majority of the women interviewed. Some women used them only rarely. They turned to them as a last resort, generally preferring to turn to family first because of the lesser stigma associated with exchanging aid among relatives. Often there was a particular time in a woman's life when she was worse off than at the time of our interview, and felt she had no other choice than to turn to charity: initially leaving an abusive partner; moving to a new community; getting the first apartment; or waiting to receive food stamps or a cash grant after a job was terminated. Doreen, a 31-year-old African American woman who is currently married but separated from her husband, turned to charities and social services when they were still together, as her husband had lost his job.

> Yes, I got help. That was before we moved in this house, when we were staying out on the place by the highway. My husband had lost his job, and the agency paid my light bill for me. And I couldn't get the kids nothing for Christmas, so I signed up for "Hope for the Holidays." My mom helped me sign up. They gave us bunk beds and stuff like that. And they gave us food. I have been down low. I've really been down low.

Certain charities or social services were mentioned frequently by women. Food banks were among the agencies mentioned most often, although few women used them on a regular basis. They felt that food programs were stigmatized; use of them indicated that they were poor mothers because they couldn't plan their family's food budget adequately. Irene, an African American woman with four children, commented on the stigma associated with using charities, food banks in particular.

> About four months ago we went to Catholic Charities and got a referral for some food, but I didn't like to do that so good. I just felt like, there's people out there that might need it more than me. You know what I'm saying? So I said no. Then when I found out that drug addicts are going there and getting it, so I said no. Because they get their money and they use it for drugs, and then they go there and take advantage of that, and that ain't so good. So I try not to go there that much.

Like others, Irene did not want to be affiliated with a program servicing drug addicts. She created a hierarchy of needy people, and she, as a poor mother, was at or near the top of the hierarchy. Drug addicts, in contrast, were at or near the bottom.

Instead of routine help with food, women tended to be more comfortable seeking formal help with their rent or utilities. According to the annual report of the local United Way's Information and Referral Services, which offers a 24-hour referral hotline to callers who need help with housing, food, medical services, and shelter, nearly a third of their 15,000 calls last year were for help in paying rent or utilities. "We're doing a better job all the time in making sure people get fed. But one of the big areas we're not able to help is finding someone, or an agency, that can help them pay a utility deposit, and there is only limited help in just a small number of cases with paying a utility bill," said Jan Wright, Program Coordinator of the referral program (*Gainesville Sun*, Nov. 22, 1997). Programs that paid a family's utility bill were very popular, despite the fact that they were limited to one payment per year. Nonetheless, respondents regularly mentioned these as an important source of help. They saw this as a program uniquely created for them. It was not viewed by recipients as a program for drug addicts and other less respectable needy people. In fact, some women reported to use no charity other than one that would cover their utility bills. Several failed to even know of any other charities in the community to which they could turn. It is not altogether clear how they knew of this assistance—whether this agency was mentioned formally by their caseworkers or if information was passed informally among family members and friends. Another frequently mentioned set of programs were those that help to buy gifts for children at Christmas time (most likely related to the fact that these interviews were conducted close to the Christmas holiday season). "Hope for the Holidays" is a large-scale community event designed to provide Christmas presents for poor children. It was a sought-after honor to be selected for one of the "grand prizes," such as new living room furniture, a new bedroom set, or even a used car.

Women who are new to welfare, or new to the community, often reported difficulty in finding out what services are available to help them. Accessing "the system," as it was referred to, is not altogether straightforward, I was told on several occasions. "I had no idea where to go, and just stumbled on things here and there."

From these interviews, I surmise that most women use social services only occasionally, primarily to help them during a particular crisis or a financially difficult period. However, I did interview a small number of other recipients who relied regularly on private and public charities and social services to help them through each month. Unlike other recipients, they tended to have few family members to rely on. They regularly used food banks, shopped at thrift stores and day-old bakeries, and used programs to assist them in paying utility bills. Janie is an example of a resourceful woman who relies on a variety of services to help her make ends meet. She is a 19-year-old white woman who has one young child.

> Before I found out I was pregnant, I was living in my car or living at different people's houses. Or the Covenant House, or shelters, you know. I had a list of resources and I used every one of them. I still do. I've gone to the Salvation Army for dinner a couple of times when it got to the point where I didn't have enough food in the house. They always have a hot meal. Sometimes I don't have to buy my diapers. There are agencies:

Right to Life, Catholic Charities, and Crisis Pregnancy Center, where if you bring your clothes that you can't use, they will trade them in. So sometimes I don't have the extra bills. Look around my house—that box, that table, all of those came from the Salvation Army. This . . . that . . . and that table came from other people who knew I needed help.

Working Side Jobs: Is This Fraud?

Welfare recipients depend on multiple sources of assistance to supplement their welfare checks. They must piece together these important sources because their cash grant and food stamps do not provide enough money on which to live and raise their families. Those who live in subsidized housing can generally stretch their welfare assistance further than those women who pay full rent for their apartments, but even they usually have trouble making ends meet at the end of the month. Utility bills, clothing, diapers, school supplies, transportation, laundry costs, and routine household cleaning supplies, are some of the many items that deplete meager cash grants. Two hundred forty-one dollars a month, plus a couple of hundred dollars in food stamps, does not adequately cover even the low cost of living for an adult with one child. It also comes nowhere near lifting a family from poverty. Consequently, as I have shown here, women and their families turn to other relatives, if available, to help them out. They also turn to boyfriends, friends and neighbors, and to the fathers' of their children. Yet, it's important to note that these sources of assistance are unpredictable, and are not available to all women. To round out their budget, women also turn to private and public charities and social service agencies for at least occasional assistance.

These interviews revealed that even charities and social services agencies did not completely fill the gap between income and needs. Consequently, some women on welfare also work on the side, and often they did not report this income to the welfare office. Approximately one-quarter of the women interviewed informed me that they had recently worked at least sporadically to earn enough money to allow them to meet their monthly bills, buy food for their children, purchase the diapers or washing powder that food stamps cannot cover, or to buy their children a special treat in order to keep their spirits up. These findings echo those reported elsewhere. For example, estimates of unreported side jobs in the range of 20 percent were noted in the state of Wisconsin before Governor Thompson began his controversial welfare reform experiments (*U.S. News Online*, Oct. 20, 1997). Edin and Lein (1997) report that 39 percent of the 214 women in their study reported to have worked jobs on the side during the past year.

Jasmine, a 35-year-old African American woman who is divorced from her husband and has two children, bluntly explained the necessity of supplementing her welfare assistance so that she can maintain a reasonable standard of living for her family.

I may have some extras, like my telephone or cable bill, or something like that, but living these days and time, children need those things. We need a phone for emergencies and things, instead of having to walk to a neighbor or use a pay phone. To tell you the truth, I've been working little odd jobs on the side, like cleaning somebody's house or something like that to make ends meet. Also, there's a neighbor around the corner, and I've been taking him to the grocery store. He pays me $10 to take him up there to the grocery store, and I make money that way. Then, I also may go out in the fields, or something. You just have to do that to survive.

Sarah's story also reveals the necessity of side jobs in order to make it. Sarah is white, has three children, and is divorced from their father. The divorce was emotionally and financially complicated, and the difficulties are continuing as her husband attempts to gain custody of all their children. The children, some or all of them, divide time between Sarah and her ex-husband, who lives in a larger city approximately 70 miles away. Sarah currently works part-time at a fast food restaurant, and has informed her caseworker of her job. Her welfare benefits have been reduced accordingly, given her employment earnings. Sarah told me that it took her considerable time to find this position, despite having several years of experience working in the fast food industry, including experience as a manager. Before she found this position, and during a period when only one of her children lived with her, they relied on a variety of other "odd" jobs to make ends meet. These were not reported to her caseworker. She and her daughter could not survive on welfare alone: Her rent for her trailer, which is subsidized through a program at the community college, is $250 a month. Sarah's utilities average $100 a month, and she has a telephone and a small car payment. Therefore, her bills run approximately $500 a month, yet her cash grant for herself and her daughter was only $241. How did she make ends meet? First, she relied on a neighbor, Mrs. Janson, who let her stay at her place for a few months rent-free while Sarah saved her welfare checks. This allowed her to eventually move into her trailer.

> If it wasn't for the school, and for my neighbor, me and my daughter would have been in the streets. But, between the school, AFDC, and Mrs. Janson letting me stay at her place, we could get this trailer. Otherwise we had no money and we would have fallen right through the cracks. But a lot of people don't have that extra help. And so that's what they do, they slide right into them cracks because there is nowhere else to go. They become homeless and draw inward because there is nowhere else to go.

Once in her trailer, Sarah faced the difficulty of trying to earn enough money on the side to continue to pay her recurring bills each month. She and her daughter, who wasn't yet in her teens, worked together in order to earn enough money to live. Her daughter's after-school hours were not spent in school sports, in clubs or organizations, or playing with friends. Rather, they were spent helping Sarah earn money to pay the utility bill.

> We cleaned houses; we raked people's yards. We did everything to get that extra money so they wouldn't turn off the utilities. We didn't have any money left over. If we had $5 or $6 at the end of the month, we went

bowling. That was our one thing we did together. If we didn't have any money we went to [a specific park in town] because if you're on welfare you can get in for free. We did a lot of walking. For holidays, birthdays, or Christmas they got food.

The dilemma that many women face is whether to report these earnings to their caseworker. Legally, they are required to do so. In reality, some do, and some do not. I was told that caseworkers vary in the rigor in which they pursue such information, and vary in their likelihood of documenting temporary earnings. Some women told me that caseworkers were aggressively searching for evidence of fraud. Other women told me that some caseworkers will "let you get away with it." Leah told me how she handles trying to get additional money for Christmas, or other special occasions:

> Most of the time I try to do some temporary work. If I'm not employed, I try to get a lot of hours doing temporary work. Sometimes AFDC will let you get away with it. And sometimes, if you work during holidays, then come January and February, when you're not working anymore, they cut your AFDC and food stamps. So, if you do it, it depends on the caseworkers. They might just say, "Hey, since it was only a couple of months, we won't add it." And then again, some people add everything.

Some women are not willing to gamble with the generosity of a caseworker who may or may not break the rules to allow a woman to keep her earnings. Recipients know that if they earn something and report it now, it may take a month for the paperwork to go through the proper channels and reduce their grant. But, more importantly, if they are laid off, or if the temporary employment ceases, it may take another month for the paperwork to go through the system to allow their benefits to resume. During this time they will have no aid, and may experience considerable financial hardship. Women are well alerted to the fact that reporting employment, especially if it is unstable or temporary employment, can leave you and your family vulnerable. Therefore, many women choose to forgo telling their caseworker about extra income. I was frequently told about side jobs involving baby-sitting, hairstyling, doing nails, and providing transportation to others. A few other women worked in the formal sector, holding part or full-time jobs in the fast food industry, or a nursing home, and did not report the income to a caseworker. This is risky, as Dawn, who was profiled in Chapter 3, found out. She was caught and convicted of welfare fraud. Yet Jo Lynn, a white woman with two children, believes working in the informal or formal sector or receiving benefits from friends or family that go unreported is commonplace. This is because of, she told me, the restrictive requirements and the low benefits afforded to recipients. She suggested that they simply cannot live on what they are given, and therefore must find a way to augment it.

> The system makes us fraudulent. It makes us fraudulent. I can tell you right now it makes everyone that is on the system fraudulent. They might as well tell you. They might as well tell you the truth. I'm fraudulent, and

everybody else that I know is. Because to get by, you have to do things that they're not going to allow.

Some women reported receiving extra income from boyfriends, or children's fathers, and most failed to report it to their caseworker. Legally, welfare recipients are required to report such "gifts," but most did not, especially if they saw the gift as a one-time or infrequent occurrence. They told me they could not afford to survive and raise their children without these gifts—they were one of the many ways to subsidize their meager cash grants. Some acknowledged, sheepishly, that they were breaking the rules, "I just hope they never catch up with us." Others rationalize it as a smart survival strategy. Coreen is a bright and ambitious 21-year-old African American mother of a toddler who "never thought I'd be on welfare." Her pregnancy was unplanned, and she lived with her mother, even sharing her mother's bed, until the crowded conditions became intolerable. She applied for welfare and moved into a small subsidized apartment, where she has resided for only a few months. Unknown to her caseworker, Coreen also works 30 hours a week at a fast food restaurant. Why is she cheating the welfare system? "I want to get ahead, and make something of myself," she tells me. She sees her "double dipping" as the only way to get off of welfare permanently. It will allow her the financial cushion she needs to continue college with the goal of being a teacher. It will allow her to move out of the housing projects, which she desperately detests. It will allow her and her boyfriend, who plan to marry soon, to save money so that they can have a fresh start. Welfare, she tells me, doesn't allow for this.

> As long as they give you money, they don't want you to better yourself, that is to say, have a job. This is how I truly feel. They cut your money as soon as you get a job. You can't have a bank account; you can't save money. I feel the system traps women. But I'm in school, and I'm not dropping out until I finish. . . . And I haven't told them I'm working yet because I feel like, it's not enough. With the money I make at [restaurant] that will only be enough for me to pay my bills and buy Pampers for my baby. That's not including clothes, socks, and stuff that she needs. They give you ten days; the last time I had a job they gave me 10 days to report that I had a job. And then I lost my job, and I couldn't get a check for a whole month. That's not good. Me and my baby had to borrow, borrow, borrow. If they knew I was working they would take away the whole thing. And I have a boyfriend, and we are trying to move and get married and stuff. I mean, I feel good, because I know I have a future.

Coreen is clearly committing welfare fraud. She is taking money that she is not legally entitled to. Yet, despite the seriousness of her crime, many readers will not be altogether angry with her. As will be shown in Chapter 7, one of the major concerns with the welfare system is that it does not allow women the opportunity to amass the assets needed to exit welfare for good. Assets can cushion the difficulties that may seem to be minor irritants to the more affluent, but become unbearable on a minimum wage budget. Having assets can soften the blow when initial wages are held for a pay period; a car needs to be repaired; clothing or a uniform needs to be laundered or dry-cleaned regularly; or when a sick child cannot go to day care or school and a baby-sitter must be hired. Coreen, like others, knows that exiting welfare will be difficult. She feels that committing fraud by "double dipping" will at least give her a shot at it.

Each day, millions of welfare recipients piece together a broad array of strategies that allow them to meet the basic necessities of life. A fortunate few, like Kate, who was introduced at the beginning of this chapter, have extended families who give help generously and graciously. Others are not so lucky. Living month to month, they resort to a variety of legal and illegal tactics to support their children. They live a tenuous existence between hope and despair.

7 Insiders' Perspectives on the Welfare System

"We gripe and we gripe about the fact that we are paying all this money for people who don't seem to be doing very much for themselves. But if you looked at the system from an insider's point of view, you would see that there are actually penalties built into the system for someone with initiative, going out to get a job, or doing something to try to better themselves. I speak from personal experience," Stephanie told me, her eyes and voice full of spark and passion. When talking, she revealed a flood of pent-up emotions about the welfare system. She knows the system well; she has received aid for four consecutive years. This time period is now considered to be too long according to recent welfare reform mandates; she is wasting taxpayers' money. People like Stephanie must be removed from the welfare rolls. "People like Stephanie?" Who is Stephanie, anyway, and what exactly is she "like"? And why is she so critical of a welfare system that she has, at least on first glance, benefited from?

This chapter explores recipients' views of the welfare system. These women explain, contrary to popular belief, that they have a passionate disdain for the system. Although recipients are often criticized as lazy and unmotivated, glibly taking free money from hard-working taxpayers, this research uncovers a far different portrait. Women are grasping at ways to get off welfare. They are virtually begging for help and begging that the system be reformed in such a way that it helps them get off welfare once and for all. Sometimes it appears to onlookers that welfare recipients just want a free hand-out from the government. It appears that way because so many types of assistance are needed in order for welfare recipients to be able to exit the system permanently. Their needs exceed what the public and politicians are often willing to pay.

Stephanie is a university student who lives with her seven-year-old daughter Megan in a student apartment on campus. The complex in which she lived had a generic army-base look to it, with row after row of identical and drab cinderblock apartments. The sidewalk was cluttered with children's toys, and grass areas were well worn from children playing and riding their bicycles in their safe and sheltered "yards." The directions she gave me were good, and I found her apartment quickly, even though it was indistinguishable from all the others. I knocked, and when she opened her door and smiled at me, I was startled. I knew her—fairly well as a matter of fact. Yes, her name had a familiar ring to it, now that I thought of it. Stephanie had been a student in one of my courses several semesters before. I remember her because she was outspoken, vocal, and passionate about issues pertaining to social inequality. Therefore, it was with some surprise and some understanding when I saw who it was who had agreed to be interviewed.

Being on welfare was very unexpected, 26-year-old Stephanie told me. She grew up in a middle-class family, and although there were some lean years after her mother's divorce, her mother's subsequent marriage to a man of some wealth ended those difficult times. Stephanie had been taught about hard work and motivation— "the Protestant work ethic" she called it. She had been a good student, and she was a hard worker at the several jobs she had as a teen. She was promoted quickly and given increased responsibility. While working at a hotel as a cashier, she met her husband-to-be. In her youthful idealism and with a quest for adventure, she eventually left this job to join him in working for a circus. "This is the part of my life that I just hate. I actually joined him—the idiot that I was. I actually ran off and joined the circus," Stephanie chided herself. With the circus, they traveled all over the western United States.

It was soon thereafter that Stephanie discovered, or "acknowledged" as she put it, that she was four months pregnant. As she prepared for the birth of their child, she began questioning their lifestyle. "How in the hell are we going to raise a child in this atmosphere? I had no health insurance, nothing."

Her soul searching led her to leave the circus and to move back home to live with her mother. Because neither she nor her husband had health insurance, and because they were separated, she applied for and received Medicaid to cover the birth expenses of her daughter. As it turned out, her daughter Megan was born with a congenital abnormality of her kidneys. She needed corrective surgery at birth, and has had several surgeries and other kidney treatments since, at costs that Stephanie could never have afforded without some assistance.

Eventually, she and her husband divorced. She has not seen or heard from him in four years, and has no idea where he is living. "It's as though he is dead, although I presume he's still alive. I don't really know," she told me. During his absence he has not contributed to the support of Megan whatsoever, nor has he ever contacted her.

Since their divorce, Stephanie has taken considerable measures to ensure that she and Megan will eventually have more financial security. These measures, for the time being at least, have been difficult. She moved more than 100 miles away from her family to enroll in a state university and work towards a bachelor of science degree in nursing. At the time of the interview, she had finished all her prerequisites, and was taking coursework in the demanding nursing program. She looks forward to being able to support herself and Megan within the next couple of years without assistance from welfare.

Stephanie and Megan's financial situation is difficult, although they are considerably better off than are other recipients who are not in school. Stephanie receives a $241 cash grant for Megan and herself, $212 in food stamps, and receives several thousand dollars in grants and student loans each semester to cover the costs of tuition, books, and some of their living expenses. "I'll practically owe the costs of a house when I'm finished with school," she told me. In addition to receiving no support from Megan's father, she receives no regular financial support from her family either, except for a car they bought and keep in their name, but which she has in her possession. As I found to be relatively common among welfare recipients, the car is registered in her parents' name in order to circumvent stringent asset limitations imposed by the welfare office. Her parents pay for the insurance on the vehicle, an arrangement also undisclosed to the welfare office, while Stephanie provides the gas and maintenance.

Stephanie does not have the leisurely lifestyle that so many of her fellow students are able to have. She told me that her day normally begins about 3:00 or 4:00 A.M. so that she can do her laundry, housework, get herself and her daughter ready for school, and drop off Megan at before-school care, so that Stephanie will be on time for her 7:00 A.M. classes. Her classes, and the work associated with them, often last all day. On her open afternoons she does her homework or library research. She tries to squeeze in a work-out at the school's athletic club three times a week, her only real "mental health break—I get rid of a lot of stress that way." She picks up her daughter from school at 6:00 P.M., after she has been there for at least 11 hours. Stephanie spends much of her student loan on tuition for a private Christian-oriented school for Megan. The safe environment, small student–teacher ratio, and the more personalized attention at the school helps soothe Stephanie's fears that she is neglecting her child, or is in other ways a "bad mother" by having Megan stay at school for so long each day. Indeed, she is grateful and relieved that her daughter enjoys school and does not complain about the long hours away from home. She scarcely minds that the $300 dollar per month tuition precludes her from ever buying new clothes or spending money on herself.

Evenings are spent making dinner, working on homework, watching a little television, bathing, and then, by 8:30, it's time for Megan's bedtime story. Stephanie usually falls asleep soon afterwards, only to get up again the next morning at 3:00 or 4:00 A.M. and begin the routine all over again. She does it because she feels that a college education is her ticket out of poverty. She hopes that her nursing degree will provide her with the job security needed for a brighter future. Consequently, she studies diligently and receives top grades. In many ways, Stephanie is a "model" student.

Because so many students in her student housing complex do not have parents or other relatives nearby, Stephanie and her neighbors have developed their own social support network and exchange baby-sitting and carpooling regularly when it is needed. "You have to," she told me. Although she rarely goes anywhere socially without her daughter, this help from neighbors is particularly important on weekends when she needs to study or when she has an important exam or paper due.

After being on welfare for four years, Stephanie knows the system well. And she detests it. It does little to help women help themselves and their families, she told me. With such low-paying benefits, "some live in squalor," and she is particularly concerned about the effects of this on children. She wonders if they can grow up to be physically and mentally healthy, without appropriate food, shelter, and clothing. "I fail to understand how we can allow people to suffer like this, without a second thought," she said.

It is a popular belief that benefits must be kept low as an inducement for women to get a job; the general public doesn't want women to get too comfortable on welfare. Yet, ironically, Stephanie suggests that the welfare system itself penalizes women who try to "better themselves" by seeking work. "Go get a job," it is decreed, but unless women are able to land high-paying jobs for themselves—jobs which include benefits such as health insurance—they will continue to need some help from somewhere. If the assistance will not come from the fathers' of their children, then it must come from the government. But, instead, if a woman gets even a low-paying job, she will have her benefits reduced or completely eliminated. Even those women working in low-paying minimum wage jobs will likely lose their Medicaid. Moreover, their food stamps and housing subsidy, if they have a housing subsidy to begin with, will be reduced or eliminated. And as Stephanie put it, "You can't survive on minimum wage. That's ridiculous!"

Little did Stephanie know that welfare reform would soon make persons like her ineligible for aid. She may be a model student, but she is no longer a model welfare recipient—despite working hard to gain the education she needs in order to exit welfare for good. Instead, "people like Stephanie" are seen as burdensome, and are no longer welcome on the welfare rolls. Paying for a four-year university degree is considered extravagant and a drain on our public resources.

Yet, as we pause to reflect on Stephanie's case, and the millions of women like her, we should ask, "who benefits from welfare reform?" Are the recent changes designed to benefit poor women and their families? Or are they instead designed to benefit the rest of us? Perhaps they are designed to give us a sense of security—albeit a false one—that poverty has somehow been reduced simply because fewer families receive aid.

Embedded in the sweeping welfare reforms of 1997, when Temporary Assistance to Needy Families (TANF) replaced Aid to Families with Dependent Children (AFDC), are two critical philosophical undercurrents. *First, we as a populace apparently no longer believe that children, especially those with only one parent, are best cared for in the home by that parent.* A single mother's priority should rest in the economic realm; she should be a wage-earner first, a care-taker of her dependent children second. Welfare reforms decree that it is better for a child to be physically cared for by strangers and financially supported by its mother than vice versa. This is contrary to the well-touted "family values" discussion dominating much of the media, which extols families in which women stay home to care for children. Women on welfare are excluded from these discussions. As "manless women," as referred to by Dorothy Miller (1992), they are a subset of the undeserving poor, are suspect, and we question their right to care for their own children at taxpayer expense.

Second, we apparently assume that women on welfare do not want significant changes made in the structure of the welfare system, and therefore, we must force these changes on them. The Individual perspective suggests that the poor are largely responsible for their economic plight through their own laziness, immorality, or lack of human capital, as indicated in Chapter 2. Considerable concern is expressed over what "to do" with these women—women who seem satisfied living on the public dole and apparently do not want more for themselves or their children. Thus, welfare reform is based on the idea that we must force change on recipients of the system, because they will not embrace reform efforts of their own accord.

These philosophical underpinnings are at the root of both federal and statewide initiatives, and can be seen in the state of Florida, the site of the data collection for this study. Using Florida as a case example provides a glimpse of the government impact on the lives of poor women and their families.

Florida WAGES: A Case Example

Following the leads of Wisconsin and Michigan, Florida was the third state to receive federal clearance to carry out its own welfare reform plan. On October 1, 1996, Florida implemented its own welfare reform law known as Work and Gain Economic Self-Sufficiency (WAGES), replacing the former federal AFDC program. WAGES is a "welfare-to-work" rather than a "human-capital-investment" program, unlike the Family Transition Program (FTP), the former experimental welfare reform program in the state of Florida. WAGES does not provide case management services designed to coordinate services to meet the physical, social, or emotional needs of recipients. As a "welfare-to-work" program, its stated purpose is to "end entitlement, require work, support individual initiative, and protect children" (The Florida Legislature, 1996:1), but many onlookers suggest that the supportive and protective functions are secondary to simply ending entitlement and requiring work.

Closely following the federal mandates, or at other times becoming more stringent than new federal requirements, WAGES initiates several critical changes (The Florida Legislature, 1996). *First*, participants, with few exceptions, are limited to 24 months of benefits in any 60-month period, and sets welfare total lifetime limits at 48 months (one year less than federal mandates). This requirement is based on the concern that large numbers of women choose to remain on welfare for extended periods rather than secure employment. Yet most women are on welfare for short periods of time. Long-term continuous welfare use is rare. Harris (1996) did find, however, that 42 percent of recipients who left the system returned to welfare within two years. Women worked outside the home, then, because of reasons related to low pay, inadequate child care, lack of medical benefits, and other constraints, they often return to the welfare system (Edin, 1991; Edin and Lein, 1997; Hagen and Davis, 1994; Jarrett, 1994).

Second, WAGES requires "able-bodied" adults to work or engage in activities leading to eventual employment. The assumption is that they must be forced to obtain employment, because most will not do so willingly. However, as will be shown in Chapter 8, finding a job is not always an easy proposition, and when found, a near minimum wage job is not necessarily a ticket out of poverty. Equally important is the fact that approximately one-half of these minimum or nearly minimum wage jobs fail to provide health insurance for their employees, an increase of 56 percent since the 1970s (Seccombe, 1996; Seccombe and Amey, 1995).

Third, WAGES requires teen parents to go to school or find a job, and they must live with their parents or another responsible adult. Unmarried mothers who head a household and who are without a high school degree must now get their diploma or General Equivalency Diploma (GED) in order to continue receiving assistance. This change stems from the concern over the increase in the number of young unmarried women who have children, and thus find it difficult to complete their education and thereby reducing their job prospects. Hoynes and MaCurdy (1994), for example, using data from 1,301 female heads of household from the 1968–1989 Panel Study of Income Dynamics (PSID), found an increase in younger women on welfare, an increase in single never-married women, and an increase in recipients lacking education and job skills. Moreover, these groups of women were likely to remain on welfare for a longer duration than were other groups.

But is teenage childbearing the cause of welfare use, as such studies suggest? Other research indicates that it is not. Hotz, McElroy, and Sanders (1996), using data from the National Longitudinal Survey of Youth (NLSY), which followed teen mothers until age 34, found that teen mothers, as compared to teens whose pregnancies ended in miscarriage, are no more likely to participate in welfare programs throughout their early lives from age 17 to 34 than are those women who had their first live births as adults. Teen mothers were somewhat more likely to use public assistance while they were young, but by age 25, they relied on welfare less often than did the women who had children as adults. They found that welfare benefits received by teen mothers would be lowered by only four percent had these women postponed childbearing by at least two years. However, these savings are more than offset by what teen mothers earn and pay in taxes, resulting in a net gain to the government. These findings are consistent with the growing literature indicating that the costs of teenage childbearing are not as great as generally believed (Bronars and Grogger, 1995; Geronimus and Korenman, 1993).

Fourth, the WAGES program in Florida places caps on benefits for children born after a mother begins receiving cash assistance. This is predicated on the widely held assumption that women on welfare have large numbers of children irresponsibly. Yet Rank (1994, 1989) reports that the fertility rate for women on welfare is considerably less than for the rest of the population (45.8 per 1,000 women versus 75.3 in Wisconsin and 71.1 nationally). Moreover, he found that fertility rates decline as the length of time on welfare increases. In 1994, 79 social scientists issued a press release refuting the idea that childbearing decisions were based on the availability of welfare (Danziger, 1994). Yet, despite this evidence of a lower than average rate of fertility, the state of Florida has decreed that benefits received for the first additional child born to a mother on public assistance be reduced by 50 percent, and a second additional birth brings no increase in benefits at all. Proponents of "family caps" as they are called, suggest that a cap would remove the financial incentives for AFDC recipients to have more children out-of-wedlock. Opponents argue that an additional birth does not dramatically increase a welfare check; checks increase by $24 to $147, depending on the state, with a national average of only $60. Is this really enough money to encourage someone to have a child? If so, then why is there no public outcry that dependent tax exemptions, the Earned Income Tax Credits to lower income working parents, or proposed tax credits for children, induce women to have children beyond which they can afford?

Donovan (1995) examined the fertility rates among welfare recipients in New Jersey and Arkansas, two states that initiated family caps, and found no difference in their fertility rates compared to those states without caps. Initial findings, which implied that caps on aid for additional children did reduce fertility rates, was later explained by a delay in the reporting of additional children. Many women on welfare had no incentive to rush and report a new birth under family cap policies, or feared that they would lose already existing benefits with an additional child. Other researchers report similar conclusions using a nationwide sample of welfare recipients from the 1990 Survey of Income and Program Participation (SIPP) (Farlie and London, 1997). They find that the potential effect of family cap policies on the fertility of welfare recipients is likely to be small or nonexistent for the following reasons: (1) incremental benefit levels may appear quite small relative to the cost of raising an additional child; (2) because a large proportion of the welfare population receives a cash grant for less than two years but will spend at least 18 years raising a child, incremental welfare benefits are likely to be inconsequential to them; (3) many births are unplanned among certain subgroups of welfare recipients; and (4) past ethnographic research suggests that pecuniary factors are unimportant for at least a portion of the welfare population. Researchers Farlie and London conclude:

> Overall, our estimates suggest that the potential effect of family cap policies on the fertility of AFDC recipients is likely to be small at best. There are many possible reasons for this finding. First, incremental benefits levels may appear very small relative to the costs of raising an additional child, thus weakening AFDC participants' sensitivity to changes in incremental benefits. Second, a large proportion of the AFDC population receives AFDC for less than two years. Because these women have to pay the costs of raising their children for a much longer period of time, the effect of changes in incremental benefits on fertility is likely to be inconsequential to them. Third, economic theory proposes that higher incremental benefits increase the probability of planned births; however, many births are unplanned among certain subgroups of the AFDC population. Finally, past ethnographic research shows that nonpecuniary factors are very important in the birth decision for at least a portion of the AFDC population. (1997: 591–592)

Some onlookers suggest that family caps are simply another method used to control women who pose a threat to our patriarchal system (Abramovitz, 1996a,b; Miller, 1992). Efforts to control poor women's reproduction have been fueled by a concern that they violate the traditional "family ethic" by having children without a husband. A woman's proper role, according to societal expectations, is to marry and have children while being supported by and subordinate to a male breadwinner. Poor women on welfare flagrantly violate this ethic, and therefore must be controlled and punished (Abramovitz, 1996a, p. 3). They are suspect, and as such, their children do not deserve to be supported.

Fifth, although the program does not offer the comprehensive services of Florida's previous Family Transition Program (FTP), it does allow "bootstrap" training to upgrade skills for up to two years after a participant leaves the program. However, education and training must be directly related to employment. Most women will no longer be allowed to go to school full-time without working at least part-time. The WAGES program limits full-time education without simultaneous employment to 12 months for any person and to no more than 20 percent of the welfare caseload at any given time. This will undoubtedly slow their progress towards their college degree and stifle real hope for securing jobs providing a living wage. Thus, people like Stephanie, who is pursuing a bachelor's degree in nursing, would lose their eligibility for assistance if they remained in a four-year degree granting program. The fact that finishing her degree program would virtually guarantee success after leaving welfare, and that she would, over the course of her life, pay back in taxes far more than she received in welfare seems to be given little consideration.

Several additional features of the new Florida WAGES program are particularly noteworthy. These include the provision of transitional child care for two years after recipients leave the program, and transitional Medicaid for up to one year. Adult men who are aged 21 or older and who impregnate girls aged 16 or younger will be charged with statutory rape, regardless of the romantic feelings shared by both partners within the relationship. Moreover, given the increased emphasis on child support obligations, welfare benefits will be reduced by one-quarter if the father of the child is not identified. As indicated in Chapter 6, women sometimes avoid seeking child support from noncontributing fathers at times in order to minimize conflict-ridden interactions between themselves and the children's fathers.

This is only one example of the ways in which welfare reforms have been implemented at the state level. One can clearly detect the underlying currents that society does not value the maternal labor of welfare mothers; and that we think they are swindling the American taxpayer and will continue to do so until they are forced to stop.

It is important to note that those who are at the forefront of writing welfare reform legislation generally have little direct experience with the system, and most likely never will. One notable exception is Lynn Woolsey, a Democrat from California, who received welfare many years prior to serving in Congress. She recently told the *New York Times*, "I know what it's like to lie awake at night and worry about not having health insurance. I know how hard it is to find good daycare. I had thirteen different baby sitters in one year. I know what it is like to choose between paying the rent and buying new shoes. Like so many American families, we turned to AFDC" (Woolsey, 1994). Ms. Woolsey not withstanding, the representatives who spearheaded welfare reform efforts largely represent white, upper-middle class males, the group least likely to ever need or use welfare. The participants of social welfare programs, primarily poor or working class women, have had little input into the welfare reform process. Their needs, desires, and suggestions have not been uniformly sought. I suggest that the stigma associated with welfare and the dominant paradigm of Individualism have prevented fruitful discourse from occurring in critical national or statewide contexts.

But women who receive welfare have numerous ideas about how the system could be changed to better meet their needs. They enthusiastically shared with me the ways that the system should be changed. First, I explore the views of women on welfare toward government and the role that it should have in improving the lives of poor women and their families. Second, I examine recipients views of the welfare system, including their opinions on the specific reforms that have come to characterize the welfare debate: (1) time limits on welfare, (2) work requirements, and (3) "family caps" that limit or deny additional benefits for children born to mothers on welfare. Third, I share their visions of meaningful reform that require changes in the structure of work in our lowest tiers as well as changes in the welfare system.

The Role of Government

Most people, rich or poor, believe that our government owes its citizens some degree of protection and care. But it's not clear exactly how much and of what nature this care should be. Nonetheless, many people are feeling abandoned by their government—their jobs and wages are vulnerable, they cannot provide health insurance for their family, and they cannot afford the down payment on their first home. These concerns are not spread evenly throughout the population; they are felt most acutely by the working-class and the poor members of our society (Rubin, 1994). Lillian Rubin's study of working-class families in the early 1990s showed us that these concerns are prominent in the minds of many people and they look to government, sometimes reluctantly, for some degree of protection.

These interviews reveal that many poor women on welfare also feel abandoned by our government. They were concerned that politicians did not care about them and the lives of their children because politicians did not really know of their experiences. Stephanie commented on the distance between those on welfare and those who make the laws about welfare:

> It's very easy up in Washington to sit on their throne, as it were, to say "Oh, they're lazy," and this and that. But, it doesn't hit home until you are in this situation. I think it would do them good to go and visit these people themselves, and see what kinds of houses people are living in. It's about compassion.

Politicians were seen as a far-off group of people who make policies to meet their own needs, and are generally unconcerned about the plight of the poor. Government was seen as "run by white males. White males have the status." Women didn't feel that their voices were given an avenue for expression, and suggested that the government was generally unaware or uninterested in their needs. Both African Americans and whites shared this opinion: Government is run by a distant and far-off group of people who do not represent them.

Laura, a well-educated white woman with three years of college behind her, expressed this sentiment that the government does not reflect her interests. Despite the fact that she resembles her state legislators more closely than most other welfare recipients, at least in terms of education and race, she feels little kinship with them as she tells me, "I think it would be nice if the government were totally different. Yeah. It would be nice if the government helped people. The government needs to shift entirely to being less for the politicians and more for the people."

Marissa stands in stark contrast to Laura. She is an African American woman with a 10th grade education and has given birth to four children, the first of which was when she was only 16. Yet, like Laura, she echoed this concern that the government was generally unaware or disinterested in average families, particularly those who are poor and who receive welfare. She suggested that, although the government complains of deficits and high welfare expenditures, the tax structure favors wealthy Americans. They pay very little in taxes, while the middle classes are forced to subsidize the poor.

> The rich people, they ain't kicking in enough damn taxes, if they even is kicking in some. Like I told you before, it's the middle class that is doing it all. The middle class can't take care of their families and us, and the prisoners, and all that too. The rich people just sit there and try to donate, but really not giving up nothing. But the government has a lot to do with it. Look at minimum wage. I thought it was going up? The government has a lot to do with it. They're not really helping. When you get off AFDC, you're still going to be poor because the jobs around here aren't paying too much.

Despite their educational and racial differences, Laura and Marissa join the other women interviewed here, and the countless others among the working poor, who feel that somehow, our government has abandoned them (Rubin, 1994). Their concern about the tax structure is not unfounded. Data published by Citizens for Tax Justice, a nonprofit organization that monitors the tax system in the state of Florida, indicate that the poorest 20 percent of Florida's families—families of four living on less than $12,000 a year—average 13.8 percent of their income in state and local property, sales, and excise taxes. Conversely, the richest one percent of the state's families—those making more than $1 million a year—pay about 2.7 percent of their yearly income toward taxes. Middle-class families—those averaging approximately $35,000 a year—pay 7.6 percent of their income in state and local taxes. Florida, as do many other states, relies on regressive sales and excise taxes, rather than on a progressive income tax, where payment is directly related to one's ability to pay (Eisler, 1991). Florida has one of the largest gaps between rich and poor in the nation. The top one-fifth of Florida families received an annual income 14 times that brought in by the lowest one-fifth between 1994 and 1996. Nationwide, income disparities widened in 44 states during this period (Williams, 1997).

But, notwithstanding the common concerns of Marissa and Laura, it is critical we note that the poor are not a homogeneous group. I found that a tremendous diversity of opinion existed on the role and responsibility of government, as would be the case in the more general population. Contrary to popular opinion, not all recipients believe that the government has a responsibility to help the poor, or that it has shirked that responsibility. Some recipients subscribed to Individualist philosophies themselves, and therefore not surprisingly, they believed that the poor are ultimately responsible for helping themselves and should not be reliant on public aid. Several women forcefully argued that people are responsible for their own economic plight, and the government is doing enough, or perhaps even too much to help women on welfare. These sentiments were reflected in my conversations with Kim. She an African American mother of three, and has been on and off welfare for 10 years. She now works part-time and is searching diligently for full-time work. Kim is ambitious and is focused in her plans for a better life. It just hasn't quite "happened yet." She replied to my query as to whether the government should do more to help poor people:

> I don't think so. Because I say you got to want to help yourself. A lot of people don't want to help themselves. Why should the government keep helping them? Because a lot of them keep getting this handout, and aren't going to help themselves.

Others voiced that the responsibility ought to be shared by government and families. "It should be fifty-fifty," according to Tanya, a 35-year-old African American mother of five. She has been on welfare off and on for five years, and also received welfare as a child. Her need for aid notwithstanding, she feels strongly that individual initiative is important, and the role of government is to help people help themselves. She continued, "The government should subsidize, and people should try to help themselves. With all the opportunities out there, people can help themselves."

These interviews expose the diversity of opinion among welfare recipients. Although most do indeed feel that their families have been abandoned and left behind by the federal and state governments, a significant number expressed opinions that differed substantially with what we would first expect. That is, opinions on government responsibility represent a spectrum that we might find with a survey from any other part of the population. Welfare recipients are not demanding that government should design policies to help them stay on welfare. They are, instead, asking that government be concerned about poverty and the problems associated with trying to raise a family on a welfare budget, and provide a helping hand in solving these problems.

Opinions of the Welfare System

I asked that women describe, in one word, what life is like on welfare. "Hell," "difficult," "miserable," "challenging," "degrading—very degrading," were just a few of their choices. Comments such as these contradict popular folklore, which suggests that women on welfare enjoy being on the system, are purposefully lazy, and enjoy the "free ride" that they receive at taxpayers' expense.

These interviews revealed a considerably different and contradictory impression of welfare recipients than the popular opinion expressed by the media. Welfare recipients do not like welfare. They described life on welfare as "a strain," "depressing," "rough," "a struggle," "aggravating," "a trap," and "scary."

Patrice, an African American woman who receives a small check for $91 to augment her income from a part-time job, describes life on welfare as "a challenge."

Prior to her employment, she received $305 per month for herself and her two children. Now, with her job, her check was reduced and her food stamps were reduced from $276 to $167 dollars per month. Yet, despite the difficulty of living on reduced aid while raising her two young children, she told me that she would rather work than be on welfare. What is life like on welfare, I asked her? "A challenge. You have to try and budget every little thing, trying to survive with a minimum. It's a challenge, and it's really pitiful."

Strengths of the Welfare System

I asked women to describe the specific strengths or the positive features of our current welfare system. I wanted to know what aspects of the system worked well for them, and should be retained. Elected officials fail to ask the users of the system these crucial questions when they design social policy.

Few women had quick or enthusiastic answers to my query about the positive aspects of welfare. When asked, respondents tended to laugh, grimace, shake their head in disbelief, stare back blankly, comment that they need more time to think about an answer, or curtly retort, "There are none!" Despite the initial shock with the questions, some women eventually conceded that there are some positive virtues with the welfare system. Three themes emerged in our discussion. First, a number of women commented that welfare provides an important floor for poor families, albeit a marginal one. Without welfare, several women told me that they would have no recourse other than to be living out on the streets, in a homeless shelter, or remain married to a physically or emotionally abusive spouse. "It keeps me out of dumpsters," I was told. Welfare may not be much, but at least it's something. Janie, who bore a child conceived during a rape, has experience living out on the streets before her daughter was born, and is thankful that those days are over. Janie has been on welfare for a little over a year since her daughter's birth, and sees welfare as a lifesaver. First, it has given her the opportunity to bear her child, rather than having her pregnancy aborted. And now, she elaborated on its importance in providing a stable home environment:

> It's been really helpful. Because of my current situation, without it, I would be highly lost. I really would be. Because without it, I've got nothing. I'd have no house, I'd have no money, and I'd have no baby. They could take her away from me for not being able to take care of her. My daughter and I would probably be on the streets.

Second, several specific programs were mentioned repeatedly as being particularly helpful. Medicaid was mentioned most often as a highlight of the welfare system, "because poor people, they can't afford all these high-priced doctor bills." When they were asked to prioritize their benefits, and which they would choose if they could have only one, Medicaid emerged most frequently as the benefit of choice. It was followed by food stamps, and then "the check" itself. Other research has also documented the importance of Medicaid to the lives of women on welfare. Social workers

Hagen and Davis (1994), using a focus group format with 16 AFDC recipients, also found that Medicaid was prioritized as the most important benefit received. Interestingly, Medicaid is also the service that women used least often. Most women do not need Medicaid daily, weekly, or monthly, as is the case with food stamps, their cash grant, or subsidized housing. Nonetheless, it appears that women are acutely aware of the catastrophic results that could happen if they were without health insurance and one of their children needed medical attention. Having health insurance of some sort emerged as synonymous with being a good mother, as shown by Dawn's comments. Her four children have not been particularly sickly over the years.

> Medicaid. My kids' health has always been more important to me than anything else I ever did. And we had a couple of periods where we didn't have health insurance, Medicaid and stuff, and the kids didn't get their checkups like they should have. And that bothered me. Medicaid is definitely the most important.

Unlike Dawn's relatively healthy children, Stephanie's daughter Megan has not been so lucky. Megan has required extensive medical treatment over the past several years. To Stephanie, Medicaid is a lifesaver.

> Oh, I've never had to use my Medicaid myself, but my daughter couldn't do without it. So, yeah, Medicaid is the most important benefit to me. I tend to not think about the Medicaid all that much; I think about food stamps because it puts food on my table. I see that everyday. But if I didn't have my Medicaid, I don't know what I would do. And it's an *ad hoc* thing. You never know when you are going to get sick. I may not use if for the rest of the time I'm on welfare, but at least for my daughter, I don't know what I'd do without Medicaid. There would be absolutely no way that I could pay for the medical care that she has received.

The third strength noted with the welfare system is the favorable review given to several reform efforts. In particular, *voluntary* programs designed to assist women's transition off welfare that were available during the interviewing period were applauded by a considerable number of recipients. The most comprehensive of these programs, the Family Transition Program (FTP), was a two-year "human-capital-investment" program that included numerous features designed to assist participants toward self-sufficiency. It was an experimental program available in only six counties in the state of Florida. Women were randomly selected to participate in FTP, but participation was voluntary. Those who were selected were free to decline the program, if they desired. FTP's underlying philosophy was that women on welfare face a multitude of disadvantages (e.g., education, economic, health, mental health). In order for women to be successful in the transition off welfare permanently, all of these issues must be addressed. As such, FTP addressed the human capital needs of women; further education and training were key components to the program. The "downside" to this program, from the point of view of some recipients, is that participants were limited to 24 months of AFDC benefits in any 60 month period after entering FTP. Time limits made some women uncomfortable because they were not confident that they could truly be self-sufficient after the two-year period ended.

The FTP program included several major components. First, the program amended several traditional welfare rules to create stronger incentives to work. For example, recipients were allowed to keep a greater portion of their earnings before losing eligibility for welfare. In addition, FTP allowed families to accumulate more assets than normally allowed, such as a higher valued automobile. Child care benefits were also increased to make it easier for women to work. Second, FTP streamlined and enhanced supportive services for recipients. Each recipient is assigned a case manager, whose job is to work with other social service agencies to meet the social and health needs of program participants. Case managers develop closer relationships with clients and provide the moral and social support necessary to build women's self-esteem and in other ways increase their likelihood of success in employment. Third, FTP enforced parental responsibility by, for example, requiring that mothers with school-age children ensure that their children stay in school, by speaking with their children's teachers, and by verifying that their children have received proper immunizations (Bloom, 1995; Bloom, Kemple, and Rogers-Dillon, 1997).

Many recipients, at the time of the interview, were taking advantage of FTP and other voluntary programs. Dee, for example, describes her experiences. She is in school at the community college and plans to eventually transfer to the university to study accounting.

> There are a lot of strengths. They have programs for single parents. They have programs for teen parents. The system tries to help those who help themselves. It is helping me pay for my schooling now because I didn't get aid this term. They are paying my tuition, they are paying my books, and they are paying my child care. They give me my bus passes for free. So they help me out right there.

Clearly, FTP had many positive features, particularly with respect to enhancing human capital. But, as I suggest in Chapter 8, human capital alone is not the panacea to permanently exiting welfare.

Although several positive features of the welfare system were identified when probed, many weaknesses remain.

Weaknesses of the Welfare System

Criticisms of the welfare system were vast and widespread. Women spoke with a heightened sense of concern and passion as they relayed their firsthand experiences with a system they called frustrating, demoralizing, and in need of considerable change and repair. The women interviewed here were anything but complacent about the system. They had firm ideas about the dysfunctions of the welfare system, ideas that had been fermenting since their introduction to it. Three critical themes emerged from these interviews: (1) welfare simply does not provide enough money to live on, (2) services are delivered inappropriately, and (3) benefits are eliminated prematurely.

First, a significant number of women lamented that the welfare system provides benefits at such a low level that it is virtually impossible to maintain a decent standard of living for their children. An AFDC grant in the region where the interviews were conducted was $241 a month for a parent with one child, $303, $364, and $426 for a parent with two, three, and four children, respectively, in 1996. Food stamps ranged from $212 for a parent with one child, to $371 for a parent with four children.

Jasmine, a 35-year-old African American mother of two children, is employed part-time, but continues to receive a partial welfare benefit because of her low earnings. She would prefer to work full-time, as she has done in the past, but when her two children began having severe asthma attacks, she cut back her hours so that she could take care of them. She feels uncomfortable leaving them with a baby-sitter, she told me. Luckily, she has relatives who can watch them during her reduced work hours who are knowledgeable about asthma, and how to treat it, in case an attack were to occur. Like others, Jasmine is frustrated by the size of her welfare grant and her reduction in food stamps, believing that they are inadequate for taking care of children:

> I simply don't get enough food stamps. And the AFDC, at $54 a month, are you kidding? They keep asking me, "How are you paying your rent, how are you paying your rent?" It's like, hey, if you'd give me more money, I could answer that. And she's like, "But this doesn't add up. Your income and your outcome don't add up. You just don't have enough money." And I'm like, "Why do you think I'm here? Yes, I don't have enough money. They are implying what? That I'm selling my body, or what? You know? I bounce checks, there's your answer."

Stephanie supports herself and Megan on a grant of $241 a month while supplementing it with student loans. She acknowledges that, compared to other recipients, she is relatively affluent. She feels, however, anything but affluent. Stephanie expressed anger that a country as wealthy as ours spends so little to take care of its children. She began this conversation with a discussion of substandard housing that low income people may reside in:

> . . . is something going to come out and bite me? This is the equivalent of the Black Plague, with all the rats. How can anyone grow up normal, intelligent, and become a productive member of society living like that? I don't understand. And when you're hungry at night, or when your child goes to bed cold, how can you expect them to go to school the next morning and learn anything? You know, Maslow's hierarchy of needs. If you don't meet the very bottom ones, how are you supposed to be anything on top? We're humans, and will resort to survival skills. And I'm sure that's what many people are doing. Just surviving. I've known a lot of women who live in these villages [student family housing at the university] who

are not as fortunate as I am. I mean, I had a house full of stuff when I moved in here because I already had a house. I mean, how can any child grow up and be stimulated in an environment where they may or may not be able to heat the house, or be able to afford the extra $20 or $30 that I hand over at the end of the month to buy food? Or they may not be able to go out and buy the clothing that their child needs when they outgrow it, or the shoes. Most of the time I can swing it. But, like I said, if it wasn't for family housing and living on campus, and my financial aid, there would be no way.

When mothers on welfare complain about the amount of money they receive, they are not just bleating for the sake of it. Children who are deprived of adequate financial support suffer long-term consequences. McLanahan and Sandefur, in their award-winning book *Growing Up with a Single Parent* (1994), report that income is a significant factor, although certainly not the only one, in explaining the deleterious effects of growing up in a single parent household. Using several data sources from nationally representative samples across the United States, they found that children in single parent households are less likely to graduate from high school; they are less likely to enroll in and graduate from college; they are more likely to be out of work; and girls are more likely to become teen mothers than are those children who have grown up in two-parent households. Income itself accounts for approximately half of the differences between the two groups. Thus, our government tradition of supporting children inadequately has serious long-term consequences.

A second concern with the welfare system was over the way in which services were delivered. Women repeatedly described many problems: they complained that the system is far too impersonal; caseworkers are unhelpful; there should be more "one-on-one help"; child support should be more closely enforced and monitored; and that the delivery medical services through the Public Health Unit were problematic. Moreover, women repeatedly told me that the system is cumbersome and complicated.

Alexandra, a 29-year-old white woman who has been on welfare for four years, describes the "maze" she encountered when she lost her job and turned to welfare for help:

> I mean, when you start on welfare, you have to start depending on people that are already on welfare to get you into the system because nobody is there to help you and there are no guidelines to go by to tell you how. I just needed some assistance at the time and I wanted to go back to school and stuff, but I couldn't get assistance because I couldn't figure out how. I kept going down for appointments, and I couldn't get in there. It's just like you have to know somebody to be able to get on it and get through it. It's like a maze; it's like a puzzle, and you have to fit the pieces together and you have to start learning how to work the system, basically. It's like a job learning how to do it, and I was real naïve. I never saw a food stamp in my life. I never saw a WIC check, you know. I didn't even know what an

AFDC check looked like. I had never even known a person who used them.

Becky, a 23-year-old white woman who works nearly full-time cleaning houses, summarized the concerns of many when she complained that services are delivered without individuals' needs in mind. If people are on welfare because of varying circumstances, then their needs are likely to differ as well. They may need different things in order to help them get *off* welfare.

> There needs to be more individual one-on-one help. Meet the individual's need, instead of forcing them to conform to some generic lot and saying take it or leave it. I feel like a hypocrite being on AFDC because I don't agree with it and its way of treating people. It treats everybody the same, but it needs to stop and look at the individual and try to help each individual person according to what they need. No patch solutions.

The third weakness of the welfare system that was repeatedly emphasized is that welfare benefits are significantly reduced or eliminated prematurely when a recipient acquires a job. Given the options of low-paid work for welfare recipients, their incomes are not sufficient to pull them out of poverty. Moreover, when working, they face a new host of challenges and difficulties, such as needing transportation, child care, or requiring additional clothing or frequent laundering of uniforms. Many women would be willing to take on these extra challenges but find that, with their cash grant, food stamps, housing subsidies and Medicaid cut, they are in a worse financial predicament than they were while they were home receiving welfare. Is it worth it, they ask themselves? This issue is addressed further in Chapter 8, which explores why some women are apparently hesitant to take jobs.

Welfare Reforms

All of the women interviewed wanted substantial reforms made to our welfare system. They were adamant: The welfare system needs reforming because it does not help them get off welfare. Dee questions whether welfare, even in the wake of reforms, actually tries to help women.

> They give you just enough money to keep you going with helping with rent and the utility bill, just enough to keep you going and looking forward to that next month's check. So therefore, you look forward to next month's check. In a sense, they baited the hook and you done took a bite out of it, and now they are fighting to keep you there. Even though they talk about reform and everything. I think that as long as people stay on the welfare system, they know that these people are not going to be in the job market.

In this next section I examine how respondents felt about three reforms in particular: (1) time limits on welfare, (2) work requirements, and (3) "family caps" that limit or deny additional benefits for children born to mothers on welfare. These three features are some of the more controversial changes made in welfare law in 1997. They illustrate our uneasiness with appropriate roles for single mothers, and our underlying contempt that welfare recipients are smugly satisfied with, and would like to remain on, the public dole.

Time Limits

Time limits would impose an arbitrary limit on the number of years that recipients could receive welfare, both consecutively and overall. The majority of women interviewed either opposed time limits or suggested that they would support them reluctantly, but only if certain specific conditions were met. Women who opposed time limits generally suggested that they are arbitrary, and that they fail to take personal needs into account. They believed that there are a variety of legitimate reasons why women, including themselves, may need to rely on cash programs for longer than two or three years; "Too many things could go wrong once the two or three years passed," or "you can be up on your feet one day, and down the next." Because they often felt that they were on welfare because of circumstances that were beyond their control, many believed that they had little control over the circumstances that would get them off welfare. An example of this sentiment was expressed by Jasmine. She is employed, but her income was not enough to pull her above the poverty line. When asked if she thought time limits of two to three years should be imposed, she responded:

> No, I don't. Because sometimes it takes people a little longer than that to get on their feet. Like me with my children. Like I say, it's pretty much medical problems that will keep a person on. . . . There's got to be a reason why the person is on the system in the first place and there's got to be a reason why that person is still on the system later on down the line, maybe four or five years later on down the line. There's got to be a reason for that.

Stephanie also strongly opposed time limits. She also argued passionately that they were arbitrary and unfair, and further, she suggests that they would ultimately increase the crime rate. Several respondents echoed this idea:

> Oh God, that is amusing. How can you put a timeline on someone's life? I see what they are trying to do. They are trying to get those individuals who they feel aren't making efforts to get off the rolls. But I don't agree with that. Setting an arbitrary time limit on a system that is so dysfunctional to begin with that, you know, it's amazing that anyone gets off it. . . . Even with the current system we are suffering, and now they want to cut us off after three years? What do they think that is going to accom-

plish? Yeah, it will accomplish an incredible rise in crime because that is what people are going to resort to in order to survive. I mean, hell, if it was me, I'd probably push drugs too. Even though it is totally against my beliefs. Or I would rob. I mean, if it means the difference between me eating and having a halfway decent place to live or not, I'd do it. So, if that's what they want to accomplish, then hey, go ahead.

This concern that crime may increase as welfare eligibility becomes more stringent, was alluded to by both white and African American women. They felt that strict time limits could result in considerable hardship for many families, and at least some of these families would resort to crime to make up for the lost income, "and they can't put people in jail forever, you know? They're going to have to take care of people some kind of way."

Amy, a 23-year-old white mother who has been on welfare for two years, elaborated on this theme:

> Once you start having people that are poor, or homeless, or hungry, you're going to have a lot more crime. We're going to see a lot of crime because they are going to do what it takes to support the family, whether it's drugs, or stealing, or burglarizing. We're going to see a lot of this if we yank people off. What are they going to do, you know? People say you can get a job anywhere, but you can't. And a lot of people aren't qualified to work. So, you know, we can't just say "We're taking this from you and next month you're not going to have a check, you're not going to have food stamps—go out there and find a job." They can't go out there and find a job. They have no job skills. They've been on welfare for ten years taking care of children and their home, or sitting home doing nothing. And, nobody's going to hire them right now. So it's just going to cause problems.

Other women supported time limits reluctantly, and only if certain specific amendments were included to ensure that allowances were made for specific circumstances and needs. These most commonly included allowing additional time for women whose lives are especially difficult or disorganized, giving women additional time for schooling or training, and ensuring that women are guaranteed a job above minimum wage. Women on welfare may experience a high degree of disorganization in their lives. Day-to-day living is a challenging attempt to pay the bills on time, to put food on the table, to juggle child care, to find a job, to locate donations and charities to help benefits stretch further, to nurse sick children, and to earn additional income that can be hidden from one's caseworker. Time limits made many women nervous: How can they ensure that their lives would progress smoothly through the stages necessary to be off welfare in two to three years, when their lives are a constant struggle today? Women referred to the concern that they have in trying to find a job or their ability to keep a job. How can they really guarantee that they will be able to secure a good paying job for themselves with medical benefits during this relatively short time period and not need any further aid? Many women reported that they have submitted numerous applications to no avail. Doreen is a 31-year-old African American woman who receives $241 a month for herself and her 15-year-old daughter Latasha, who is seven months pregnant with her first child, and requires complete bed rest after going into early labor. She is being home schooled so that she can continue high school. Doreen said that she would like to get a job, and has earnestly looked for work in the past, but usually can only turn up part-time pay in the fast food industry. So, instead, she baby-sits occasionally for extra money, but does not report this income to her caseworker. And now, without a car, with Latasha needing full-time care, and with a new grandbaby on the way, finding a job seems a near impossibility. She summarizes the concerns of many regarding time limits when she says:

> If they can get a job within that time, then yeah. But if they can't get a job within that time period, then allow another three or four years until they can. Because if you go out and put out applications, that doesn't mean that person is going to hire you. You know, you can get out there and do it, but there's no guarantee that the person is going to hire you. They might hire the next person, or the next person. . . . You know, actually it would be really good if they guaranteed that you would get a job. It's my opinion that if they can go and guarantee you a job, then get off welfare. But if they can't guarantee that they're going to get you a job, then leave them alone because it's going to hurt the kids in the long run.

Other women voiced concern that their education may take more than two or three years, "because when you got five kids, there's no way you can sit down and study all the time." One example is Dawn, introduced in Chapter 3. She has been on and off welfare for most of her childhood and adult life, and recently began an educational program at a community college. She was enthusiastic about her future possibilities, but recognized that her training may take more than two years, given her other family and household responsibilities:

> I guess if somebody just sat around those two or three years and didn't do something then cut maybe those people. But a person like me, you are going to cut it when I'm not through with my education? Wait, hold on, give me a few minutes, you know? I don't think you can say, "Just cut everybody at the same time. Just cut it off."

Despite the well-stated opposition, not all women opposed time limits for receiving welfare. Some voiced their support, and suggested that time limits would prevent young teenage girls from getting pregnant and subsequently relying on welfare. Others believed that two to three years was ample time to develop the skills to become self-supporting or to find a job. Not surprisingly, these women usually had been on welfare for one year or less, and were optimistic that their financial situation would improve very shortly. They maintained that welfare should be a short-term helping hand, and therefore it was reasonable that aid be discontinued after this brief amount of time. One mother, Janie, aged 19, who had been on welfare for one year after giving birth to a daughter conceived during a rape, candidly told me:

> The reason they are stopping it is because they are providing ample time for school, for work, and they are giving you all the opportunities you need, and by then you should be able to take care of yourself. . . . Two years makes sense. It gives people long enough to get their programs, to figure out exactly what they want to do, exactly what they need, and can go from there.

In conclusion, most women who were interviewed opposed time limits, or only supported them reluctantly with significant clauses attached, because strict time limits were thought to be arbitrary and would not take into account personal need. Only a few welfare recipients felt that the limitations were necessary to stop the abuse and fraud that is assumed to occur with the system. Most welfare recipients did not see time limits as a useful way to reform welfare because they did not perceive that they themselves were abusing the system or that they were careless in looking for work or trying to get off welfare. They felt that time limits would increase their stress level, potentially harm their children, and that it would make their attempts to get off welfare more difficult rather than easier.

Work Requirements

Unlike time limits, work requirement reforms received overwhelming support among welfare recipients. Despite the persistence of the idea that recipients must be forced into work, I found that most women enthusiastically supported reforms requiring employment. Furthermore, they suggested that if recipients could not find jobs, they should do volunteer work in their community in order to be eligible to receive a check. Most women contended that requiring work would improve women's self-esteem, would provide them with needed skills and experience, would allow them to serve as an important role model to their children, and last but certainly not least, would get them off of welfare. These findings contradict popular notions that welfare recipients prefer to live off the public dole. Instead, I found that they want to get off welfare. Carrie, a white 39-year-old mother of three who currently attends school and has been on welfare for five years, summarized the views of many women when she commented:

> I think they ought to do something. Either like volunteer work at a hospital, or go out and help old people, or there's a lot of work to do. I don't think that people ought to just sit around and do nothing. Unless there's something wrong with them, people who are incapacitated in some way. . . . There's no reason why they should sit home and watch soaps all day. I think everyone should have something to do outside the home. Even people who have little kids. There should be some kind of group day care for kids so that mothers can get out and have some kind of outlet.

Carrie was not alone in her ideas. Leah agrees with her. Leah is a 24-year-old unemployed African American mother who has four children, ages 10, 8, 6, and her youngest not yet a year old. On first glance she looks like an unlikely candidate for work. Although she has a high school diploma, she has never held a job. Leah has been on welfare since she turned 18. Yet, even she concurred with the vast majority of women interviewed: women on welfare should have some sort of job, even one that doesn't pay wages.

> At least, if they can't get a paying job, they should have volunteer hours. They should have to go somewhere and volunteer so that if there are small children in the house, so the children can see the person do something— leave the home and go be involved in something. That they aren't always just surrounded by people who don't leave the house and who aren't doing anything. Hopefully it will be a better role model to see your parents get up and do something.

The majority of women—white, African American, young, old, those with either school-age or young children—embraced work requirements for women on welfare. Yet women also said that children should be over the age of three or should be in school; that recipients should be allowed to finish school if they were already enrolled; that the job should pay above minimum wage; and that benefits should not be automatically and immediately eliminated, "or else it just wouldn't work." Jo Lynn expressed the sentiment held by many who support work requirements, but only if these other conditions are met. Otherwise, she suggests, working becomes prohibitive. She tells us of her dilemma, of wanting to work, but wondering if work will enhance or detract from her meager standard of living. She is frightened by the prospect of working, and worries that employment will reduce her already meager standard of living.

> Yes, depending on the situation. Depending on your youngest child's age. Maybe on how long a person has been on AFDC, and depending on how much money that person gets from a job, or what benefits are going to be cut. I think a lot of people would be willing to go to work, even want to work. It's a scary thing, where, like me, okay, I have $241 a month, and I want to get a part-time job. And they say, "Okay, you can take the job, but we're going to start cutting everything off." You know, it takes a little while to establish yourself. I think if they would help establish people, like give them six months to keep their AFDC check and their work check, where they could put some money aside maybe or build up for their own apartment, or whatever they need to build up. With health insurance, if you get a job and make over a certain amount of money you lose your Medicaid completely and everything. And I think that's a really serious situation for a lot of people.

Women worried about their children. First and foremost, the women I interviewed wanted to ensure that work would be compatible with motherhood and would better their family's lives. If it did not, either financially or psychologically, then work was less enticing.

Alexandra is divorced and has one child. She's been on welfare for four years, although she anticipates being off welfare shortly. She has an Associate of Arts (AA) degree from a community college and would like to transfer to a four-year university for a bachelor's degree in art. The walls in her home were decorated with her own art work, revealing keen talent. Alexandra also suggested it is unrealistic to expect women to simply go to work without some assistance from the government. She questioned the benefits of putting infants and toddlers in day care for nine or 10 hours a day. She also brought up the cost of child care, and questioned whether a job would even cover these costs. Although she supports work requirements in theory, she doesn't feel like it is desirable to work full-time when her child is young, nor is it even possible to work unless her child care needs are taken care of:

> Work or go to school is good. I wouldn't mind having a part-time job or something. But how much money can I make at a part-time job? And how much does a sitter charge? A lot, you know? Is your entire paycheck even going to be able to pay for a week or a month's baby-sitter? So, I don't know. It's a good idea, but they would have to pay child care. You see what I mean? Otherwise, it just wouldn't work.

Several women opposed work requirements outright, primarily because they felt that women who are single parents should not be required to work and leave their children to strangers for care. Although opportunities for employment were applauded, they opposed mandates that apply to all women *carte blanche*. They adhere to the adage that it is better for children to be taken care of by their own parent rather than by a stranger. They expressed concern, as did several other mothers, about leaving their young children to be cared for by strangers in an impersonal daycare setting. Relying on their own mothers, sisters, or other female relatives was a common strategy for child care. But many women indicated that even relatives could not be relied on to provide full-time child care on a regular daily basis. Furthermore, they acknowledged that they didn't *want* to relinquish the care of their children. They wanted to care for and nurture their own children, and they felt that they should not be denied this experience simply because they are poor and receive welfare. Although they may not be familiar with the nuances of the multiple scientific studies that indicate the importance of parental social support and interaction for the resiliency and adaptation of at-risk youth (Bowen and Chapman, 1996; Harris and Marmer, 1996; Resnick, Harris and Blum, 1993), somehow they knew intuitively that as sole parents, their physical presence and nurturing are critical to their child's social development. Stephanie, eager to work as a nurse, nonetheless referred to work requirements as "indentured servitude." Another woman, 29-year-old Laura, who has two children, a toddler and an infant, said:

> I think that it's more beneficial for my family that I be home than to compromise our lives in other ways, in sending them out to be cared for by somebody else. I would rather have a system that helped people take care

of their kids and take care of their kids well. To teach them to grow up and to have more of a community aspect of people helping each other than this "for each his own" kind of thing.

Despite the concerns expressed by these few women, the vast majority of welfare recipients enthusiastically endorsed work requirements. Many were visibly delighted by the prospect that the government would give them a job. However, although largely supportive of work requirements, many women also exercised caution. They were concerned about the kinds of jobs would they get, whether their benefits would be immediately affected, and, most of all, they worried about their children. They were adamant that work should not come in the way of motherhood—after all, they are the only parents that their children have to rely on.

Family Caps

"Family caps" are designed to limit or deny additional benefits for children born to women on welfare. This policy is based on the assumption that women have additional children carelessly, or perhaps even purposely, in order to increase the level of welfare benefits received. It is assumed that women will cease having children if they are no longer "rewarded" for it.

The majority of women interviewed opposed this reform effort. They believed that family caps unfairly penalize innocent children "from something that they need." Yet there is significant disagreement as to whether women on welfare deliberately have children to increase the size of their benefit level. Some women argue that yes, other recipients will be influenced to have more children if their welfare benefit is increased. However, even some of the women who believe that women do have additional children to augment their welfare check still opposed family caps, arguing that children should not be punished for the decisions made by their parents. Jessie, a 42-year-old African American mother, spoke for most women when she said, "Increase. You shouldn't jeopardize a woman for having a baby or make children suffer because of their parents."

Reference was often made to the additional costs associated with having a child, and that the current benefit probably could not realistically be stretched to cover these costs. Again, the child would ultimately suffer as a result. Marissa spoke of inflation, and that a child's needs cannot be squeezed out of an already low welfare grant.

> There's inflation, you know, and prices go up. I think it should be increased. You know, the basics of buying clothes and stuff. That's another family member, and you can't live off the amount it is. Well, you can live, but as far as buying Pampers and stuff like that, you couldn't do it without an increase.

Other women were more ambivalent regarding whether benefits should cover an additional child born to women while on welfare. They may oppose family caps in principle, but they acquiesced that caps may be necessary if women continue to have many children while on welfare. The threshold varied as to when caps should be implemented. Some claimed that if a woman had one or two additional children while on welfare she should still receive benefits for that child, but caps should be imposed for subsequent births. Others were more tolerant and allowed three or more additional births. Not surprisingly, their tolerance closely mirrored their own experience with nonmarital births. For example, one woman, who had one child while receiving welfare, maintained that caps should be applied only to the second pregnancy:

> I feel that if they do it this one time, okay. I don't see to give them more money if they have more than one child on AFDC. Because one time, it could have been an accident, or whatever the case may be. But if they have more than one child when you're on AFDC—if you see a pattern there— you shouldn't get any more.

A small number of women endorsed family caps wholeheartedly and without any qualifiers. They believed that women have additional babies simply to receive a greater level of benefit, and felt that this reform would curtail this behavior. Tanya, a 35-year-old African American woman on welfare for five years and who herself recently had a child while on welfare, felt that caps are fair and reasonable. She felt that it is not unusual for other women on welfare to have a child for the sole purpose of increasing their check, unaware of the empirical evidence indicating that women on welfare have lower fertility rates than other women (Rank, 1989). She subscribes to the stereotype nonetheless, and believes that family caps will stop women from having additional children. Distancing her situation from these other women, she says that their benefit level should not increase:

> I would say, stay the same. A lot of people out there are saying, "The more children we have, the more money we'll get." I would say, after two or three years, it should stay the same, whether they have another child or not. They should know that the system can only do so much for them and their children.

These few women's concerns not withstanding, the majority of women interviewed opposed family caps, which would deny or limit additional aid to women who have children while on welfare. They felt that the costs associated with having another child could not be absorbed easily within the previous benefit, and that the child would ultimately suffer as a result. Most felt that caps would not reduce the birth rate significantly, and that this program would do little to really help women exit from welfare.

Ideas for Reform

What reforms, then, do recipients perceive to be in their best interest? Soliciting ideas about welfare reform generated spirited conversations. Women expressed a desire for a system that is proactive, rather than reactive; one that supports and encourages women, rather than punishes and threatens them; a system that provides incentive for self-help, rather than one that discourages women from trying to help themselves; one that protects children, and doesn't harm them in either the short- or long-term.

The interviews revealed several specific ideas for welfare reform, falling into two broad themes. The first focused on how the welfare system itself could be improved so that women would have more security in raising their children on it. For example, they suggested that benefit levels should be raised, because it simply is not enough to live on. Contrary to rhetoric espoused by welfare critics, raising a benefit level would not encourage women to remain on the public dole, they told me. Instead, it would help them terminate welfare more quickly by providing them with an opportunity to save money and acquire a few additional assets, such as a reliable automobile, that would ultimately make it easier for them to seek and maintain employment. The paltry benefit levels keep them impoverished, while the ambitious often resort to fraud so that they can realistically improve their financial status.

They also asked that the welfare system more vigorously enforce the collection of child support from fathers. Although some women clearly stated that they wanted nothing to do with the fathers of their children, often because of physical or emotional abuse, they generally did want the government to intervene on their children's behalf. Many expressed resentment that they alone shouldered the burden of child care while fathers were off playing, working, in jail, or had the luxury of simply disappearing from sight. Some women preferred the fathers' absence because they would then not have to hassle with visitation schedules, engage in custody battles, or put up with sexually or emotionally harassing visits. One woman likened herself to a prostitute—providing sex to her son's father so that he would give her occasional child support money. Overall, the women wondered why the system treats them with suspicion and contempt, while apparently doing little to chase down fathers who do not financially support their children.

Recipients also told me that they wanted a system that was customized to individual needs. They felt that the "one size fits all" model will not work, and that they would benefit from welfare workers that take a case-management approach. Case managers should have a personal interest in the needs of recipients and assist them in finding employment. I was reminded that not all women have the same needs, come from the same background, or have the same reasons for needing welfare in the first place. One woman, Sarah, suggested that recipients be allowed to choose from an array of benefit options in order to customize their welfare package with what they truly need. She told me that she received far more food stamps than she needed, for example, and used them as Christmas and birthday gifts for her family and friends. She acknowledged the waste, felt badly about it, and suggested that what she really needed instead was help with her rent. The unsubsidized rent on her small and run-down trailer consumed nearly all of her $241 welfare grant. Another woman told me that she would rather not have a cash grant at all, but she wouldn't be eligible for Medicaid without it.

Recipients also clamored for a system that distinguished between those who want to work hard to improve their economic circumstances and those who do not. They asked for a system that recognized that some women (i.e., themselves in particular) do not fit the stereotypes of welfare recipients that are so prevalent. Although they exaggerate the differences between themselves and other recipients, their concern that the system tends to punish those who are trying to improve their circumstances does contain merit. For example, educational programs for welfare recipients are significantly curtailed under recent reforms. Women asked that the system allow those who are making strides toward self-sufficiency to continue to receive needed benefits. They felt that benefits should be ended for those who are cheating or manipulating the system or who are making no effort to improve their economic circumstances through school or work. They also stated that those who are making satisfactory progress in school should not be arbitrarily dropped from welfare after some predetermined two-year time limit. In other words, women like Stephanie, working towards a bachelor of science in nursing (BSN), were viewed as model welfare recipients, not as someone who should have her benefits eliminated.

The second set of suggestions for ways that the welfare system could be improved, surprisingly, had little to do with welfare itself. Rather, recipients pressed for changes in the way that our society structures low-tier work, and asked that policymakers reexamine the interplay between work and welfare. Women asked that low-tier work be made less tenuous and more secure so that they could get off welfare once and for all. They considered changing the structure of low-tier work so that they could exit welfare permanently the best reform of all. For example, they asked for help in finding jobs, particularly jobs that paid sufficiently so they could support a family. They know that the current minimum wage will not allow them to take care of their children adequately; it leaves them in a more desperate situation than they were in while on welfare. They suggested that jobs in and of themselves were difficult to get, and finding jobs paying at least $8 an hour were nearly impossible to locate on their own. Many told of submitting job application after job application without ever being called for an interview. They asked for help finding employment, particularly jobs that would lift them above the poverty level. Several suggested that it was high time to raise the minimum wage so that they could support their families on it.

Recipients also suggested that, when they do get jobs, they should be allowed to keep part of their welfare check and part of their benefits, for a short period of time at least, to enable them to accumulate the capital necessary for stability. They complained of intermittent employment and welfare use, but attributed it to the vulnerability associated with suddenly having a huge housing bill, or startling food bills, or expensive child care, or the need to buy an automobile for transportation, while earning wages that were only slightly higher than they made while on welfare. They found that their financial security did not improve. Their lives became even more difficult and disheartening as they tried to juggle a new job paying at or near minimum wage with the newfound bills they were required to pay, all the while trying to locate dependable and affordable child care. They asked for interplay between work and welfare, and suggested that if they could keep part of their check, and part of their benefits, such as housing subsidies or food stamps, for at least three to six months, they could begin to accumulate the capital needed to cushion themselves when the unforeseen emergency inevitably occurs. It was felt that this would improve their confidence that they would not, once again, have to return to welfare.

Moreover, they asked that educational benefits be continued and strengthened. Many noted that their ticket out of welfare and minimum wage jobs was through greater education and job training. Although more than half of our sample had at least a high school diploma, most recognized that this is simply not enough to compete in today's job market. Moreover, they felt that teenage women on welfare must be encouraged, or perhaps even forced, to finish their high school education. It was commonly expressed that, in order to receive benefits, teenagers should remain in school. Or they suggested that wages be tied to education; those with high school diplomas or GEDs would earn higher wages than would those without degrees. Some women requested remedial help in basic skills such as reading, writing, and arithmetic, believing that their skills were deficient. But more often, women asked for substantial training that would be directly tied to higher wage work and job opportunities. They were suspicious of short-term training programs; many had experience with them already and still felt ill-prepared for the labor market. They know that there are higher paying opportunities beyond the service sector, but many women do not yet have the skills to compete for these jobs, and they hoped that a component of welfare reforms would be devoted to helping them acquire work-related skills.

And finally, they asked that their medical benefits be continued. They expressed fear and trepidation that future jobs were unlikely to offer health insurance to themselves or to their families. When asked to rank the importance of all the different types of aid they received, Medicaid was at the top of their list. The need for medical benefits kept many women on welfare longer than they would like. But accepting a job without medical benefits was seen as behaving irresponsibly by jeopardizing their children's health and well-being.

We can conclude from these interviews that welfare recipients wanted a welfare system that was based on an incentive, rather than on a punitive approach. They asked for both a welfare system and an economic system that supports families, encourages them, invests in them, makes them more secure, and reinforces their duty and motivation to provide for their children. They wanted welfare to be a temporary helping hand—not a permanent fixture in their lives.

These in-depth interviews with women on welfare reveal a complex set of beliefs with respect to the welfare system. They want the government to help them off of welfare; they do not simply want hand-outs. Moreover, recipients are not opposed to welfare reform. On the contrary, the women in this study embrace ideas for change. They are passionate that the welfare system is in disrepair and needs to be fixed. They expressed eagerness to work; but they needed assistance in finding good paying jobs, and they needed support mechanisms such as education, child care, and medical benefits that would enable them to continue working. Most importantly, their children's needs came first, and they were not willing to jeopardize their children's well-being by inadequate day care. Recipients were less enthusiastic about strict time limits and caps denying additional benefits for children born to mothers already receiving welfare. They pleaded for a system that takes personal needs into account and suggested that a "one size fits all" model will not work. They wanted a system based on positive incentives, one that provides support and encouragement and strengthens the security of work for those employed in jobs within the bottom tier of our economic system. They don't want help to stay on the system, they want help to get off of it.

Why does Stephanie, introduced at the beginning of this chapter, despise welfare, despite seemingly benefiting from the system for four years? She suggested that its supposed help is really a facade. Because of our society's heavy emphasis on individual personality traits as the root cause of poverty, many people do not respect poor women. Consequently, lawmakers are not really motivated to create policies to help them. Welfare's policies and programs are punitive in nature. Welfare critics lament about women "dependent" on the system. The unspoken but inherent view is that people are lazy by nature, and thus, welfare must be kept low to prevent women from getting too comfortable on the system and to serve as a warning to others who may be looking for an easy handout. But, Stephanie suggests, in the quest to cut costs, policymakers refuse to make the initial investments needed in both the welfare and economic systems to help women jump successfully from welfare to work—a jump that most recipients undoubtedly want to make. She reminds us that these things may be costly, but as a society we can pay now or we can pay later in terms of increased crime and other social problems:

> The only thing I see with many of these things that they are trying to do today is that they are trying to cut their costs—in the short term. What they don't realize is that, in the long term, sooner or later it's going to end up costing more in lost property, crime, and you know, drug abuse and drug selling. Sooner or later it is going to come out in the wash. I understand that they are trying to reform the welfare system. It needs it. It really does. From a person who is on it, it really needs it. They need to do something so that people can get off welfare. People need to think about investing in women and children. Give people the opportunity to work or give them an education. Do not penalize them. Give them a little extra for child care. Help them make the transition from being on welfare to getting off. We need to make sure that people are living in decent, clean housing, with clean water, and decent air and good food. You can't do anything if your body is undernourished and you're living in a bad environment. I think that's the way we need to go.

CHAPTER

8 Getting Off Welfare

By 2002, most of the 3.5 million families who receive Temporary Assistance to Needy Families (TANF), the replacement for Aid to Families with Dependent Children (AFDC), are expected to get off welfare and fend for themselves. Some exemptions will be granted to those who cannot work because of their health status, their age, or other conditions, but these exemptions will not likely exceed 20 percent of those currently on welfare. Instead, for the vast majority of "able-bodied" recipients, the welfare reform signed into law by President Clinton mandates that they find jobs and become self-supporting—quickly. Many of these adults, mostly mothers, have already begun looking for work. This chapter explores the outlook for these women. What kinds of jobs are they likely to find, and at what pay? It asks whether communities can absorb this many new workers, and looks at the obstacles they may face in finding and holding onto jobs. Unable to move back and forth on and off welfare, as recipients often have in the past, how can we ensure that women will not need the extra assistance from welfare? Politicians and the public will measure the success of welfare reform by the rate recipients are eliminated from assistance and put into jobs. Whether women and children remain impoverished in their new jobs is of less interest.

Welfare recipients are often lumped together into one large homogeneous group. In reality, many different kinds of persons receive welfare, and they receive it for different reasons. Passell (1997) highlights three types of recipients, all of whom have different backgrounds and needs, and whom will fare differently under reform legislation. The first group consists mostly of women who are impoverished because of bad luck, temporary illness, or divorce. These women often need a short-term "helping hand" to boost themselves back up to independence. Their stays on welfare are short, especially if they have family, friends, and other social supports from which to draw. Their lives are temporarily disorganized, and usually are sorted out enough to leave welfare fairly quickly. Stays of only a few months are not uncommon. As indicated in Chapter 1, 19.5 percent of welfare recipients are off the system in six months or less (U.S. House of Representatives, Committee on Ways and Means, 1996). These women would find jobs on their own quickly without the prod of welfare reform legislation.

The second group of recipients, and the most numerous, are on welfare for an interrelated set of individual and structural reasons. Some are on welfare because they lack job skills, experience, education, or other types of human capital. One-third of the AFDC caseload scored in the bottom decile on the Armed Forces Qualifying Test (AFQT), which is a measure of basic skills (Olson and Pavetti, 1998). As it stands now, these women may not be desirable employees, except perhaps in the lowest tier service sector positions where turnover is high, wages are low, and benefits are virtually nonexistent. Women in this group, it has been argued (Passell, 1997), can have their marketability enhanced with further training, counseling, and financial incentives in a strong job market. Although it is acknowledged that in a weak market their chances of finding work will be more difficult, the importance of the labor market itself is sometimes downplayed. Yet it is of critical importance in understanding the plight of these recipients. Policymakers assume, with additional training or with a graduate equivalency diploma (GED) in hand, women in this group will find employment in which to support themselves and their families. But can the labor market absorb all of these additional workers, even with their newly earned GEDs, and additional job training? It is this group of welfare recipients that will be most affected by welfare reform legislation. Potentially, they stand much to gain and, realistically, will have much to lose by federal and state reforms. Whether they are winners or losers is dependent on whether they are allowed to attend, or remain, in school long enough to learn high-paying marketable trades, or whether they are processed through superficial job training programs quickly and then turned loose to fend for themselves and compete in a saturated service-sector labor market that pays minimum wages and offers few of the benefits that higher paid workers have come to rely on.

The third group faces severe obstacles to employment. Their physical health may be extremely poor. Or they may have deep-rooted psychological problems that simple short-term counseling or job training cannot overcome, and therefore are of little interest to most employers. For example, 13 percent of AFDC recipients have been found to suffer from near constant depression (persisting at least five out of seven days per week) (Olson and Pavetti, 1998). In all likelihood, a sizable number of these individuals will be exempt from work requirements, particularly those with physical ailments, because they will be certifiably unemployable. However, many of these women, particularly those with mental or emotional problems that are less visible, will not be exempt. They will be forced to compete with thousands of other individuals for low-wage jobs—jobs that they will have difficulty obtaining in the first place, and jobs that they will have more difficulty keeping. National data indicate that 23 percent of AFDC recipients have extremely low basic skills, coupled with severe barriers to employment in two or more of the following areas: physical disability or health limitations; mental health; health or behavioral problems in their children; alcohol or drug use; domestic violence; child welfare; or housing instability (Olson and Pavetti, 1998). Despite rhetoric that says otherwise, not all adults are psychologically, intellectually, and physically capable of financially supporting themselves and their families, given the demands and challenges that poor families face regularly.

Pearl is one of the women who will face relentless obstacles to finding and keeping employment to support herself and her sons, yet her disabilities are largely psychological, and therefore will likely go unnoticed by officials. It took several attempts before I could reach Pearl at her home. She had no telephone, so I could not call in advance. Maybe it was her beautiful flower garden that drew me in and encouraged me to return time and again. Beautiful and well-kept gardens are not common sights in the housing projects that I visited. The second time I stopped by her house, and she was still not home, I wrote her a note, and stuck it in her door. I introduced myself in writing, briefly explained about this book, and told her I would stop by again. On my third attempt I still did not catch her in, but two boys who were playing outside told me that she was their mom, and they indicated that she had my note, and wanted to talk with me. On my fourth visit I found Pearl at home.

After so many attempts to locate her, after seeing her lovely and well-tended garden, and after talking with her children, I felt that I knew her even before we met. I envisioned a young, vibrant African American woman, frequently off visiting friends or running errands. I was wrong. Pearl was very different than I expected. First, she was older than I had imagined. She was 48 years old, but looked considerably older than her age. Her teeth had all been recently pulled, adding to her aged looks. As it turns out, Pearl has eight children; the two I met were her youngest boys, ages 9 and 12. Two more boys, ages 14 and 17, also live at home; and one 18-year-old girl comes and goes at her own convenience. Pearl's oldest three children are grown and out of the house. Pearl looked tired and worn out. According to her own account, that's exactly how she feels.

> I have a lot of pressure. It's like a bruise, you know, all my life. By staying down and worrying about kids. I've had to raise them all myself. Stress. I've been under a lot of stress for a long time. They put me on Prozac. Sometimes I have so much pressure sometimes I don't take them. I just sit there and let the pressure worry me. I had fainting spells, and the doctor said, "I can't see anything, just get it together." Like I want to. But I tried, but with the kids, it was like, throw me back. It's hard being with such pressure all the time. I let myself go down by worrying about them.

Pearl's children have been a constant source of tension for her, especially since the divorce from her second husband because of his frequent infidelity. He is now in prison. She tells me that she loves her children dearly, but acknowledges that she has little control over them. On the weekday morning that I interviewed her, two of her boys were home from school; the 14 year old was home because of a "cough," although I didn't hear him cough once during the 90 minutes that I was there. Her 12-year-old son was home because he had been suspended from school for two weeks because of a sex-related offense, of which he claimed innocence.

Her life, as she tells it, has been terribly disappointing, "I feel like I've been mistreated, held down, you know?" Her two oldest sons, ages 28 and 26, have been in and out of prison for drug-related offenses and burglary. One stole money from her—nearly $100, which represented a major savings effort on her part—so that he could buy crack cocaine. None of her children have graduated from high school; all dropped out in the 9th or 10th grade. "They just quit. I think it's because of drugs. You know, in this neighborhood, they get with other kids, and they are doing drugs, so they want to do the same thing," she told me. Nor does the future look bright for the boys who are still in school and living at home; "I've got one kid suspended out of school for ten days. And the 17 year old is giving me lots of problems. He doesn't want to go to school. I've got a whole bunch of pressure," Pearl says. All she really wants, she tells me, wistfully, is to be able to move out of the housing projects—away from the crime, the drugs, the noise, and to keep them in school. She wants to move out of the city to the countryside, where she envisions a slower and more relaxed pace of life, and a more positive environment in which to raise her three remaining teenage boys. "I've been trying to get money to get out of here," she reveals. "I want to move far out of the projects. There is too much drugs. They're messing everywhere you go. Lots of drug dealers in this neighborhood." But sadly, a move is not likely to happen. Pearl has lived in the same public housing unit for nearly 25 years.

Pearl is no stranger to hard work. She's cleaned houses, has worked as a maid in hotels, and worked in a meat packing plant. She quit these various jobs because of problems with her children or health problems related to the stress her children cause. "The kids really worry me. They call me on the job, one of them is in trouble, and the police are here. So I get so upset I give up. I'm too easy to give up." But Pearl is not a quitter. She has worked very hard over the years, including as a farm laborer off and on during much of her life, spending hours hunched over picking vegetables so that she could earn $20 for her family. "I've been working all my life like a boy." She left school in the 8th grade in order to help support her family by picking vegetables during Florida's long growing season. As a mother, Pearl has tried to teach her children the value of hard work and the rewards that can be reaped from it by taking them with her to work in the fields. "I try to teach them how to earn a dollar, you know?" She suggested that they could keep all of the money they earned, and put it towards the high priced sneakers or other clothing that they have been begging for. However, they scoff at the idea of toiling for hours of backbreaking labor only to make less than minimum wage at the end of the day. "Those drug dealers put ideas of easy money into their heads . . ." she tells me. From her sons' perspective, why not sell drugs? It is glamorous, easy, and profitable work. Working in the fields, in contrast, is none of these.

If Pearl has worked before, why do I anticipate that it will be difficult for her to work again? Pearl suffers from a wide variety of physical ailments, but probably none of these are severe enough to excuse her from work requirements. She had recently broken her foot, although it has since healed. She has back problems that she claims prevent her from doing any heavy lifting. She gets tired easy, and has asthma. She also has arthritis, and experiences pain when using her hands. She's applied for Social Security Income (SSI), but has been turned down twice because her physical health problems have not been evaluated as serious enough for disability insurance. More serious, perhaps, are Pearl's emotional and psychological limitations. She is under so much stress from her children, "pressure" as she repeatedly called it, that she would have extreme difficulty finding or holding a job. She told me that she would like to have a job, or go back to school after her children grow up. And over the past few years she has started working towards her GED several times with the assistance of the welfare office. But she quit because of the pressures associated with her children, and because of the numerous household chores that come with five children living in the home. Trying to keep them out of drugs, keep them in school, and cleaning up after them is a more than a full-time job in and of itself. It is, for all practical purposes, more than she can manage on many days. Adding a work requirement to her life would seem to be an impossibility:

> I wash clothes 24 hours a day, hang them up, fold them, and put them in the room. I mop the floor and clean up the house all the time. When I broke my foot I had a cast on to my knee. And I couldn't get them to mop up the floor, pick up paper, keep the yard clean or fold clothes. They don't want to do nothing like that. If you don't have any money, your children don't want to help you nowadays. I feel so much pressure that I can't go to sleep at night. If I lay down early, I might go to sleep. But in 30 minutes I'm up. At three or four or five o'clock in the morning I never go back to sleep. I might go out there in the yard and work and rake.

Pearl is one of the most difficult cases I witnessed, in terms of her employability. She faces tremendous obstacles to finding and keeping a job. Short-term training programs will be of little real benefit to Pearl. She is not on welfare simply because of lacking job experience or lacking a GED. A quick-fix job-training program or enrollment in school for a GED will not, miraculously, make Pearl significantly more employable than she is today. Pearl is on welfare primarily because of deep-rooted emotional and psychological problems that are caused by, or at least exacerbated by, the arduous task of raising eight children at a meager poverty level existence. She was poor whether or not she was employed. Living in poverty is not a trivial event, and some families experience more serious problems than others do. Moreover, some families have better coping skills or more social support in times of crises. Pearl's coping skills are not well developed, and she has no friends or extended family to turn to for social support—support that I found to be crucial to the improvement of the lives of most women on welfare and their families, as noted in Chapter 6. Instead, her aging mother, siblings, and adult children make incessant demands on her. She receives only a sporadic $50 check from the county welfare office as a child support payment for her youngest children. Without the material, financial, or emotional assistance that most other women reportedly had from extended families, neighbors, friends, boyfriends, or from the fathers' of their children, Pearl is poorly equipped to handle the stress of day-to-day living, let alone take on the added dimension of paid employment.

Although perhaps Pearl's case was more extreme than it was for other women interviewed here, her limitations and concerns were not entirely unusual. I saw several other women whose sense of self-worth and self-determination had been eroded to the point that I wondered how they would possibly find the inner strength to leave welfare, despite telling me that they desperately wanted to do so. Their wounds and disabilities are on the inside, not on the outside. And as such, they will likely go unnoticed by welfare authorities. They will be forced into a labor market that they are, to put it mildly, poorly equipped to handle. Who will be there to help the many of them when they fail and fall through the cracks?

My guess is that there are thousands of women like Pearl all across the country. They do not represent all women on welfare, or even the majority of women on welfare. They are, however, a sizeable population that must be recognized and treated with fairness and dignity.

Amy represents the other end of the spectrum. In contrast to Pearl, her employment options look bright and her future contains tremendous optimism. Amy has one five-year-old daughter, who was conceived during a rape. She has been on welfare for three years. She is also attending a university, is very motivated academically, and has nearly completed the requirements for a bachelor's degree in occupational therapy. Her intention is to enter a master's degree program in physical therapy. If she is successful, which I have every reason to believe that she will be, Amy will make $50,000 a year at her job within a few years. No more welfare, ever. She will pay in taxes, over the course of her working career, far more than she ever received while on welfare.

Amy does not yet feel defeated. She receives financial aid to augment the $241 she receives in welfare, and consequently has a somewhat higher standard of living than do others who receive welfare alone. Equally important, she has a very strong extended family that helps her emotionally and financially, unbeknown to welfare officials. Amy's mother and father tend to many of Amy's day-to-day uncertainties: they baby-sit their granddaughter every weekend so that Amy can study; they have loaned her a reliable automobile; they give Amy money at the end of the semester when her financial aid is running low so that she will not have to live solely on AFDC; they buy virtually all of their granddaughter's clothing, toys, and pay for her weekend entertainment when she is at their house. Amy's parents also support her emotionally in her endeavor to earn a college degree. They provide the praise and the moral support that is so necessary for her to continue the frantic pace that comes with a demanding course of study, required internships and volunteer hours, and single motherhood. Moreover, Amy has no particular health problems, has only one child, and is highly intelligent. Given her circumstances, she will, undoubtedly, be a success story. Nonetheless, even for Amy, life is far from easy. She suffers from a number of stress-related disorders, including panic attacks, in her quest to juggle school, motherhood, and paying the bills.

The Women in the Middle: Why Increasing Human Capital Is Not the Only Answer

Most women on welfare are neither as successful as Amy nor as despairing as Pearl. Instead, they are somewhere on the continuum between these two cases. It is likely that these other women, too, will find it difficult to locate work. It is, of course, correct that the dearth in human capital characteristics are important to understanding the lives of many welfare recipients, and in grasping their needs to get off the system. Many women on welfare lack high school diplomas and have limited marketable skills and work experience. These, of course, have a bearing on their employability and opportunities. Persons with more education, more marketable skills, and extensive work experience will have an easier time finding a well-paying job than will someone without these human capital assets.

But the challenges that women on welfare may face are not solely related to a lack of human capital, as we are led to believe. After all, many women leave welfare, permanently or temporarily, while doing nothing to improve their human capital standing, *per se*. Although additional job training, particularly if the training was to come in the higher paid skilled trades, such as carpentry, nursing, or electronics, would be useful and enthusiastically endorsed, this alone is not enough. Instead, other problems in the employability of women on welfare are more *structural* in origin. These major structural difficulties include: (1) not enough unskilled, semiskilled, or skilled jobs to go around for all the women who want them or will need them; (2) jobs that do exist for welfare recipients are largely low paying and do not provide critical benefits; and (3) job training programs are not designed to significantly improve women's job prospects. These three work-related concerns are rooted in limitations of our social structure. They are not related to individual attributes, and the full array of quick-fix job training or motivational programs in the world will not resolve these fundamental problems. Even if we successfully raised every former welfare recipient's educational level to a GED or beyond, the reality is that there are not enough jobs to go around, and the wages and benefits of existing jobs do not permit the jobholder to be lifted from poverty.

Despite these structural obstacles to welfare reform, policymakers continue to draw on the age-old notion that the problem with women on welfare is that they are personally deficient. Their deficiency in human capital, such as education, job skills, and job experience, or their lack of motivation and a socially acceptable work ethos are blamed as the primary factors associated with welfare use, and the primary obstacles to getting off the system. During the 1960s, the War on Poverty, the preoccupation with deficiency in human capital and a concern with a subcultural anti–work ethos—major premises of Individualism and the Culture of Poverty perspective—dominated reform efforts, as shown in Chapter 2. Then, an emphasis on education and job training as a route to self-sufficiency—a "human capital enhancement model"—dominated the political ethos.

Today we are also seeing these individualistic and cultural concerns as the dominant drive behind reforming welfare. But this time around, as compared to the War on Poverty era, fewer dollars are being put into human capital training programs, and those that do exist are of shorter duration and are less comprehensive. However, the underlying philosophic current remains: Welfare dependence is bad, work is good, and we can solve our welfare dilemma by giving people some rudimentary training and putting them to work—forcibly, if need be.

Education and Employment Training

Although significantly less prominent than in the past, current reforms place a small emphasis on education, skill enhancement, job training, and general efforts to increase the level of human capital that women on welfare can offer to potential employers. States may modify federal mandates, but generally, recipients can now only count 12 months of vocational education towards work requirements, and only 30 percent of the caseload can pursue vocational training or education full-time, counting these activities towards work requirements. Education and "bootstrap" training—short-term courses on resume writing, interviewing skills, and other how-to-get-a-job tips—are limited to those directly related to employment. Two- and four-year college programs used by many of the women in these interviews, such as in nursing, accounting, teaching, occupational therapy, and computer programming, would, in most cases, no longer qualify.

What are the educational and job training needs of welfare recipients? My analysis reveals a complex situation. Certainly additional education and more extensive employment training opportunities are better than less education and training. Many recipients—at least the 20 percent of welfare caseload who are without a high school diploma or GED—would benefit from more extensive training in the previously stated occupations, as well as in the skilled trades, such as auto mechanics, welders, or electricians. And in all likelihood, many more women would benefit from further training. Low basic skills may be more common and problematic than other potential barriers to employment, including physical or mental health problems, substance abuse, domestic violence, involvement with the child welfare system, or housing instability (Olson and Pavetti, 1998). For example, not only do one-third of AFDC recipients score in the bottom decile for the women's distribution of the Armed Forces Qualifying Test (AFQT), but one study found that 30 percent of AFDC recipients were reading at the 6th grade level or below (Olson and Pavetti, 1998). Furthermore, somewhere between 25 and 40 percent of AFDC recipients may have learning disabilities (Nightingale, Yudd, Anderson, Barnow, 1991).

But it is not altogether correct to assume that all welfare recipients are deficient in their education level and job training. Although the average education level of recipients is lower than for the population as a whole, many have finished high school and some have attended or graduated from college. Moreover, approximately 13 percent of welfare recipients nationwide were enrolled in job training in 1994 (Committee on Ways and Mean, U.S. House of Representatives, 1996). This does not mean, of course, that only 13 percent have *had* training. Many welfare recipients received training years ago, but found that the training did not lead to a permanent job that paid wages high enough to support their families.

Interestingly, several studies have actually concluded that programs allocating substantial funds to education and training may do no better and sometimes fare worse than do those that focus primarily on immediate job placement. Studies conducted in Alameda County, San Diego, and Riverside, California, for example, report that the earnings gain for recipients was lower than where training was not conducted (Lerman, 1995). The reasons for this are not altogether clear, but I suspect that it is not training in and of itself, but the *type* of training that is important. Women in short-term, superficial, quick-fix training programs do not gain the knowledge and skills required to make appreciably better earnings, at least in the short run. It is not surprising, then, that research by Edin and Lein (1997) report that women on welfare place little faith in these programs. Instead of a superficial examination of how to write a resume and practicing interview skills, women preferred in-depth educational and training programs that were directly linked to higher wage work.

The percentage of women in this study who were enrolled in educational or training programs was significantly higher than the national average—40 percent of the women were engaged in education or job training at the time of the interview. This is likely because of two reasons. First, the interviews took place in a town that contains a major state-funded university, a community college, and two for-profit colleges. More than a half-dozen of the women interviewed were concurrently taking advantage of these educational opportunities: Dee was at a community college studying accounting; Amy was at the university studying occupational therapy; Stephanie was in school at the university preparing to become a registered nurse; Molly was finishing her prerequisites at a community college so that she could transfer to a university to study to become a registered nurse; and Coreen was taking her prerequisites at the community college so that she could enter the College of Education at a university. Several other women were in two-year programs at the community college studying business, computers, or nursing.

Other women had completed training programs in the for-profit schools located in the community, but complained that their "diplomas" did not help them get jobs for which they were trained. These proprietary schools are often built in poorer neighborhoods and court an impoverished clientele with offers of training that will lead to high-paying jobs, ". . . and all I actually got was about a four thousand dollar student loan that now I need to pay."

Treena, a 42-year-old African American mother, earned her GED, and then attended a for-profit school where she studied to become a secretary. It did not lead to a job. She is now back at the local community college to further her studies in business. She was one of four women interviewed who had attended a for-profit proprietary school. Like the others, she felt that their program had been a waste of time. She told me that she was led to believe that her degree would lead to a high-paying clerical job, perhaps earning $7 to $8 an hour. Instead, she found that potential employers did not value her degree from a for-profit college without work experience in that field. She now owes several thousand dollars in student loans, and blamed the school for encouraging her to borrow money for deficient job training.

> I was going to business classes, but I had just injured my back. That was in early '87, '88, '90. But I couldn't continue to walk there because of my back. You know, I fell, and reached out, and I could hear the pinch. I was in a neck brace and everything. So I transferred to [proprietary] college. It was closer. I completed college. It took a year. And that was in word processing, secretarial word processing, but I could never get a job in it. Everywhere you go to fill out an application, they said you haven't had any experience on the job. But you know, if you're just getting out of school, I can't understand why people can't give you a chance to try and show them what you can do. No one gave me that chance. Nobody. [Proprietary] college didn't give me any help at all. No, no help in finding a job whatsoever. None. So I spent a lot of money. I'm still paying them back.

The second reason for the higher than expected rate of enrollment in training or education programs is that the county in which the interviews were conducted was the site for a significant welfare reform experiment by the state of Florida, introduced in Chapter 7, called the Family Transition Program (FTP). Women were randomly selected and offered the opportunity to participate in more intensive job training or a GED program, and under the guidance of a case manager, were given a variety of additional forms of assistance, such as higher allowable asset levels, bus passes, child care assistance, and mental health counseling. As a result of completing the program, welfare recipients would have time limits on their eligibility for cash assistance. A sizeable number of women interviewed had been selected, and some agreed to be in this program. FTP was controversial, however. Some women didn't understand the welfare department's concern with obtaining a representative sample and, like Jo Lynn, were disappointed that they weren't selected to be in FTP:

> I begged them! I was gung-ho. You know, they help you with transportation costs. I mean, now I don't have enough money to drive my car across the city to [community college]. I have to take the bus. I mean, a lot of times I walk to pick her up from school because I don't have enough money for gas and stuff. Please, just give me the training, and something to help me get there, and some child care while I'm going. After I get a job, I will pay for my own child care. Help me get a job that makes enough money, but I'm not talking about $10 an hour. Just something I can live on. I don't want anybody to have to give me anything. But I wasn't selected. They wouldn't put me in it. So instead, they picked somebody that's going to drop out, and the taxpayers are going to be wasting their money on somebody who quits.

As we saw in Chapter 7, the FTP programs have much to offer respondents with respect to enhancing their levels of human capital. Many recipients could most likely benefit from increased opportunities to furthering their education or upgrade their job skills. But a dearth of human capital, although problematic for many recipients, is not the only problem that they face. They face other structural obstacles to finding and keeping work that pays enough for them to support themselves. They fear these obstacles, and consequently some women turned down the offer to join FTP, knowing that they must agree to the stipulation that they will be off welfare in two years.

Coreen was randomly selected to participate in FTP, and turned officials down. She, like others, reasoned that the risks were too high. How could she ensure that she and her daughter would not need welfare any time soon after the program was completed? Women who turned down the opportunity to join FTP told me that they did not feel comfortable gambling with their children's future; to do so would be irresponsible. Instead, Coreen for example, is attending the community college on her own, with the hopes of someday being a teacher.

> They have a Family Transition Program where they help you get a job. Now this is what they tell you. They will give you school training for a

job, and they will help you find a job, and then they will still give you assistance at the same time. Okay, that's good. But once you're in this program, you can't get no more. If you lose that job, there is no way you can get anymore assistance in the county. That's just like saying, if your supervisor doesn't like you for some reason—maybe they don't like you because you look better than them—then they fire you for that, and then you are stuck. Say you can't find another job for a month. Then you and your kids have to live without food and stuff because you were in that program. They send me a letter every week, and I've turned them down. I'm not going to do that because you never know how your life is going, what kind of struggles you will have in life. So I just turn them down. It's too big of a gamble.

Women revealed that they valued education and training, either through FTP, other welfare programs, or on their own through the local community college or university. However, many women intimated that it was not altogether clear that education and training by themselves would lead to a job. Many had high hopes, but then found that it was very difficult if not impossible to find a job in their field because of the high numbers of other qualified applicants.

Latasha, a 29-year-old African American mother, has been diligently looking for full-time, permanent employment. She did not complete high school, but recently went back and received her GED through a program sponsored by the welfare office. She's been off and on welfare since her first child was born nine years ago. She has worked a variety of low-wage jobs, primarily in fast food restaurants, and then quit when her hours were cut, or work seemed to particularly interfere with her role as a mother. She's concerned about "the perverts" in her housing project neighborhood, and therefore refuses to let her children, ages nine, eight, and six, outside alone. Latasha doesn't like welfare. She is very ambitious, and hopes to have a full-time job soon and be off welfare altogether. But despite her newly granted GED, she has not been able to secure the employment she desires:

> I'm trying hard, but it's like I'm kinda held down or something. I'm not sure the more education you get will necessarily get you a job. So I might need to move out of state. I might need a new start. It's extremely hard to get a job, there are so many students here. I'm really praying, and hoping the man up above is looking out for me.

In spite of the perceived and real value of education and job training, recent changes to the welfare laws actually make it more difficult for welfare recipients under TANF to get quality training than in the past under AFDC. These now placed restrictions on the kinds of education or training that count toward the states' work participation rates. Amended and liberalized in 1997, it still remains that only 30 percent of those adults who are aged 20 and older and who are engaged in work activities are allowed to participate in vocational education. There are no restrictions for teens until the year 2000, and then the 30 percent limit will be applied to them as well (Center for Law and Social Policy, 1997; Children's Defense Fund, 1997b).

Although there is a stated concern with increasing women's level of human capital, the training programs, for the most part, appear to be doing very little to significantly help women in the arduous search for well-paying work. Instead, training programs are generally short-term and superficial attempts to teach women how to "market themselves" to an employer. Or they are designed to teach women the academic skills necessary to pass an exam to receive a GED. Training programs, overall, do not provide the vocational education in order to give women the skills needed to command higher wage work. Women commonly told me that they wanted real training and real education—not simply a GED or training in resume writing. A GED does not translate into a good-paying job, they told me. They wanted vocational training that would teach them a specific set of skills, and would eventually lead them to a specific well-paying job. The skills and jobs most sought after were in nursing and working with computers.

Some women were busy working toward these goals at the time of our interview. Nonetheless, I was struck by the alarming number of women who had no real firm grasp on how to get from "here to there." Some women, for example, had no idea that they would be eligible for financial aid, such as Pell grants, if they went to college. Because they had no savings and no credit cards, they believed that college was not an option.

Other women luckily stumbled on a path toward their goals, but admitted that they needed extra help in following it. Beth, a 27-year-old woman with one daughter, has her high school diploma, but was not finding the type of job that would lift her and her daughter out of the depths of poverty. Given the additional problems of finding adequate child care, affording transportation, and the risk of losing her Medicaid, she found it more conducive to sit home and collect her small welfare check than work in the low-paying service sector. But Beth, like most other women I met, had a dream. She wanted to be off welfare, and specifically, she wanted to be a nurse. She happened to discover a program at the community college designed to help women like herself turn her dreams into realities. But, again, like so many of the other woman I met, Beth was scared, and needed extra assistance:

> I went to [community college] for one of their classes—it was just like for a week. Like career opportunities. And I liked it. I started to, you know, go through the process of taking tests and everything. But it was like, they rush, rush, rushed me, and I got scared. My life was stressed out at that time, and I didn't need no more stress. I just quit. I was going to go for nursing. I've always wanted to go for nursing, but I kind of feel like if I can't have somebody right there helping me through it, instead of rushing me and pushing me, I just don't feel like I can do it.

Will job-training programs provide the vocational training and moral support that many women making the transition off welfare are likely to need? "Welfare Mothers Prep for Jobs, and Wait," the headline in the *New York Times* reads (Swarns, 1997). The four-week job-training program in New York City, known as Job Clubs, is helping women "learn to dress professionally, to write resumes, to give an employer a firm, confident handshake and to believe in the prospect of financial independence and newfound self-respect." This is one of a number of statewide job readiness programs. Yet, of the thousands of women who have completed the short Job Club program and have been turned loose to find jobs in New York City, the vast majority have failed to find jobs (Swarns, 1997). A sizeable number of women on welfare need more than these types of cursory services in order to be able to support themselves and to be independent of public aid.

Work Experience

Proponents of both the "welfare-to-work" and "human-capital-enhancement" approaches to welfare reform suggest that recipients' lack of work experience is a primary obstacle to finding quality employment. But the vast majority of women interviewed had held multiple jobs over the course of their lives. National data also suggest that most welfare recipients have been employed, often weaving employment with their stays on welfare. So, at first glance, welfare recipients do not lack work experience, *per se*. But unfortunately, if we look at the types of jobs recipients have held, we find that their jobs tend to be low-paying ones in the bottom tier of the service sector, are often temporary, and do little to improve their financial circumstances over welfare. The Institute for Women's Policy Research examined the work experiences of AFDC recipients using data from the U.S. Bureau of the Census' Survey of Income and Program Participation (1995). They used a nationally representative sample of 1,181 single mothers who received AFDC for at least 2 out of 24 months sometime between 1984 and 1989. The data reveal that 43 percent of AFDC mothers work substantial hours (950 per year, on average), and another 30 percent were looking for work. Their jobs paid an average of $4.29 per hour in 1990 dollars, and tended to be concentrated in women-dominated occupations within the lowest tier of the service sector. Thirty-seven percent of recipients worked as maids, cashiers, nursing aids, child care workers, and waitresses, which is three times the rate for all women in the United States. Thus, although recipients, overall, are not lacking in work experience, it is the *type* of experience that is critical.

Like many other women on welfare, 23-year-old Tamela has worked in the fast food industry. She had two children while still in high school, and it was at this time that she also tried to work at McDonalds. She earned minimum wage, and like so many others, found the stresses of juggling work and family to outweigh the small wages she received:

> When I was in high school and had my two kids, I worked at McDonalds, and didn't see that I was benefiting by working. I mean, I liked working with the public and everything, and I had a lot of fun doing it. I could say, "I have a job," and that gave me pride, but it was not beneficial by no means. At the time I did not have transportation, so I had to find my mom to keep my kids, making sure she could do it or finding someone else, then finding a way to work and getting back home. It's stressful. I think its crazy for the simple fact that you don't benefit from it, from work, unless

you have a job that's going to pay you more than minimum wages and the system would help you with child care.

Amy's employment history is also not unusual:

I worked in an electronics factory assembling little electronic things, parts, like resistors and transistors and things. It was for minimum wage. It was really nasty work. It was terrible. And when I was in high school I worked as a secretary–stenographer type person in a medical records office. I did well. But, it also was pretty dead-end, you know, minimum wage.

Molly describes her work experience:

I've done all kinds of things. I've worked at a hardware store, I've worked at department stores, at restaurants, I've waitressed, I've ridden a mobile munchies truck to construction sites and sold food out of a truck. Lots of different things. But when I had Jeffrey, my first child, we talked about it. And my husband Tom wanted me to stay home with Jeffrey. And I had William 15 1/2 months later. So I was a stay-at-home mom. I took care of them. Sure I could go to work now. I can work. But it would be pointless if I'm making minimum wage. Who is going to take care of my kids? I might as well go to school and further my education so when I do go to work I get paid something decent so I can take care of my family the way they should be taken care of. Not from a minimum wage job.

Rhonda tells me about her employment history, which again, is familiar:

In Maryland I had a lot of jobs. I wasn't on welfare. I worked at the hospital back home in Maryland, and I've done cashiering and housekeeping. But then I came down here to help my sister because she got sick and had two kids. But there are no jobs. I've done whatever temporary jobs that agency gave me, like housekeeping at the hospital and a warehouse where I sorted lids for a printing company.

Americans cherish the belief that hard work pays dividends. If one simply works hard enough, one will prosper. Each year of continued effort would yield progressive economic improvements, the theory holds. Unfortunately, for many people, this is not the scenario they encounter. Despite a vast array of work experience, the women interviewed here generally found that hard work rarely leads to anything better. Their past on-the-job experience, even when they worked diligently, did not lead to advancement. At best, their pay increased only very slightly, even after years of employment. Moreover, their employment did not significantly improve their level of human capital by giving them additional education or training; nor did it significantly increase their "social capital," by allowing them to make connections with others that could eventually lead to better paying or permanent jobs with fringe benefits attached to them. No matter how hard or diligently they worked, they remained within the lowest tier jobs. There was very little upward mobility into the kinds of jobs where higher pay and benefits were standard. These findings are similar to those by Edin and Lein, who, in their study of 214 welfare recipients, also report:

> In short, these women were unable to build careers; if they chose to work, they were much more likely to move from one dead-end job to another. Thus, women learned that the kind of jobs available to them were not avenues to success or even to bare-bones self-sufficiency; they were dead-end jobs. (1997: 70)

Yet, despite hard work rarely leading to anything better, women repeatedly had high hopes for work. Those with less experience were the most hopeful: They were still holding out that they would find the job that would let them move out of the housing projects, buy them a car, provide day care for their children, allow them to buy name-brand clothing for their children, and in a multitude of other ways offer some semblance of a middle-class lifestyle. Older women, or women with extensive labor-market experience were often more cynical; some had lost their hope because of one dead-end job after another. Yet, even among this group, I was intrigued with the high interest in employment, despite the likelihood that their jobs will not significantly improve their standard of living. Most continued to be hopeful despite the odds against them. Most hoped for practical jobs that they felt were within their reach: nursing, day care, and secretarial work. Dee, who is attending school to become an accountant, told me, poignantly: "I've always wanted to go to college. My goal is to get my CPA license. My dream is to open my own firm. And my fantasy is to be bigger than H & R Block."

Several factors increase the likelihood of women finding work, according to research by the Institute for Women's Policy Research. The most significant factors, according to national data from 1,181 single mothers who received AFDC, are: (1) the ability to work (e.g., not having a work-preventing disability), (2) availability of jobs (e.g., living in states with lower unemployment rates), (3) not having toddlers or infants, (4) family support (e.g., receiving child support or earnings from other members), and (5) having greater amounts of human capital (e.g., having past work experience, having a high school diploma). Meanwhile, factors that were found to have no association with the likelihood of finding work include: (1) average state benefit levels, (2) the amount of time spent looking for work, (3) the mothers' age, (4) mothers' welfare history, and (5) race. Several of these findings are critical to our discussion here. First, human capital factors are only one of several relevant considerations in explaining the propensity of welfare mothers to work. Second, despite arguments to the contrary (Murray, 1984), according to these data at least, the relatively higher benefit levels in some states do not deter women from seeking employment; instead, a more important factor in the likelihood of procuring employment is the statewide unemployment rate. Third, these data suggest that structural factors are critical to understanding how and why women leave welfare and why they do not.

The Importance of Our Social Structure

If increases in human capital, such as in education, job training, or job experience, are not enough to ensure that women leave welfare and find quality jobs in which to support themselves and their families, what else is needed? I suggest that a dearth in human capital itself does not necessarily cause one to turn to or to remain on welfare. Rather, it makes one more *vulnerable* to needing assistance when faced with other circumstances such as job layoffs, seasonal employment, illness, employer cost-cutting devices, and changes in family structure. Women with lower levels of human capital have a more difficult time navigating beyond these daunting personal and structural barriers to self-sufficiency and well-being. Therefore, they may have to turn to public welfare programs in the interim. Their stays on welfare may be short, or they may be long, depending on a variety conditions—including their level of human capital; the severity of the event or structural condition; and their degree of social support. Reliance on welfare is not simply the result of individual choice or personal failure. Instead, this reliance is largely a consequence of vulnerability to factors embedded in our social structure. Some of these structural factors are more specific to women (e.g., dependence on men for financial support; negotiating childcare), whereas others transcend gender (e.g., too few jobs paying living wages; an inadequate set of social service programs designed to provide a safety net for low-income families). It is the interaction of human capital, structural factors, and social support that prompt the need for welfare assistance.

A thorough discussion of the many aspects of our social structure that contribute to poverty and welfare use is obviously beyond the scope of this book. I do, however, focus on issues pertaining to employment—both the amount and types of jobs that are being generated in our economy, and relate these to the plight and needs of poor women on welfare.

Not Enough Jobs

In large cities and small towns across the nation, there are not enough jobs available to absorb the influx of people looking for paid work because of the cessation of their welfare benefits. Despite recent hoopla over a low unemployment rate in the United States overall, not all citizens can find work easily. Some groups, in fact, are experiencing dizzying rates of unemployment. Although overall unemployment averaged 5.2 percent for the nation in 1997, unemployment among African American women ages 15 to 25 with a high school diploma was 19.7 percent, and 22 percent for those who had not completed high school (Bernstein, 1997; Herbert, 1997). In this era when Affirmative Action programs are criticized for giving minorities and women supposedly unfair advantages, it is unfashionable to allude to white privilege. But it is undeniable that, in a society such as ours, which is so heavily focused on race, being white has its advantages in many realms. Yet those who have privilege rarely notice or comment on it. It is simply taken for granted.

Given the imminent cuts in the number of women and children eligible for aid, the unemployment rate among many segments of the population is expected to soar. Jared Bernstein, a labor economist and author of a recent report by the Economic Policy Institute in Washington, notes that the continued job squeeze for unskilled or semiskilled jobs has ominous implications for the welfare-to-work initiatives that politicians are pushing (Herbert, 1997). There are not enough jobs to go around, and the traditional safety net is being eroded. This puts our nation on an inevitable collision course.

In New York City alone, there were about 470,000 people on welfare in 1997. Many of these individuals, although certainly not all, have low levels of education, few job skills, and little or sporadic work experience beyond the service sector. A sizeable portion of recipients will be forced to compete for jobs, yet only 88,000 new jobs have been created there since 1992 (Chartrand, July 13, 1997). Competition for these positions will be stiff, particularly when the other 250,000 unemployed people in New York City are factored in. They are not on welfare, but many will be competing for the same positions. In the fierce competition for these jobs, individuals who are young, African American, and without a high school diploma will fare the worst.

A survey in New York City, conducted by the State Department of Social Services between July 1996 and March 1997, reports that only 29 percent of former welfare recipients have found full- or part-time jobs. For the purposes of the study, anyone earning at least $100 in three months after leaving welfare would have been counted as employed. The statewide statistics are somewhat better, but still uncouraging, when slightly more than one-third are counted as finding employment. Professor Marcia Myers, in the department of Social Work at Columbia University, notes "This really gives us the first glimpse of life after welfare, and it is alarming" (Hernandez, March 23, 1998).

What does it feel like to look for work week after week, and turn up with nothing? When even the lowest tier jobs in our economy have stiff competition, many women feel psychologically wounded. What is the point, they ask themselves? Although unemployment statistics paint an ever-glowing rosy picture in this period of economic upswing, the real faces behind those statistics reveal the hurt and frustration that comes with being unemployed—wanting work, but not being able to find it, let alone maintain it.

Illustrating this scenario is Sheila, a 40-year-old woman who is supporting her 12-year-old daughter on her $241 a month AFDC check. She is enrolled in FTP and is working on her GED, and at the same time is applying for jobs. She acknowledges that her math and reading skills are not very strong. "I can do some math—I'm not real good at fractions yet, and I don't read real well, but I'm hoping to find a job." But her search is not going well. Despite submitting numerous applications, she has not received an interview, let alone a job. Yet her two-year contract with FTP was in full swing, and the clock was ticking. At the time of the interview, she had only five months of welfare left, and she could not apply again for several years. "It's depressing," she tells me. "You can apply and apply, but you can't make someone hire you."

The shortage of unskilled jobs has not gone unnoticed by welfare officials and the media. "Welfare Job Needs Worry Officials," declares the headline of a newspaper in North Florida where the women interviewed for this study reside (Rausch, Feb. 19, 1997).

> Alachua County will need more than 3,100 new jobs to employ local welfare recipients as a result of Florida's welfare reform rules, state officials say. That has local officials worried. "And they're not there," says Commissioner Brown. More than 90 percent required to work are women, 40 percent have less than a high school education, and 38 percent have no work history in the past two years.

A study by a Pennsylvania economic forecasting firm reports that, nationwide, there are only enough new jobs to employ about half (54 percent) of welfare recipients who will need work (Children's Defense Fund, 1997b). Some states have considerably fewer jobs and they estimate that California will only be able to employ 42 percent of recipients, Maine only 25 percent, and New York only 13 percent. Florida is expected to do comparatively well; it is estimated that they will be able to employ 93 percent of welfare recipients because of its growing service-sector economy. They estimate that only 13 states will have enough jobs to accommodate the welfare recipients that will need to find work over the next two years. Harvard Public Policy professor Nancy Newman studied 200 fast food jobs in the Harlem area of New York and the workers who held them, and reports that adults who came from households on welfare had less luck getting these types of jobs than those who didn't. She found that there were generally 14 people applying for each job opening in Harlem restaurants, indicating that there is a limit to how many welfare recipients the fast food industry can absorb. And while there is some upward mobility for workers, there are significantly fewer management positions than there are applicants (*U.S. News Online*, Aug. 18, 1997). Another study conducted in Ohio by the Midwest Job Gap Project found in that state that there were 23 would-be workers for every job that paid poverty level wages ($12,278 annually in 1995, for a family of three), 66 job-seekers for every job that paid wages at 150 percent of poverty ($18,417), and 100 contenders for every job that paid $24,907, the amount estimated as a livable wage for a family with children residing in Ohio (Children's Defense Fund, 1997b).

Types of Jobs Available for Women on Welfare

Typically, then, what types of jobs are available to welfare mothers? American industries have undergone rapid restructuring in the past few decades in response to technological changes and global competition. Social scientists establish broad occupational categories by distinguishing between primary, secondary, and tertiary sectors in the labor market. The primary sector consists of jobs in which raw materials are harvested, such as in timber, agriculture, or mining. Jobs in the secondary sector transform raw materials into manufactured goods. The tertiary sector, or service sector, is the fastest growing sector of our economy and focuses on providing a wide variety of services, such as salesclerks, attorneys, cashiers, and waitresses. Within each sector we can distinguish between tiers of workers. The "primary labor market," is characterized by having relatively high benefits and job security. Relatively low pay, few benefits, and little job security characterize the "secondary labor market." Within this labor market, women leaving welfare often occupy jobs within the lowest tier.

In recent years the number of workers needed in manufacturing has declined considerably. These disappearing jobs tended to pay relatively higher wages because of union protections. Instead, our economy is experiencing an explosion of jobs in the service sector. But compared to manufacturing jobs, those in the service sector, particularly within the lowest tiers, are generally without union protection, tend to be poorly paid, and offer few fringe benefits to workers. The protections offered by unions are well established; for example, union workers averaged more than $14,000 more in wages than their nonunionized counterparts in 1992 (Feagin and Feagin, 1994). Women who were union workers averaged weekly wages that were 1.3 times that of nonunionized women workers. But Goldfield (1987) documents the steady decline in union membership in the United States. He states that, during the early 1980s, collective bargaining agreements covered less than one-quarter of workers, a decline from more than one-third in the 1950s.

The minimum wage in the Unites States, at $5.15 per hour in 1998, comes nowhere near lifting even a small family out of poverty. Yet almost two-thirds of workers making the minimum wage are adults aged 20 or older, and 40 percent of them provide the sole income for their families (*U.S. News Online*, April 29, 1996). Adjusted for inflation, the value of the federal minimum wage has dropped by more than a dollar since the 1960s and 1970s. Based on 1996 dollars, the minimum wage ranged between a low of $5.65 and a high of $7.21 during this period, usually hovering around $6.25. The erosion of the minimum wage began in earnest during the mid-1980s (U.S. Bureau of Labor Statistics, No Date). Some onlookers suggest that the minimum wage level should be raised by $2 to $3 per hour so that full-time workers would be above the poverty line for a family of three, which was $12,516 in 1996 (U.S. Bureau of the Census, 1997a, Table A-2, p. A-4). This would have the benefit of aiding welfare recipients and nonrecipients alike. However, when discussions of raising the minimum wage surface, business leaders often cry "foul" (*U.S. News Online*, April 29, 1996; Wilson, M., 1996). They argue that increasing the minimum wage will harm the poor by raising prices and destroying more than 200,000 entry-level job opportunities by 1999, and that it will cost consumers and workers about $2.2 billion per year as the higher cost of entry-level jobs is passed on through higher prices and lower real wages:

> Proponents defend a minimum wage increase by declaring it to be a moral issue and moral imperative—not just an economic or political consideration. The minimum wage, however, epitomizes government paternalism as its worst. It presumes that politicians are morally justified in destroying some people's jobs in order to inflate other people's wages. The American principle of economic freedom has been replaced by the principle of "government knows best." . . . Government must share the blame for stagnant wages. . . . Employers, as well as workers, operate within a competitive labor market in which wage rates broadly reflect the productivity of workers—less the costs of government-imposed mandates and taxes associated with employing a worker. But instead of addressing the impediments to wage growth imposed by government, proponents prefer to blame employers for stagnating wages and curry favor with voters by proposing another hike in the minimum wage. (Wilson, 1996: 3–4)

But these are age-old complaints that have been used against all minimum wage increases, including the creation of minimum wage itself. Instead, many economists and other social scientists argue that the income gains from a minimum wage hike would outweigh the job losses and price increases. Recent academic studies suggest that job losses would be negligible, and raise the larger questions of fairness and social justice (*U.S. News Online*, April 29, 1996).

Yet the concept of paying a living wage is taking hold. Boston, Baltimore, Denver, and Portland, Oregon, are several cities around the country that make particular companies pay their employees wages in line with the cost of living in the area. Boston, which passed the law most recently, requires that companies receiving city contracts or subsidies worth more than $100,000 must pay employees a minimum wage of $7.49 an hour. This is more than $2 higher than the minimum wage in place in 1998. "In these prosperous times for our city, our state, and our nation, it is incumbent upon us to ensure that the rising tide does in fact raise all our boats, not just the yachts," said Boston mayor, Thomas Menino (*Gainesville Sun*, Aug. 13, 1997).

Another concern is that many of the jobs that are being developed are part-time, subcontracted, or temporary in nature. Many offer irregular work schedules. Employees working in these types of jobs represent the fastest growing category of workers in the United States. Since 1982, temporary employment has increased almost 250 percent, whereas all employment has grown less than 20 percent. Statistics are imperfect, but part-time and temporary workers made up about a quarter of the labor force in 1988, and by the year 2000 it is estimated that they will constitute one-half. In other words, 35 million women and men begin the work day not knowing if, and for how long, their jobs are likely to continue (Castro, 1993; Morrow, 1993). Their job security is vanishing before their eyes.

Some part-time and contingency workers prefer this arrangement; especially highly paid professionals who value their freedom and independence on the job. Physicians, accountants, attorneys, and financial planners are among the professionals who can make a lucrative business in part-time consulting. But most Americans prefer the security of a steady job with an established pay scale and fringe benefits. Former Labor Secretary Robert Reich commented on the development of a two-tier work force, in which the contingency worker gets a different pay and benefit package (or no benefits at all):

> As the contingency work force grows—as many people find themselves working part-time for many different employers—the social contract is beginning to fray. . . . The first step, in the mid-'80's, was to reduce some of the benefits packages for the lower-tier workers, and that continues. The next step was to fire middle-level management. The third step was to reduce benefits packages across the board for all employees. And now, we're at the fourth step, which is to do much more business by contract, whether it is with contingent workers and part-time workers or by contracting out. . . . It's an enormous stress. The anxiety level is very high, regardless of the kind of job you hold. Nobody is safe. (cited in Castro, 1993)

There is also a growing trend towards jobs that require weekend, evening, or variable nonfixed schedules, particularly those found in the lower paying service sector, which many welfare recipients will look to for employment (Presser and Cox,

1997). Recent analyses of national data indicate that women with a high school diploma or less are most susceptible to nonstandardized work hours. Most women with children do not want this arrangement; more than half the women surveyed whose youngest child was between ages 5 and 13 reported that the main reason they worked these shifts was because it was a requirement of the job, and that they could not get any other job (53 percent). Only 30 percent of women listed beneficial reasons for working these shifts, such as it allowed for better child care arrangements (18 percent); it allowed better arrangements for care of other family members (7 percent); that it offered time for school (2 percent); or that it provided better pay (3 percent). Sociologists Harriet Presser and Amy Cox summarize the conclusions from their study and pose an important dilemma for getting women off of welfare:

> The results . . . show that low-educated mothers are disproportionately represented in occupations with high rates of nonstandard schedules, that many of these women who work nonstandard hours do so primarily for labor market rather than personal reasons, and that job characteristics are stronger determinants of employment during nonstandard times than are family characteristics. To a substantial extent, then, low-educated mothers appear drawn into working nonstandard hours by a lack of options. Finally, the study shows that these trends are likely to increase given current occupational projections, thereby increasing demand for child care during evenings, nights, and weekends. Accordingly, to achieve the primary objective of welfare reform—moving mothers permanently from welfare to employment—child care will need to be expanded markedly during nonstandard times, including evenings and weekends. Generating new jobs and expanding child care will go a long way toward meeting that objective if the scheduling of both can be better synchronized. (1997, p. 33)

President Clinton has called for more "good jobs at good pay" for workers. Rhonda is one of many women who is looking for one of these jobs that President Clinton referred to. She would like to raise her young son, Bobby, without welfare, and recognizes the need for a permanent full-time job. Instead, however, she has been stymied by the tremendous growth in part-time, temporary positions.

> Hopefully I can get me a job. A permanent job. My sister's trying to get me a job where she works. I put my application in last week. And it would be a permanent job. When you go through those agencies, it's just temporary work. It's just whenever they need you, and it's unfair too. Every job I've found is through this temporary agency, like Manpower, but it's only temporary. And they cut my check and my food stamps, and when my job ends, it's like your stuck again. So I'm trying to find a permanent steady job. But it's hard around here. I've been out looking for work, and hoping that something comes through.

Rhonda may be surprised to learn that Manpower is the largest private employer in the United States, with 560,000 workers (Castro, 1993). Every morning, its workers scatter into factories and offices around the nation, looking for a day's work. As other industrial giants shrink their payrolls, Manpower and the multitude of other temporary agencies such as Kelly Services are booming and dispatch up to 2 million workers daily.

Turnover rates in many low tier jobs, even those considered to be "permanent," are high. Sometimes women quit work in hopes of finding something better or to return to welfare. However, women in these jobs are also considerably more likely to be laid off—three times more often than other workers (Blank, 1995). They are the expendable workforce. They work in the service industry, in clerical work, and on assembly lines performing routine tasks. To the management, people in these largely unskilled or semiskilled jobs are interchangeable. A high turnover rate is not a problem for management, and in fact may even be considered desirable so that health insurance premiums and other benefits can be avoided. These disposable or throwaway workers generally earn less than those on the regular payroll, and must live with the uncertainty that their jobs may permanently end today when they clock out at 5:00 P.M. Their anxiety is high. And for many of these workers, unemployment insurance is not an option. One recent study reports that only 11 percent of welfare recipients with substantial work hours were eligible for unemployment insurance (Spalter-Roth, Hartmann, and Burr, 1994).

Eliza, a mother of four children, epitomizes the plight of many women who are looking for work but find that they are at the mercy of job employers who care more about profits than in providing stable employment, reliable and sufficient work hours, and benefits for their employees. Eager to work, she was delighted to find a job in a fast food restaurant, joining the 3 million others who work in this industry (*U.S. News Online*, Aug. 18, 1997). She told them up front that she was looking for 30 to 40 hours of employment per week. Knowing this, they hired her, but instead of meeting her needs, they routinely ask her to leave work early, unpaid, during the slow periods. She was hired to fill an organizational need, and released as soon as their need for her labor lightened. Because her income was so much less than she anticipated when being hired, Eliza found that the job did not pay her bills. In addition, she felt that the long commute was not worth her while, and she therefore quit to return to welfare.

> That's something I need is a job. I've been looking. I just can't find the right one. I used to work at [fast food industry], but I wasn't making much money. By the time I caught the city bus, went out there, by the time I got to my kids, I spent all the money that they gave me. I liked the job, but it was just that I had to pay 75¢ to get to work, and paid 75¢ to get back. If I missed the bus I had to give somebody $3 or $4 to take me. And they wouldn't give me enough hours. I told them when they gave me this job that I needed at least 30 to 40 hours a week. I just can't afford to work less. But I was wasting my time going out there. I had to be at work by 11 o'clock, but they would send me home by 2 o'clock. I didn't even get 20 hours a week. You hear what I'm saying? Ten or 12, maybe. I think what they was doing was hiring you for the busy hour, and once the busy hour passed, you was sent out of there. I had to quit because it was costing me too much to go way over there.

Eliza's frustration with businesses that put profits above employee well-being was not unusual. Many others expressed this frustration, including Patrice. By most welfare recipients' standards, Patrice is a success story. Although still receiving a small AFDC check at the time of the interview, Patrice was also employed 20 hours a week by a hospital in the community and earned a wage of $7 an hour. She has some training in nursing, although failed to get a degree when she became pregnant and quit college. Despite her relatively high wage compared to others in similar circumstances, she has more trouble getting off of welfare than one might imagine because of the piece-meal nature of the job. She provides home personal care, and travels extensively from client to client each day, but she does not get paid for her travel time. Thus, a considerable portion of her workday goes unpaid.

> I do personal care through the hospital. I'm not a nurse. I was attending LPN school and I became pregnant so I had to withdraw. But I do personal care. I usually go in and take vital signs and assist them with their shower, and if they need any assistance with feeding I'll do that. Usually I'm only there for an hour or so. I comb their hair, and pretty much that is it. I get paid usually for 20 hours a week. Usually I get $7 an hour. But I don't get paid for time between clients. My driving time is really blank time, as far as they are concerned. It doesn't really exist. But in my job I have to commute from one side of town to the next and to different little cities. But without a job I'll be pitiful again with that fixed welfare income.

The new low-tier and low-wage jobs created in the service sector that welfare recipients are likely to fill, provide few, if any fringe benefits. Research indicates that, in addition to lacking health insurance, women who received AFDC in the past are less likely to work in jobs that provide paid sick leave or paid vacations. These are two important benefits that help to meet the many unpredictable time demands made by children (Heymann and Earle, 1997). Using data from the National Medical Expenditure Survey (NMES) and the National Longitudinal Survey of Youth (NLSY), both based on large representative samples in the United States, Heymann and Earle examined the working conditions of parents who are employed 20 or more hours per week. They found that 59 percent of women who had in the past been on welfare for five years or more had jobs that provided no paid sick leave, as compared to only 30 percent of women who had never been on AFDC. In addition, 41 percent of recipients who had been on AFDC at least five years had no paid vacation from their job, compared to 20 percent of other women who had never been on AFDC. They report that long-term welfare recipients were almost five times as likely as those who had never been on AFDC to have a combination of no paid sick or vacation leave, and were without flexible work schedules to accommodate the needs of work and family (19 percent vs. 4 percent). The increased odds of having a job that does not accommodate family needs among a population who is vulnerable to begin with, increases the likelihood that women will have intermittent labor-force experience. Because they do not have flexible hours, or receive no paid sick leave or vacation pay, they have few alternatives but to quit when their own children get sick or need special attention.

Why Some Women on Welfare Are Hesitant to Take Jobs

In Chapter 7, I indicated that one of the criticisms of welfare is that benefits are significantly reduced or eliminated prematurely when a recipient acquires a job. Given the low wages of their work, recipients cannot support their families with so little net income. Therefore they often find that they are in a more precarious financial situation when employed than when they receive welfare. Work does not provide security. Instead of proving a secure economic base, women who are employed in low-wage work report that they get further and further behind in their bills. Low-wage work cannot sustain a family, yet at the same time, welfare benefits such as food stamps, subsidized housing, and Medicaid will be severely reduced or eliminated completely. In the quest to be a "good mother," leaving the security of welfare voluntarily for the insecurity of low-wage work is considered to be risky and even irresponsible; too risky for some. This is one important reason why some women on welfare are hesitant to accept these jobs.

Patrice purposefully limits the number of hours that she works so that she will not become ineligible for various forms of welfare assistance. She is willing to have her cash grant reduced, but wants to ensure that she will continue to receive food stamps, housing subsidies, and Medicaid. Is she simply greedy? Not really, because she knows that her job, even if full-time, and even at $7 an hour, will prohibit her from purchasing these things on the open market. Her salary would be below what she would need to pay full rent, pay all her own food costs, and purchase health insurance for herself and her two sons.

> Pretty much, the bottom line, being on the system, everything depends on your income. While you're on AFDC, everything works for you. You got free Medicaid. You got free food because you get plenty of stamps. Then, you get your check once a month, which once you pay your rent, utilities, and buy Pampers for your baby, or whatever, your money pretty much be gone and you're broke. But once you start working, your [welfare] check depends on your income and it may stop. Then your Medicaid becomes a question—depending on your income they'll cut it. Then your stamps be decreased or either cut off. Then, being in the projects, like me and many other welfare moms, your rent depends on your income and your rent goes up. Then usually I end up paying so much for child care that I don't have nothing left. So, I have a harder time than when I'm not working! And therefore, you don't really benefit any. The majority of people out here [in the projects], they found that it's better to stay home and do nothing and receive AFDC.

But when asked further why she doesn't then stay home full-time and receive welfare, she commented on her conscious choice to work to augment welfare. She has found, for her family, the delicate balance between trying to survive on minimalist welfare benefits and having all her benefits eliminated without a job that pays enough to make up the difference. Finding this balance improves her self-esteem and makes her feel that she is a "good mother" to her sons. She continues:

Sometimes I used to think, I'd say, "Maybe I do better off staying on wel-fare." You have plenty of food to eat. You can sit home all day and play "Mom." But, me, I have a certain, you know, look at life. I believe in pros-pering because I like nice things, so I don't think welfare will work for me very well. So I just feel more, you know, secure about myself and it builds my self-esteem when I can be more independent, you know, do for myself and my children. I look out for them. They didn't volunteer to be here. So they're my responsibility. Things didn't work out with me and their fa-ther, so they are totally my responsibility. So I want to provide the best for them that I can.

Remaining on welfare is not an irrational choice. Rather, women weigh the costs and benefits associated with employment. If they believe the benefits outweigh the costs of employment, be they psychological or material in nature, they are likely to choose work. But if they believe that the costs outweigh the benefits, or begin to believe this during a spell of employment, they are likely to quit. For example, women who work full-time will receive significantly more money each month than if they received welfare. Earning $5.25 an hour, for 40 hours a week, 52 weeks per year, would bring in approximately $900 a month before taxes. This is considerably more than a $241 monthly grant for a family of two, the $303 dollars received from welfare for a family of three, or the $343 received for a family of four in the state of Florida. From the looks of it, it behooves welfare recipients to find, and keep, even low-wage work. But the financial picture is convoluted. Earning $900 a month, before taxes, a family of three would no longer be eligible for cash assistance, they would have their food stamps reduced, and would likely to lose all, or at least part, of their low income housing subsidy. Moreover, they would lose their Medicaid after one year. To pur-chase these items on the open market is expensive. This family would be eligible for the Earned Income Tax Credit ($3,556 in 1996), but most of that would be offset by the new financial costs associated with child care, transportation, clothing, and laun-dry needed for work (estimated at $3,000, U.S. House of Representatives, Committee on Ways and Means, 1996). Because most welfare recipients do not have the skills or education that allow them to find and retain well-paid jobs, and because so few of these jobs exist, even relatively modest expenses associated with employment, such as a $2 daily bus fare, may represent a formidable obstacle to working. Most families would have a difficult time supporting themselves on $900 a month, or $10,800 a year; for a three-person family—a mother and her two children—their income would be $2,000 below the poverty line, which stood at $12,516 in 1996. A family of four would be living at $5,000 below the poverty line, which was $16,036, in 1996 (U.S Bureau of the Census, 1997a, Table A-2, p. A-4). Edin and Lein (1997), based on their detailed budgets with women on welfare, surmise that the typical woman on welfare assistance would need to take home $1,300 a month in order to maintain even the meager standard of living that she had on welfare. This translates into approxi-mately $16,000 a year, or $8 to $9 per hour at her paid job, depending on the number of hours worked per week or number of weeks worked per year. Most women who leave welfare do not make anywhere near this much money. Using a large sample of women from the Panel Study of Income Dynamics (PSID), Harris found that women who voluntarily left welfare for work over a 10-year period earned an average of $6.11 per hour in 1991 dollars (Harris, 1996). But these are the women who voluntarily left welfare; those women whose welfare benefits are involuntarily terminated are likely to earn significantly less than this. Unless a woman locates incredibly cheap and well-insulated housing, free baby-sitting, finds a job that provides medical benefits, and can easily walk to work, the odds are that she will not be able to earn her way to self-sufficiency. Carrie, a 39-year-old white woman with three children, told me:

> You know what ticks me off? I know you want to know. If I go out and get a job, it's going to about kill me to work because I'm already about to die because of the stress and responsibility I have. But in order to get a little bit more money I would go and get a job. But then they take away my grant. It's like dollar per dollar that they take away. So what's the point of killing yourself?

Lynda, a 35-year-old African American woman, has worked many jobs, but agrees wholeheartedly with Carrie.

> I have been on AFDC, off to work, on AFDC, off to work, and on AFDC my whole life. I'm not one of the people who just raised my kids constantly on AFDC. I always try to show them that you can do better. But every time I come up with a perfect plan to get off the system, I only find out the system is there to work against me. I had plans in September to get off the system again. But then, as soon as I got a job, I find out my food stamps are fixing to get cut to virtually nothing. That happened when I worked at the [convenience store]. When I worked there I started in January, and they allowed me to get my grant in February. But then in March my grant was cut off. And my food stamps was cut from almost $400 to around $170, which means I had to start taking money to buy food for the rest of the month. And then my rent went up. It was just too much.

Twenty-seven-year-old Roseanne, who also has had a number of different jobs, reveals:

> And then like, okay, if we get a job and start working and stuff, they just want to drop everything. But you still got your bills and stuff. So that's kind of a strain, and that makes some people say, "I shouldn't bother." Because everything goes up too. Your rent goes up, like maybe a hundred and something dollars. Maybe two hundred; it depends on how much you're making. And then they want to drop you from stamps. So things are hard when you just have that one income coming in.

But, as shown here, many workers today have trouble even securing full-time permanent work. Consequently, their earnings are likely to be considerably less than

$900 a month, or $10,800 a year featured previously. Eliza, for example, was routinely sent home during the slow periods in the fast food restaurant where she worked. She could barely assemble 20 hours a week, despite repeatedly asking management for increased hours. When women earn sporadic wages, their financial security crumbles. Their welfare benefits will be reduced or eliminated based on the initial wages earned, and it may take a month or longer for benefits to be reinstated when the earnings fail to materialize. This is a very dangerous period for families. If they have family or friends to rely on, they often moved in with them or borrowed money and food in order to get by. Many relied on food banks or other social services. Most women interviewed experienced at least one episode of being between a job and welfare benefits, and firmly said they want to avoid this predicament again.

In addition to the financial costs and rewards associated with work, there are also psychological ones. Work can enhance one's sense of self-esteem and self-efficacy. Women had dreams of returning to work when their children were older, when their schooling or training was completed, and when their lives were more orderly. But, at this point, even if they could earn adequate wages and benefits, they worried about the implications of leaving their children to strangers, or worse yet, leaving them home alone. They are keenly aware of the possible dangers lurking in their neighborhoods: molestation, drugs, vandalism, truancy, delinquency, unprotected teenage sex, to name just a few. As "good mothers" they want to protect their children from these seemingly common occurrences, and feel that they, rather than strangers, are in a better position to do so. As single mothers, the responsibility is on them; it generally cannot be shared with their children's fathers. The interviews revealed that they take this responsibility very seriously. Dawn, for example, told me of her concerted effort to warn her pre-teenage daughter about the dangers of teenage sex. Other mothers refuse to let their children outside after school. If they are at work, they wanted to know who will so strictly supervise their children?

Some welfare critics interpret recipients' rational choice to mean that welfare is a luxury; welfare policy should be amended to make welfare less desirable by reducing benefits or denying them to women altogether. They further suggest that welfare programs breed dependency on the system. But I suggest a different interpretation. Welfare is not a luxury or a frivolous program for mothers who are too lazy to work. Instead, it provides some degree of predictability and *security*, or at least it has in the past, compared to the turbulent irregularities and poor pay of work within the lower tier of the service sector. If we, as a society, value and care about the well-being of children, we correspondingly should value a more stable economic and social environment in which to raise them. Like Edin and Lein (1997), I found that women were "less interested in maximizing consumption, than in minimizing the risk of economic disaster" (p. 63). Add to this their concern with "social disaster" as well.

I began this chapter by introducing Pearl. She is one of the many women who will, in all likelihood, not have a choice about whether to find and accept employment. With the recent overhaul of the welfare system, her benefits will likely run out shortly. Will Pearl and the other women on welfare be able to sustain themselves and their families, given the human capital and structural constraints that they face?

The number of families receiving AFDC or TANF has declined from 4.6 million in January 1996 to 3.5 million in September 1997. Florida has experienced one of the largest declines of all 50 states (U.S. Department of Health and Human Services, 1998). Yet the early data reveal that many families are not doing well when their welfare is revoked. Despite a strong economy overall, the number of people seeking emergency food assistance soared 14 percent in 1997, according to Chicago-based Second Harvest. They provide two-thirds of the food distributed by the nation's 160,000 soup kitchens and food pantries to 26 million people a year. "We're finding that as people move from welfare to work, they lose child care and can't feed their families at the end of the month, so they come to Second Harvest," says Christine Vladimiroff, a Benedictine nun and president of Second Harvest (cited in Bernstein, 1997). The U.S. Conference of Mayors released a survey in December 1997 that reported average 1997 increases of 16 percent in requests for emergency food, the largest jump since 1992. They found that 19 percent of those seeking help were turned away, and 46 percent of the cities reported that charities and other private programs provided inadequate amounts of food. "The economy is booming by most standards we use to measure it, and yet we're saying our demand is up," Vladimiroff said. "People come to us because their cupboards are bare. We don't want to have to say, 'Well, ours are too'" (Associated Press, Jan. 5, 1998). The startling rise in the number of people needing food is most likely traced to several factors, including cuts in welfare eligibility; reductions in the food stamp program—which reduced the value of stamps and limited eligibility; unemployment among vulnerable portions of the population; and low-tier jobs that are vulnerable to erosion of the value of minimum wage.

In addition more people are finding themselves unable to pay their rent. Demand for space at homeless shelters jumped 12 percent in the first half of 1997, according to a U.S. Conference of Mayors survey of 34 cities (cited in Bernstein, 1997). The need for housing, food, and other charitable help will likely continue to increase, as deadlines loom for welfare assistance.

Pearl commented on what welfare changes would mean for her:

> If they was to change welfare, I hope they can help me find a job. I need to go to job training. I've been through job training, but then you fall behind when you don't get a job. Because I know now that you've got to have the education, you know, to get a good job. Because you need writing. Okay, I'm 48. I'd rather be out there on a job if I had my health and strength like I used to. So I'd be able to accomplish something, you know, instead of sitting around here worried all the time. I can look back at myself and say I've been working since I was 14. I learned to work. Learned to earn money. And I look at my young neighbors, twenty, twenty-six, and never had a job. And I look at them and they say, "Pearl, you old." They say, "Pearl, you old now." And I say, "No, I'm not exactly old. This pressure is just getting me down."

CHAPTER

9

Conclusion

Lessons Learned and Visions of Change

Women who receive welfare have a long-standing history of being suspect or discredited as "unworthy" of assistance. Recipients are depicted as lazy and responsible for their own economic circumstances through immoral behavior and irresponsible choices. They are criticized for living outside our idealized two-parent nuclear family form and are accused of doing this voluntarily, and often flagrantly. Consequently, they are routinely denigrated, and feel the burning stigma of welfare as though its identification is etched on their foreheads. Individualistic beliefs about the causes of poverty are so widespread that, ironically, even many poor women believe them. Many were quick to berate other welfare recipients, at least in the abstract, as indolent and as not being interested in "bettering themselves."

Despite the popularity of these explanations, I found that personal attributes were not sufficient to explain why a woman is poor and on welfare, and in some cases were largely irrelevant. Women's lives are more complex than Individualist, Structuralist, Culture of Poverty, or Fatalist explanations have allowed, alone or in combination. Treatises that draw on these perspectives tend to ignore facets of women's poverty and the unique set of circumstances that surround it, and assume that the poverty experience is universal across gender. Poverty and welfare use is viewed by many as a personal problem, not a social problem connected to women's roles in the family and within a capitalistic economic structure. Ideologic hegemony operates here: Many onlookers, both women and men, have come to accept these claims as divine truth because of the enduring brainlock of the dominant paradigm that serves the interests of the more powerful members of our society. But gendered experiences, in context of the causes and consequences of impoverishment and public aid, should not be ignored.

The women that I interviewed shed new light on several important ways in which our explanations must become more inclusive of women's experience. Certainly on first glance, some women did look "lazy," in the sense that they had not looked for, or located, a job in recent months or even years. Some women, for example, were on welfare for five years or more, and it is easy to understand that welfare critics may question whether these recipients are sufficiently motivated to look for work, and whether they were making the necessary efforts to improve the financial circumstances for their families. They note, correctly, that a substantial number of women on welfare have low levels of education, poor job skills, and lack the human capital that employers would find attractive. However, most women who had been on welfare for lengthy periods did not intend to remain on welfare this long. In fact, I found considerable movement off and on welfare, reflecting interest toward paid work. The women interviewed here did not enjoy the difficulties and impoverishment associated with living on welfare. They wanted the system changed, and preferred to improve their situation with paid work. Yet many remained on welfare for significant periods of time because they believed that they are *already working:* They are taking care of their children. Being a "good mother" in impoverished conditions is a full-time job. They felt that, as sole parents, they needed to take responsibility for raising their preschool children, and they needed to be available to their school-age children before and after school so that they could keep them safe, off the streets, and out of trouble. They scoffed at the idea that they were lazy, and instead saw themselves as working diligently to ensure that their children would have a better life.

It is a profoundly sexist supposition that taking care of children rather than searching for work is evidence of immorality or a lack of initiative. It reflects the low value that is accorded to caring for children—work that has been traditionally defined as "women's work." Our society discredits the caretaking of children, despite pronatalist values that pressure couples to have them. We assume that it is better for strangers to care for children at a minimum wage, while their mothers work at other minimum wage jobs, than it is for mothers to take care of their children themselves. These sexist values are unfortunate and unintended outcomes of the broader struggle for gender equality. As more women have fought for the right to work outside the home for equal wages and opportunities, and met with some success, our society has begun to perceive women working outside the home as normative or expected. Most women with children, including preschool-age children, now work outside the home for pay. Some work out of choice, some work out of necessity, and a sizeable number can no longer distinguish between choice and necessity—they go hand in hand. Young women in high school and college today assume that they will work outside the home when they are married, and they intend to continue working if they become mothers. It is now part of our culture to expect mothers to have paid jobs, and when they don't, they often whisper defensively, or with self-deprecation, that they are "just housewives." Consequently, if most women and men come to see mothers' employ-ment as normative, there is widespread concern when others "choose" to buck the general trends, especially when these individuals are subsidized by those who are working, through the taxes they pay. If most women work, some people prompt, why can't welfare recipients work too? Many middle-class mothers who are employed out-side the home also do not necessarily have an easy time juggling employment and parenthood. They describe having role overload, role strain, and experience consider-able guilt that they aren't doing enough for their families. But, they wonder, if they work, why are other women allowed a "free ride"?

As these interviews reveal, poor mothers face additional burdens, in comparison to middle-class mothers, as they care for their children. In summary, it is simply more difficult for low-wage earners to muster up the personal, structural, and psychological resources that are needed to find and maintain a job, particularly when they know that this job will not, in all likelihood, significantly improve their meager standard of living. They will continue to be impoverished even when they work. When this is coupled with the strains associated with single parenthood more generally, some women conclude that holding a job is virtually impossible—at least until their children grow older, their job opportunities improve, other structural impediments are eliminated, and their self-confidence improves. There are always exceptions that feed our misconceptions, but again, it's not that women don't want to work, or that they are lazy and satisfied with living on the public dole. Women in this study were depressed about their economic circumstances. After weighing the costs and the rewards associated with work, many women, particularly those with large numbers of children, children under the age of six, or with few skills and job prospects, glumly concluded that work does not currently provide the security necessary to make it a rational choice.

In addition to these constraints, I found that many women were poor and in need of welfare because of labor market conditions. Historically, women's labor has often been a reserve force under capitalism. Women workers are expendable; they are called out when needed because not enough men are available for work (e.g., wartime), because men do not want to do the type of work that needs to be done (e.g., nursing), or the pay is low (e.g., teaching). When the numbers of available men are once again sufficient to meet employment needs, or when the pay increases, or unemployment increases and men therefore begin to seek out the type of work they have been avoiding, women are then encouraged to leave their jobs on the grounds that men need these jobs in order to support their families. Women may be pushed out of the labor market altogether, or relocated into other more "feminine" jobs that men still do not want to fill (e.g., clerical positions). In contrast to men, women have never been taken seriously as breadwinners. They have, historically, been trivialized as working for "extra" money to pay for family vacations or to upgrade the family's standard of living. Men's breadwinning role within the family has been used against women to deny them jobs, to pass them over for promotion, and to pay them less. As recently as the late 1960s, major newspapers in the country separated out their employment ads into "Help Wanted Male" and "Help Wanted Female" job categories. Men's jobs and women's jobs were not considered interchangeable, as men's had higher pay, better benefits, and greater chances for promotion. After all, the old adage goes, men have families to support. Women, who also support families, have never been able to amass these same types of public support, promotions, or wage increases because of their breadwinning needs. They have been expected to support their families on the wages of "women's work."

The United States economy is in another cycle of expansion. Currently, our service sector is expanding, unemployment is low, and there are not enough men willing to fill the millions of low-wage jobs that are being generated. Not surprisingly, policymakers are cutting back the welfare rolls so that poor women will take these positions. This is an age-old maneuver. However, in the past, not all women were eliminated from welfare; it was primarily African Americans, or never-married mothers, who were deemed as providing unsuitable homes and therefore had their benefits terminated. This time, however, the termination is more widespread. With few exceptions, all welfare recipients are subject to time limitations and work requirements.

A significant problem has been created. Despite the rise in service sector jobs, there simply are not enough stable, permanent jobs for all the welfare recipients who need and want them. There will be tremendous competition for semiskilled and unskilled jobs, particularly those few that pay higher level wages. The competition for these positions is expected to increase dramatically in the coming years as more women are forced off welfare. Moreover, most of these jobs do not provide crucial fringe benefits, such as health insurance or sick leave. These are not "fringe" in the sense of being peripheral to their needs. These benefits are an important part of any remuneration package and are critical to being able to raise a family off the welfare system.

Part of the reason that pay and fringe benefits are so crucial to exiting welfare is because a significant number of women on welfare face tremendous personal hardships that they did not choose and are, in an important sense, beyond their control. They need welfare's security because their lives have become sadly insecure otherwise. As revealed here, some women are on welfare because of being deserted by their spouse or partner, or because they left an unfaithful or violent partner. They need time to regroup, to assess their options, to build their self-esteem that abusive relationships so often erode, or to acquire skills so that they can support themselves. Certainly, no woman asks or deserves to be beaten or should have to live with her partner's continued infidelity. But for some women, perhaps because of other issues such as having fewer job skills or deficits in education, leaving the situation may be exceedingly difficult both emotionally and logistically. These women need assistance from somewhere in order to leave an intolerable situation. Still, other women turned to welfare because of poor health, or the poor health of their children. Those who are impoverished are more likely to suffer from a wide variety of ailments than do others. Poor children are particularly vulnerable and may suffer long-term health effects such as stunted growth or learning disabilities. To voluntarily leave welfare and risk losing health care benefits was seen by these mothers as being grossly irresponsible.

Given the vice-like impoverishment that results from an inadequate welfare system or low-wage work, the mothers I interviewed turned to others to help them make ends meet each month. Most women had developed an intricate and elaborate web of assistance among family, friends, neighbors, boyfriends, social services and charities, and perhaps even with their children's fathers. This assistance was invaluable; without it, they would be out on the streets and unable to provide any semblance of a decent living for their children. Some welfare critics have suggested that the welfare system is thus creating, or at least perpetuating, a Culture of Poverty. I would acknowledge that a subculture of sorts had developed among many of the respondents. Some held values that were somewhat distinctive from those in the middle class. They placed a high value on sharing, on the primacy of the extended family, and on the importance of women-centered aid. But rather than this subculture creating or keeping them poor, it instead served to keep them from being poorer than they would otherwise be. Women without this network or subculture of support, and there were a substantial number without it, tended to have the most despondent circumstances. They lived in the poorest housing, their children were more likely to be in trouble with the law or involved in a pregnancy, and they had the fewest episodes of work. Given paltry welfare benefits and the low minimum wage, having a supportive network on which to rely is the primary method of escaping poverty. Without this assistance, often coupled with unreported side jobs, few women would really be able to "pull themselves up by their bootstraps," as our society seems to insist on.

Our hostility toward welfare recipients is widespread and deeply rooted in class divisions in our society. We draw sharp class lines around ourselves rather than looking for the interconnectedness of our lives. I have shown that poor mothers share many of the same concerns about raising their children as do middle class mothers, but their struggles are exacerbated by not having enough money with which to provide for the children adequately. As is the case with mothers everywhere, they want to provide for their children, they want them to be safe and secure, and they want their children's lives to be better than their own. The commonalities with other women are straightforward and obvious from these interviews. I hope that their stories will enhance the "gender consciousness" among women, while at the same time not negating the importance of social class. Our position in the class structure, independently, and interactively with race, ethnicity, and gender, shapes both our objective existence and subjective conceptions of our surroundings and of ourselves.

Women's roles within the interface of work and family are in a state of flux, and women at all income levels are feeling tensions that result from rapid social change. It is not altogether clear what our society expects from women. The work/family dilemma is usually portrayed as something that can be alleviated by adjusting work schedules, managing time more efficiently, or paying for services for the tasks that women did in the past, but cannot do now because they are at work. Fathers' time in household tasks has not increased appreciably in recent decades. Despite trying to "cover" for their absences from the family, mothers feel guilty about possibly ignoring their children or their spouse's needs. Fathers, in contrast, do not feel these tensions. This is because we have an incompatible moral dilemma between motherhood and work. It is not clear to women that they can be good mothers and good workers at the same time, whereas for men, being good fathers and successful providers are virtually one in the same. Child rearing experts do not suggest that fathers take years off of work to care for their new babies or remind fathers that raising a child is more worthwhile than any job, while living in a culture that equates work with virtue, power, morality, and personal fulfillment. There is no cultural ideology that suggests that fathers split their energies, time, and loyalties between work and family, as there is for mothers. Hays (1996), describes the "ideology of intensive motherhood," as having three key components. First, a child should have one central caregiver, and it should be the mother rather than the father. Second, children and their needs should be at the heart of child rearing, and mothers should lavish their time, energy and material resources on their children. Third, the child is sacred, so that comparisons of worth between child rearing and any other activity are morally impossible. Ironically, this ideology of intensive motherhood persists in a society where most women work, and those who don't are intimidated into reporting that they are "just housewives."

Yet, it persists, she concludes, because its high value on love and self-sacrifice is a way of actively rejecting the selfish and materialistic market logic inside the family.

The moral confusion over women's appropriate roles is particularly blatant in the banner of "mother blaming" carried by psychologists to pediatricians, who blame working mothers for society's ills. Juvenile delinquency, crime, drug addiction, and teenage pregnancy are pinned on single mothers, particularly poor single mothers who intersperse work with welfare. But if they don't work, particularly if they don't have a husband to support them, then they are viewed as freeloaders. They are damned if they work, and damned if they don't. Society is confused about what it wants from women.

Poor women are besieged with the consequences of these changing roles. Unlike more affluent mothers who can purchase the services their families may need in light of paid work, poor single mothers have a more difficult time finding the tenuous balance between work and family. Society asks that poor mothers work and work harder; we ask them to be better mothers and intervene to stop these social ills; we ask them to become mothers less often; and we ask them to put off becoming mothers until they can be a good provider or are able to marry one. We ask all of these things, as welfare policy now invalidates their right to stay at home with their children. Reforms dictate that the primary responsibility of single mothers is to provide for their children's financial needs rather than their emotional ones. They should be wage earners first, caregivers to their dependent children second. This represents a major change in orientation towards women's roles. AFDC was originally created so that single mothers could stay home, because caring for children was considered to be more important than working outside the home. Although the assumptions about women's appropriate roles vary historically, reforms continue the dogmatic tradition of defining for women what is, or what is not, in their best interest. Single mothers no longer have the authority to make their own decisions about their family's needs.

Ironically, many welfare recipients would like to see the welfare system changed substantially. Unlike the imagery we may have of the Cadillac welfare queen, they would like to be off welfare altogether. Yet the negative sentiment of recipients as "freeloaders" is so strong that we assume the system must be made punitive in order for them to leave. The misconception suggests that, since they can't be shamed to get off of welfare, we need to force them off. Recent policy reforms have created a system that is far more punitive than helpful in nature. It is a welfare-to-work program; e.g., the focus is on getting women off welfare and into jobs, rather than a human–capital-approach, where the goal is on meaningful job training. Scarce resources must now be devoted to enforcing the welfare-to-work policies. I suggest we evaluate the cost of enforcement, versus the value of reinforcement—that is, reinforcing the ability of women to adequately support their families. Forcing a change that is not helpful, but simply appeases a political goal, will result in terrific manpower and financial costs. We may be creating another welfare bureaucracy that becomes unwieldy, and does virtually nothing to help those who are impoverished.

I predict that welfare reforms will meet with minimal success, and may fail completely, unless we take into account the specific needs that poor women themselves have articulated. It is critical that we understand poverty, and the welfare experience from those who have direct, first-hand exposure to the system itself. Programs created by upper class policymakers who have little real empathy towards the interplay of structural, individual, cultural, and fatalistic reasons why women may need aid, are unlikely to be tailored to meet the needs of poor women. Despite the best of intentions, it is easy to misunderstand what is needed to improve the lives of poor single women who are trying to care for and protect their children.

First and foremost, recipients are looking for *security*. Welfare is not just about money, really. It's about the security of knowing that one's family will, at least at a minimum level, be taken care of. Like most women everywhere, poor women regard having a home, stability, and protection as essential comforts. But as poor single mothers taking care of children, with minimal or no help from their children's fathers, they feel vulnerable. They turn to the government for short periods, or perhaps for longer periods, because they hope that it can provide them and their children with the security that is sorely lacking in their lives. Their marriages and relationships did not provide this security—husbands walked out on them, partners abused them, and even the best made plans sometimes do not work out. Their jobs do not provide security either—hours are sporadic, work is temporary, the pay is low, few benefits are included, and they could be fired or laid-off with little notice. The voluntary human-capital-enhancement programs offered by the welfare office prior to recent reforms also did not provide security—because of the two-year time limit attached to the assistance, many women turned down the opportunity to participate in these programs, which compared to today's policies, offered considerable hands-on help. Some women have supportive extended family or close friendship networks, and relied on them extensively, but even they acknowledged that these were not secure—maybe grandmother could baby-sit today, but that does not necessarily mean that she can baby-sit tomorrow. And finally, children's fathers were also not a source of security—child support was sporadic, if given at all. Visitation was also irregular, if there was any. I questioned one woman with three children why she relied on welfare rather than the sizable $600 child support her children's father was court-ordered to provide. Instead of keeping the child support for herself, it was turned over to the welfare office, and she was given only $50 of it. Her welfare check, coupled with her extra $50, was still $200 less than she would have received if she took the child support instead. I questioned her: Wouldn't the child support, at $600 a month and a part-time job be the more rational way to go? She let me know, in no uncertain terms, that she was appalled by my illogical suggestion because there was no security in it.

> Absolutely not. Yeah, he paid $600 last month, and $600 the month before. But what about the month before that? And what about next month? He comes and goes. I can't be keeping track of him. He ain't been by to see his kids in months. He don't care. But I've got these children, and I got to feed and clothe them. I'm all they got, and I've got to do them right. And what if they got sick? I need to be able to take them to the doctor. I can't be counting on him. Yeah, it's less money, but it's steady money. And I can count on it.

The "problem with welfare" lies not within the welfare system. The real problem lies with the structure of low-wage work in the United States. Indeed, the welfare system actually works well, compared to low-wage work. It offers the security that is sought by vulnerable families. It provides for their basic needs with food, shelter, clothing, and medical care, albeit at a minimal level. But poorly paid work within the lower tiers of the service sector does not necessarily provide a basic floor on any of these necessities. Welfare works, and that is a problem to many critics. It is a government program that provides the protection for families that low-wage work does not. The real way to eliminate the "welfare problem," then, is to restructure or enhance jobs in the lowest tiers of our labor market, rather than trying to force people off a system that, even with its faults, is a recipient's logical refuge.

These interviews, and findings from other researchers using both qualitative narratives and quantitative data from large national data sources, find a considerable movement on and off welfare, and in and out of work. Women become discouraged and frustrated with work that demands so much and returns so little in terms of security for their family. It would be poor mothering to jeopardize the well-being of their children. In fact, women take their parental responsibilities so seriously that they are willing to put up with the stigma associated with welfare; they are willing to live on a "thrifty food plan" that was designated by our own government to be for emergency and temporary use only; they are willing to live in undesirable and sometimes substandard housing; and they are willing to live on a few hundred dollars a month. Rather than lacking in motivation, women on welfare know first-hand that the conditions of work in the lowest tiers—the pay, benefits, hours, and uncertainty—are appalling, and so they opt for the security of the welfare system. Families who rely on these poorly compensated jobs lack back-up emergency reserves for when something goes wrong. They are families at-risk. They live check to check, day to day, hoping that nothing comes up to trip them up again, but something invariably does.

At the same time, there is nothing inherently wrong with these jobs that would suggest why they are so poorly compensated. Picking tomatoes, working in the laundry of a hospital, serving food, or mopping floors at the local school are important jobs. Our society couldn't do without these services; they are vital. Therefore, if the services are important and necessary, then workers in these jobs should be paid wages that allow them to continue working in them. Austria pays its service workers wages in which they can support themselves. So does Australia. Why does the wealthiest country in the world, the United States, refuse to pay living wages to its workers? Our government has a responsibility to intervene in capitalism's free-market approach. We see this intervention occur at times when it behooves our moral conscience, or when it would be in the best interests of the masses. Certainly these two qualifications apply here. It is moral, just, and fair to pay people a living wage in which they can support themselves and their families. Moreover, it may be less expensive in the long run for taxpayers to diminish a large welfare bureaucracy based on enforcement and allow former recipients to become contributing participants in the national economy. If jobs in the lowest tiers were enhanced—made more secure—then welfare would be unnecessary for most families who seek its safe and secure confines. According to these and other data, most poor women would flock to employment that paid a living wage, if benefits such as health care and child care were included. Those who remained on welfare would be those who could not, for one reason or another, support themselves. Welfare has a role in any compassionate nation, as there will always be some small segment of the population who need assistance in meeting their basic needs.

Some readers may question how the United States can afford to offer poor people these types of services, or even whether we should offer them. Workplace and family policies are controversial because they reflect moral values and cultural ideologies. Not everyone agrees about where the responsibility for individual well-being lies. The United States, compared to many other industrial nations, has wallowed in a laissez-faire approach, in which selective policies for a few predominate rather than universal policies available to all citizens. A look at how other countries similar to the United States manage their social welfare needs could serve as a powerful example as to what is feasible, and can shape our notions of what is desirable (Bergmann, 1996; Kahn and Kamerman, 1975; Smeeding, 1992).

Most industrialized nations have an interrelated set of proactive and universal programs to help families with children escape poverty. These programs are not means-tested benefits available only for those people poor enough to qualify. For example, universal family allowances are common, and they are given to parents on behalf of children as a universal right of citizenship. Day care is often subsidized so that it is free or at a very low cost. Many countries have universal health insurance systems that are financed by progressive forms of taxation—those who earn more pay more in taxes. They have these programs because residents favor structural explanations for inequality over individual explanations by a wide margin. For example, when asked, "Why are there people in this country who live in need?" 35 percent of Swedes claimed it was caused by societal injustice, and only 16 percent claimed it was because of personal laziness. The results in France were even more telling: 42 percent of those surveyed claimed blamed societal injustice, as compared to only 15 percent who believed it was caused by personal laziness. Here in the United States the explanations are reversed: 33 percent invoked structural explanations, whereas 39 percent blamed personal laziness (World Values Survey, 1994).

France is one country out of many that can provide a rich contrast to the United States. In the book *Saving Our Children from Poverty* (1996) economist Barbara Bergmann notes that there are many demographic and economic similarities between the two nations. The annual rate of growth is comparable, and both countries have similar rates of female labor force participation and births outside of marriage, and have minority populations of comparable proportions. France has a 50 percent higher unemployment rate, yet their poverty rate is considerably less than exists in the United States. The child poverty rate is 6 percent in France, as compared to 22 percent in the United States. Moreover, in 1991, about 23 percent of single mothers in France received welfare-type benefits, compared to 67 percent of single mothers in the United States. The reason for these differences is that France has made a successful commitment to enhance low-tier work. They have improved the conditions surrounding these jobs so that they are no longer necessarily associated with low wages, and they do not automatically reduce the array of benefits that are vital to an individual's and a family's well-being. This investment in low-tier work is not only monetary, but is reflected in their entire orientation to caring for their citizens. French parents at all income levels get a great deal of government assistance with child care and health care, for example. Child care is provided by an educated work force, and it is considered valued and important work. Free public nursery schools are available for children ages two-and-a-half through six, and by the time they are three years old, virtually 100 percent of French children attend. There is also a well-coordinated before and after-school care program for a nominal fee. Likewise, free health care is available to everyone by right of citizenship, and it is not lost when a person loses a job, develops an illness that is expensive to treat, or leaves welfare. The French government supplements the income of families with children by providing family allowances, housing assistance, and cash payments to pregnant women. These programs are not limited to poor families, unemployed families, or single parents. Moreover, because most of these programs are universal and available regardless of income, they have little or no stigma attached to them. They are considered to be normal facets of their social structure, much in the way public education is in our country. These programs are rights of all citizens, not privileges, and therefore there is no shame in receiving them. In contrast, in the United States we have families who need assistance, but either don't know what is available, don't know how to access it, or have been so absorbed by the Individualist perspective that their ego or guilt prevents them from seeking help that they qualify for and need.

Workers in France with low wages get even more help from these and other programs. For example, a single mother in France who moves from welfare to work retains $6,000 in government cash and housing grants. She would continue to receive free health insurance and would pay a negligible amount for child care, as do all French citizens. She would not have to face the hardships associated with low-tier work as do women in the United States. Thus, despite the fact that the welfare programs in France are more generous than are ours, women are still more likely to leave them to pursue jobs. They can do this because of the security that the French government provides to all its workers. It is wrong to assume that we must have a punitive approach and keep benefits low so that women will not abuse the welfare system. Here, as in France, women would prefer employment, and they will work, if they continued to have the security that they need to care for their families.

Critics may scoff that the costs for these programs are prohibitive. According to data compiled by Bergmann, the United States would need to spend approximately 59 percent more than it's current level to increase our spending on programs for child well-being to those of the French. As the richest country in the world, with one of the lowest tax rates, investing in our families in this fashion is not an impossibility. Instead, our money is being spent in other ways—it's a matter of priority. For example, the United States spends more than twice as much money on defense as it does for programs that promote children's well-being (e.g., child care and development, income supplements, income tax reductions, medical care for low-income children), whereas in France, the opposite occurs. We also spend an inordinate amount of money on the enforcement of our new punitive policies. That money would be better spent reinforcing the security of the vulnerable members of our society, who, despite our comfort in thinking to the contrary, could be any one of us.

I am not suggesting that the United States should blindly import the social policies found in other nations. It would be myopic to suggest that they swiftly be incorporated here; these social policies represent approaches to social inequality, family rights, and social justice that are embedded in cultures different than our own, and therefore may not translate easily. Moreover, these policies also have their own limitations and cannot be seen as a panacea for what ails us in the United States. Instead, I suggest that we study and learn from other cultures and recognize how we can adopt the relevant aspects into our own approaches, given our own cultural parameters and social needs.

Solutions to our "welfare problem" involve both short- and long-term changes in the way America structures both work and social welfare. First, it must involve investing in the human capital potential among all members of our society, including remedial education for those members of our population who currently possess limited education and job skills. Japan and Germany actively work to prevent creating an underclass with deficient skills (Wilson, 1996). They have developed policies to increase the "higher order thinking skills" among their young. Students must meet high performance standards before they can graduate from secondary school. They are prepared for work or they are ready for further technical training or a university education. And there is little or no delay in being hired by large firms immediately upon graduation. In contrast to these policies, in the United States, high school students are often aimless and many fall through the cracks. Those who are not bound for college receive little in the way of technical training; those who do go to college often have such poor academic skills that they require remedial education to qualify for basic introductory college classes in English and Mathematics. We need to ensure that our public schools are providing an equal opportunity for all students to obtain an outstanding education. Our schools should be funded by a fair formula that does not reward wealthy property holders with more elaborate schools and resources and penalize poorer property holders. Currently, school funding formulas are fixed at the local level, resulting in highly unequal allocations per pupil. Schools, even neighboring ones, can contain drastically different levels of resources such as computers, books, athletic facilities, electives such as art or music, class sizes, and teacher salaries, simply because of the variation in the collection of property taxes. Should we then be surprised that drop-out rates and needs for remedial education are more prevalent in poorer schools?

Second, we must work toward creating secure and full employment for all persons who want jobs. Let us not strive for low paid and insecure make-shift work. Sociologist William Julius Wilson (1996), Journalist Mikey Kaus (1992), and Economists Edward Regan (1994) and Sheldon Danziger and Peter Gottschalk (1995) are among those who suggest that our government should create public works jobs to rebuild and maintain the crumbling infrastructure in the United States. Although these proposals vary widely, generally they are geared to poor workers (not just those who are on welfare) and they would provide services that financially strapped cities and counties can ill afford. These jobs range from supervising children in after-school activities to rebuilding our nation's roads and bridges.

Of the various proposals, I find most intriguing those that propose to model the popular Works Progress Administration (WPA) created in the 1930s during the Depression by then President Franklin D. Roosevelt. As Kaus reports (1992: 259):

> In its eight-year existence, according to official records, the WPA built or improved 651,000 miles of roads, 953 airports, 124,000 bridges and viaducts, 1,178,000 culverts, 8,000 parks, 18,000 playgrounds and athletic fields, and 2,000 swimming pools. It constructed 40,000 buildings (including 8,000 schools) and repaired 85,000 more. Much of New York City—including LaGuardia Airport, FDR drive, plus hundreds of parks and libraries—was built by WPA.

Kaus advocates a similar program, open to every American citizen over 18 years of age who wants to participate, maintaining that there are more than enough worthwhile WPA-type-projects to go around. Jobs for men and women could include repairing potholes in our roads, serving as nurse's aides, picking up our nation's trash, building parks and recreational facilities, working in libraries to allow for extended hours, and providing a multitude of other important and sorely needed services. Because these jobs would be available to everyone—men and women, welfare recipients and nonrecipients, rich and poor, young and old—participants would not suffer from the stigma currently hounding welfare programs such as TANF or food stamps. Kaus proposes that wages be kept slightly below the minimum wage, and be supplemented by the Earned Income Tax Credit (EITC), which could be expanded to lift all poor working families out of poverty. Thus, although open to rich and poor alike, few wealthy Americans would opt for such work because the compensation package would be of little benefit to them.

As aptly noted by Wilson (1996), these jobs must be administered by the federal government, as they were under President Roosevelt, to ensure that these remain *newly* created jobs, rather than jobs that are created by localities that simply shift funding sources for previous positions. The cost for a WPA-type-program is not inexpensive; even subminimum wage jobs may cost the government at least $12,000 a year per job, or $12 billion for every 1 million jobs created. These costs would be offset somewhat by the lower TANF costs and reductions in other government budgets that may otherwise fund some of these projects at some level, such as road maintenance. But the monumental investment in our decaying infrastructure and meager social services would significantly contribute to the betterment of our society, and would ultimately enhance future economic growth. This could benefit all citizens if the program was created with care and compassion. As Kaus writes (1992: 137), "With a neo-WPA maintaining highways, schools, playgrounds, and subways, with libraries open every evening, and city streets cleaned twice a day, we would have a common life more people would find worth reclaiming."

I suggest that the special needs of single mothers should not be overlooked in the development of such a program. For example, we must guarantee that two tracks of employment do not develop (i.e., "men's work" and "women's work") with different scales of compensation. Traditionally, those occupations with high concentrations of male workers are paid higher than occupations with higher concentrations of female workers. While all positions should be available to anyone who seeks them regardless of gender, past history suggests that we must take affirmative action to ensure that both men and women are paid fairly.

Moreover, although we can debate whether the best form of compensation is with higher than minimum wages or with an improved EITC (or both), the fact remains that employment must be made *secure* for all workers. Unless jobs provide a package of benefits that include wages and EITC to pull workers above the poverty level, offer health insurance, allow for part-time work, and offer subsidies for quality child care, even a WPA type program will do little to really help women leave welfare.

Our society needs to reevaluate, from the ground up, how and why we should reform welfare. The welfare system is not full of irresponsible adults living high-on-the-hog at taxpayers' expense. This hostile image is off-target in many respects. Most importantly, perhaps, is that the primary beneficiaries of welfare are children. These children generally live with their mothers, who alone are trying to take care of their children's physical, emotional, and spiritual needs. Pushing single mothers and their children off of government assistance and forcing them to accept low-wage and insecure work will not eliminate poverty. It will likely increase the number of people who are poor and increase the myriad of social ills that are associated with economic insecurity. Children turn to drugs, girls get pregnant, and people steal, in order to ease the despair and hopelessness of impoverishment—the feeling that there is no real ticket out to a better life. They know what the bulk of Americans seem to forget—that there is very little social mobility occurring in the United States. Most people die in or near the same social class in which they were born. The United States, with its alleged compassion and sense of justice for all, coupled with its vast resources, could tackle the real "welfare problem," as the real problem is not the welfare system. The predominant problem is the insecurity associated with jobs in the lowest tiers of the American economy. Our government could enhance the feasibility of employment for millions of families by partnering with the private sector. According to a group of governors' policy advisors on welfare reform and workforce development sponsored by the National Governors' Association Center for Best Practices, private employers are willing partners in reform. They are "willing to provide child care, transportation, and other employment supports so workers will accept jobs that might otherwise go unfilled and remain in those jobs," but they do "expect government to help" (National Governor's Association, 1997:1). Enhancing work by increasing minimum wage to at least $8 an hour; creating viable and important public works jobs; expanding the Earned Income Tax Credit (EITC); providing benefits such as medical insurance to all families who do not have it, and family friendly leave policies that allow for care of a sick or needy child; subsidizing child care to make it affordable; and allowing workers to keep a portion of their food stamp and housing benefits when necessary would go a long way toward shrinking the welfare rolls. True and meaningful welfare reform is best seen as a "work problem" and approached as "work reform."

As welfare reform ages, we will see impressive data and persuasive statistics proclaiming the politically successful reduction in the number of welfare recipients. When we do, we should remember that a decrease in families on welfare does not mean a reduction in the number of families living in poverty. Furthermore, it may well mean a corresponding increase in the number of families at risk. As policies change, welfare rolls decline, and at first look, all seems well. Our attention may then shift to other social problems that are in vogue. But meanwhile, poor families are left trying to cope with enduring roadblocks only to have added social pressure to conform to America's ideals of individualism and independence.

The truth of life within our lower economic classes is often not revealed. As long as free-reigning capitalism, still incumbent patriarchy, and cultural hegemony hold sway, welfare reform's public appearance will be highly polished in the dominant media portrayals to come. Reducing welfare reliance is wonderful for all concerned, but let's also be aware of the consequences of eliminating a valuable safety net without enhancing the structure and pay of the jobs that recipients are likely to hold. We should watch and examine the situation closely to see how these working but poor and at-risk families are fairing. We know, deep down, that if reform is politically rather than morally motivated and constructed, the cruelty in the reforms will be revealed.

REFERENCES

Abramovitz, Mimi. (1996a). *Regulating the Lives of Women: Social Welfare Policy from Colonial Times to the Present* (Revised Edition). Boston, MA: South End Press.

_____. (1996b). *Under Attack, Fighting Back: Women and Welfare in the United States.* New York: Monthly Review Press.

_____. (1992). The Reagan Legacy: Undoing Class, Race, and Gender Accords. *Journal of Sociology and Social Welfare* XIX, 91–110.

Acs, Gregory, and Pamela Loprest. (1995). The Effects of Disabilities on Exits from AFDC. Paper presented at the 17th Annual Research Conference of the Association for Public Policy Analysis and Management, November 2–4.

Allard, Mary Ann, Randy Albelda, Mary Ellen Colton, and Carol Cosenza. (1997). *In Harm's Way? Domestic Violence, AFDC Receipt, and Welfare Reform.* Boston: University of Massachusetts, Center for Social Policy Research, McCormick Institute. February.

Allison, Dorothy. (1993). *Bastard Out of Carolina.* New York: Dutton.

Alter, Jonathan. (1998). It's 4:00 p.m. Do You Know Where Your Children Are? *Newsweek,* April 27: p. 29–33.

Anderson, Martin. (1978). *The Political Economy of Welfare Reform in the United States.* Palo Alto: The Hoover Institution.

Armey, Dick. (1994). Public Welfare in America. *The Journal of Social, Political and Economic Studies.* 19, 245–250.

Ashe, Arthur, and Arnold Rampersad. (1994). *Days of Grace: A Memoir.* New York: Ballantine.

Associated Press, (December 2, 1996).

Associated Press, (January 5, 1998). More People Hungry. *Gainesville Sun,* p. 5A.

Associated Press, (April 1, 1998). House OKs Drug Tests for Welfare. *Gainesville Sun,* p. 1–2B.

Axin, J., and H. Levine. (1975). *Social Welfare: A History of the American Response to Need.* New York: Harper and Row.

Baca Zinn, Maxine. (1994). "Feminist rethinking of racial–ethnic families." In Maxine Baca Zinn and Bonnie Thorton Dill (Eds.) *Women of Color in the U.S. Society.* (pp. 303–314).

Bandler, Jean Taft Douglas. (1975). Family Issues in Social Policy: An Analysis of Social Security. Unpublished Dissertation. NY: Columbia University of Social Work.

Barry, Skip. (1998). City Families Face Housing Squeeze. *Dollars and Sense* 215 Jan–Feb.: 32–36.

Belenky, Mary Field, Blyth McVicker Clinchy, Nancy Rule Goldberger, and Jill Mattuck Tarule. (1986). *Women's Ways of Knowing: The Development of Self, Voice and Mind.* New York: Basic Books.

Bergmann, Barbara R. (1996). *Saving Our Children from Poverty: What the United States Can Learn from France.* New York: Russell Sage Foundation.

Bernades, Jon. (1985). "Family Ideology": Identification and Exploration. *Sociological Review.* 33, 275–297.

Bernstein, Aaron. (1997). Off Welfare—And Worse Off. *Business Week.* December 22, p. 38.

Bernstein, Jared. (1993). "Rethinking Welfare Reform." *Dissent.* Summer, 277–279.

Berrick, Jill Duerr. (1995). *Faces of Poverty.* Oxford University Press: New York.

Bianchi, Suzanne M., and Daphne Spain. (1996). Women, Work and Family in America. *Population Bulletin.* Vol. 51, No. 3, Washington DC: Population Reference Bureau.

Blank, Rebecca. (1995). Outlook for the U.S. Labor Market and Prospects for Low-Wage Entry Jobs. In Demetra Smith Nightingale and Robert H. Haveman (Eds.) *The Work Alternative*. Washington DC: The Urban Institute Press; Cambridge MA: Harvard University Press.

Blank, Rebecca, and Patricia Ruggles. (1996). When Do Women Use Aid to Families with Dependent Children and Food Stamps? *Journal of Human Resources*. 31, 57–89.

Bloom, Dan. (1995). *The Family Transition Program: An Early Implementation Report on Florida's Time-Limit Welfare Initiative*. New York: Manpower Development Research Corporation.

Bloom, Dan, James J. Kemple, and Robin Rogers-Dillon. (1997). *The Family Transition Program: Implementation and Early Impacts of Florida's Initial Time-Limited Welfare Program*. New York: Manpower Development Research Corporation.

Blumer, Herbert. (1969). *Symbolic Interactionism*. Englewood Cliffs, NY: Prentice Hall.

Bobo, Lawrence, and Ryan A. Smith. (1994). Antipoverty Policy, Affirmative Action, and Racial Attitudes. In Sheldon H. Danziger, Gary D. Sandefur, and D. Weinberg (Eds.) *Confronting Poverty*. Cambridge MA: Harvard University Press: New York: Russell Sage Foundation.

Booth, Alan, and John N. Edwards. (1985). Age at Marriage and Marital Instability. *Journal of Marriage and the Family*. 47, 67–75.

Bose, Christine E., and Peter H. Rossi. (1983). Gender and Jobs: Prestige Standings of Occupations as Affected by Gender. *American Sociological Review*. 48, 316–330.

Bourdieu, Pierre. (1977). *Outline of a Theory of Practice*. New York: Cambridge University Press.

Bowen, Gary L., and Mimi V. Chapman. (1996). Poverty, Neighborhood Danger, Social Support, and the Individual Adaptation among At-Risk Youth in Urban Areas. *Journal of Family Issues*. 17, 641–666.

Briar, Scott. (1966). "Welfare from Below: Recipients' Views of the Public Welfare System." *California Law Review*. 54, 370–385.

Bristo-Brown, Gloria. (February 18, 1991). Letter. *Oakland Tribune*.

Broder, John M. (August 17, 1997). Big Social Changes Revive the False God of Numbers. *New York Times*.

Bronars, Stephen, and Jeff Grogger. (1995). The Economic Consequences of Unwed Motherhood: Using Twin Births as a Natural Experiment. *American Economic Review*. 84, 1141–1156.

Brownmiller, Susan. (1975). *Against Our Will: Men, Women, and Rape*. New York: Simon and Shuster.

Burns, Jodi, Meredith Ballew, Hsiao-Ye Yi, and Meaghan Mountford. (1996). "Child Care Usage among Low-Income and AFDC Families." October. Washington DC: Institute for Women's Policy Research.

Burton, C. Emory. (1992). *The Poverty Debate*. Westport CT: Praeger.

Carney, Eliza N. (1995). Taking Over. *National Journal*. June, 1382–1387.

Castro, Janice. (1993). Disposable Workers. *Time*. March 29, 43–47.

Center on Addiction and Substance Abuse. (1994). Substance Abuse and Women on Welfare. June. P. 3. Columbia University: Center on Addiction and Substance Abuse.

Center for Research on Women. (1996). *School-Age Child Care Project—"I Wish the Kids Didn't Watch So Much TV": Out-of-School Time in Three Low Income Communities*. Wellesley, MA: Wellesley College: Center for Research on Women.

Center for Law and Social Policy. (1997). "Welfare Changes Enacted." [Online] Available: *http://www.igc.apc.org/handsnet2/welfare.reform/Articles/art.876261804.htm*

Chandler, Doris. (January 8, 1997). The Shifting Focus of Welfare: Reforms Hurt Some Recipients. *The Gainesville Sun*. pp. 1B–2B.

Chandler, Doris. (November 28, 1997). Relationship to Outlast Walk a Mile. *The Gainesville Sun.* pp. 1A, 10A.

Chandler, Doris. (November 22, 1997). Housing Concerns Also Prompt Many Calls to Service Agencies. *The Gainesville Sun.* pp. 1B, 3B.

Chandler, Doris. (January 8, 1998). "Workshop Calls for Challenge to Welfare." *The Gainesville Sun.* pp. 1B, 3B.

Chartrand, Sabra. (July 13, 1997). The Difficult Road for Welfare Recipients. *The New York Times* [Online] Available: file:///D I/BRIEFC~1/ARTICLES/DIFFRO~LHTM

Children's Defense Fund. (1998). *The State of America's Children Yearbook 1998.* Washington, DC: Children's Defense Fund.

Children's Defense Fund. (1997a). *Key Facts about Child Care and Early Education: A Briefing Book.* Washington DC: Children's Defense Fund.

Children's Defense Fund. (1997b). *The New Welfare Law: One Year Later.* October 14. [Online]. Available: *http://www.childrensdefense.org/fairstart_oneyr.htm*

Children's Defense Fund. (1994). *Wasting America's Future.* Washington DC: Children's Defense Fund. July.

Clark, Ann L., and Andrew F. Long. (1995). *Child Care Prices: A Profile of Six Communities— Final Report.* Washington DC: The Urban Institute. p. 54.

Clinton, Bill. (1997a). Welfare Should Be Reformed. In C. P. Cozic (Ed.) *Welfare: Opposing Viewpoints.* pp. 20–27. San Diego, CA: Greenhaven Press, Inc.

Clinton, Bill. (1997b). Welfare Reform Must Protect Children and Legal Immigrants. In C. P. Cozic (Ed.) *Welfare Reform.* San Diego, CA: Greenhaven Press, Inc.

Colletta, Nancy Donohue, and Diane Lee. (1983). The Impact of Support for Black Adolescent Mothers. *Journal of Family Issues.* 4, 127–139.

_____. (1994). The Meaning of Motherhood in Black Culture. In R. Staples (Ed.) *The Black Family*, 5th ed. Belmont, CA: Wadsworth.

Collins, Patricia Hill. (1990). *Black Feminist Thought: Knowledge, Consciousness, and the Politics of Empowerment.* Cambridge: Unwin and Hyman.

Committee on Economic Security. (1985). *The Report of the Committee on Economic Security of 1935 and Other Basic Documents Related to the Social Welfare Act, 50th Anniversary Issue.* Washington DC: National Conference on Social Welfare.

Conger, Rand D., Katherine J. Conger, Glen H. Elder Jr., Frederick O. Lorenz, Ronald L. Simons, and Les B. Whitbeck. (1992). A Family Process Model of Economic Hardship and Adjustment of Early Adolescent Boys. *Child Development.* 63, 526–541.

Congressional Digest. (1995). *Welfare Overview.* June–July. pp. 163–165. Washington DC: U.S. Government Printing Office.

Cook, Judith A., and Mary Margaret Fonow. (1986). Knowledge and Women's Interests: Issues of Epistemology and Methodology in Feminist Sociological Research. *Sociological Inquiry.* 56, 2–29.

Cornwell, Edward E. III, Thomas V. Berne, Howard Belzberg, Juan Asensio, George Velmahos, James Murray, and Demetrios Demetriades. (1996). Health Care Crisis from a Trauma Care Perspective. *Journal of the American Medical Association.* 276, 940–947.

Dahrendorf, Ralf. (1959). *Class and Class Conflict in Industrial Society.* Stanford: Stanford University Press.

Daly, Mary. (1978). *Gynecology.* Boston: Beacon Press.

Danziger, Sheldon. (1994). Researchers Dispute Contention That Welfare Is a Major Cause of Out-of-Wedlock Births. Press release issued by Sheldon Danziger, Director, Research and Training Programs on Poverty, the Underclass, and Public Policy, School of Social Work, University of Michigan, Ann Arbor, MI, June 23, 1994.

Danziger, Sheldon and Peter Gottschalk. (1995). *America Unequal.* Cambridge: Harvard University Press.

Davis, Liane, and Jan Hagen. (1996). Stereotypes and Stigma: What's Changed for Welfare Mothers. *Affilia.* 11, 319–337.

Della Fave, Richard L. (1980). The Meek Shall Not Inherit the Earth: Self-Evaluation and the Legitimacy of Stratification. *American Sociological Review.* 45, 955–971.

Deparle, Jason. (1997). Half the States Unlikely to Meet Goals on Welfare. *New York Times* October 1. [Online] Available: file:///A1/deparle-welfaregoals.htm

Donovan, Patricia. (1995). The Family Cap: A Popular But Unproven Method of Welfare Reform. *Family Planning Perspectives.* 27, 166–171.

Douglas, J. (1993). Teen Sex. *American Enterprise.* 4, 52–59.

Dowd, Maureen. (December 15, 1994). Americans Like G.O.P. Agenda, But Split on How to Reach Goals. *New York Times.* p. A1.

Durkheim, Emile. (1947). *The Elementary Forms of the Religious Life.* New York: The Free Press. (Originally published in 1912.)

Edin, Kathryn. (1991). Surviving the Welfare System: How AFDC Recipients Make Ends Meet in Chicago. *Social Problems.* 38, 462–474.

Edin, Kathryn, and Laura Levin. (1997). *Making Ends Meet.* New York: Russell Sage Foundation.

Eisler, Peter. (1991). Taxes Hit Poor Harder. *The Gainesville Sun.*

Ellwood, David T. (1988). *Poor Support: Poverty in the American Family.* New York, NY: Basic Books.

_____. (1986). *Targeting "Would Be" Long-Term Recipients of AFDC.* MPR Reference No. 7617-953. Princeton, NJ: Mathematica Policy Research.

Enda, Jodi. (1998). Proposal Expands Child Care. *The Gainesville Sun.* January 8. pp. 1A, 7A.

Ensminger, Margaret E. (1995). Welfare and Psychological Distress: A Longitudinal Study of African American Urban Mothers. *Journal of Health and Social Behavior.* 36, 346–359.

Farlie, Robert W., and Rebecca A. London. (1997). The Effect of Incremental Benefit Levels on Births to AFDC Recipients. *Journal of Policy Analysis and Management.* 16, 575–597.

Family Economics and Nutrition Review. (1997). Cost of Food at Home. *Family Economics and Nutrition Review.* 10, 56.

Feagin, Joe R. (1975). *Subordinating the Poor: Welfare and American Beliefs.* Englewood Cliffs, NJ: Prentice Hall.

Feagin, Joe R., and Clairece Booher Feagin. (1994). *Social Problems: A Critical Power–Conflict Perspective,* 4th ed.

The Florida Legislature. (May, 1996). *A Plan to Reform Welfare in Florida: WAGES.* Conference Committee on Welfare Reform, CSSB 1662.

Forrest, Jaqueline Darroch, and Susheela Singh. (1990). The Sexual and Reproductive Behavior of American Women, 1982–1988. *Family Planning Perspectives.* 22, 206–214.

Foucault, Michel. (1980). In Collin Gordon (Ed.) *Power/Knowledge: Selected Interviews and Other Writings, 1972–1977.* New York: Pantheon.

Freidan, Betty. (1963). *The Feminine Mystique.* New York: Dell.

Gainesville Sun. (December 2, 1996a). Florida's Welfare Rolls Drop. pp. 1A, 5A.

Gainesville Sun. (December 2, 1996b). GOP Resists Changes to Welfare. p. 5A.

Gainesville Sun. (December 15, 1996). Welfare Debate Doesn't Vanish with Latest Law. p. 4A.

Gainesville Sun. (January 22, 1997). Sun's Welfare Article Insulting, Irresponsible. Letter.

Gainesville Sun. (February 23, 1997). Requirements Vary in States' Welfare Plans. p. A1.

Gainesville Sun. (August 13, 1997). Boston Will Require Companies to Pay a "Living" Wage. p. A7.

Gainesville Sun. (September 2, 1997). Officials May Gain Welfare Insight. pp. 1B–2B.

Gainesville Sun. (November 22, 1997). Report: Poor Seek Help with Rent, Bills. pp. 1B, 3B.

Gainesville Sun. (February 10, 1998). Home Life Affects Children's Health. p. 10A.

General Accounting Office. (1994). *Families on Welfare: Teenage Mothers Least Likely to Be Self-Sufficient.* Washington DC: U.S. Government Printing Office.

Gans, Herbert. (1995). *The War against the Poor: The Underclass and Antipoverty Policy.* New York: Basic Books.

Garfinkel, Irwin, Sara S. McLanahan, and Philip K. Robins. (1994). Child Support and Child Well-Being. Washington DC: The Urban Institute Press.

Gelles, Richard J., and Murray A. Straus. (1979). Violence in the American Family. *Journal of Social Issues.* 35, 15–39.

Geronimus, Arline, and Sanders Korenman. (1993). The Costs of Teenage Childbearing: Evidence and Interpretation. *Demography.* 30, 281–290.

Gilder, George. (1995). Ending Welfare as We Know It. *American Spectator.* June, 24–27.

Gilder, George. (1981). *Wealth and Poverty.* New York, Basic Books.

Glick, Paul C. (1984). Marriage, Divorce, and Living Arrangements: Prospective Changes. *Journal of Family Issues.* 5, 7–26.

Goffman, Erving. (1963). *Stigma.* Englewood Cliffs, NJ: Prentice Hall.

Goldfield, Michael.(1987). *The Decline of Organized Labor in the United States.* Chicago: University of Chicago Press.

Goodban, Nancy. (1985). The Psychological Impact of Being on Welfare. *Social Service Review.* 59, 403–422.

Gordon, Linda. (1994). *Pitied but Not Entitled.* New York: The Free Press.

Gottschalk, Peter, and Robert Moffitt. (1994). Welfare Dependence: Concepts, Measures, and Trends. *The American Economic Review.* 84, 38–42.

Gramsci, Antonio. (1971). *Selections from the Prison Notebooks of Antonio Gramsci.* Edited and Translated by Quintin Hoare and Geoffrey Nowell Smith. New York: International Publishers.

Greenhouse, Steven. (February 3, 1994). State Department Finds Widespread Abuse of World's Women. *New York Times.* p. A1.

Gubrium, Jaber F., and James A. Holstein. (1990). *What Is Family?* Mountain View, CA: Mayfield Publishing Co.

Habermas, Jurgen. (1973). *Legitimation Crisis.* Boston, MA: Beacon.

Hagen and Davis. (1994). Women on Welfare Talk about Reform. *Public Welfare.* 52, 30–40, 42.

Handler, Joel F., and Yaheshel Hasenfeld. (1991). *The Moral Construction of Poverty: Welfare Reform in America.* Newbury Park: Sage Publications.

Harrington, Michael. (1963). *The Other America: Poverty in the United States.* New York, NY: Penguin Books.

Harris, Kathleen Mullan. (1996). Life after Welfare: Women, Work, and Repeat Dependency. *American Sociological Review.* 61, 407–426.

———. (1993). Work and Welfare among Single Mothers in Poverty. *American Journal of Sociology.* 99, 317–352.

Harvey, David L., and Michael H. Reed. (1996). The Culture of Poverty: An Ideological Analysis. *Sociological Perspectives.* 39, 465–495.

Hashima, Patricia Y., and Paul R. Amato. (1994). Poverty, Social Support, and Parental Behavior. *Child Development.* 65, 394–403.

Hatchett, Shirley, and James S. Jackson. (1993). African-American Extended Kin System: An Assessment. In Harriete Pipes McAdoo (Ed.) *Family Ethnicity: Strength in Diversity.* Newbury Park, CA: Sage.

Hays, Sharon. (1996). *The Cultural Contradictions of Motherhood*. Princeton: Yale University Press.

Herbert, Bob. (November 20, 1997). The Game Is Rigged. *The New York Times*. [Online] Available: http://www.nytimes.com/1997/11/20/oped

Herbert, Bob. (April 26, 1996). The Real Welfare Cheats. *The New York Times*. p. A-31.

Hernandez, Raymond. (March 23, 1998). People Not Going from Welfare into Jobs, New York Survey Says. *The New York Times*. [Online] Available: http://www.nytimes.com/1998/3/23/news/national/welfare~nonworkers.htm

Hernstein, Richard, and Charles Murray. (1994). *The Bell Curve: Intelligence and Class Structure in American Life*. New York: Free Press.

Heymann, S. Jody, and Alison Earle. (1997). Working Conditions: What do Parents Leaving Welfare and Low Income Parents Face? Working Paper H-97-01 of the Malcolm Weiner Center for Social Policy in the John F. Kennedy School of Government, Harvard University, June.

Hoynes, Hilary, and Thomas E. McCurdy. (1994). Has the Decline in Benefits Shortened Welfare Spells? *The American Economic Review*. 84, 43.

Hotz, V. Joseph, Susan Williams McElroy, and Seth G. Sanders. (1996). Costs and Consequences of Teenage Childbearing. *Chicago Policy Review*. 1, 55–94.

Hunt, Matthew O. (1996). The Individual, Society, or Both? A Comparison of Black, Latino, and White Beliefs about the Causes of Poverty. *Social Forces*. 75, 293–322.

Institute for Women's Policy Research. (1996). Measuring the Costs of Domestic Violence against Women. *Research-in-Brief*. Washington, DC: IWPR.

Institute for Women's Policy Research. (1995). Welfare to Work: The Job Opportunities of AFDC Recipients. [Online] Available: *http://www.access.digex.net/~iwpr/wtwrib.htm*

Jansson, Bruce S. (1988). *The Reluctant Welfare State: A History of American Social Welfare Policies*. Belmont, CA: Wadsworth.

Jarrett, Robin L. (1996). Welfare Stigma among Low-Income African American Single Mothers. *Family Relations*. 45, 368–374.

———. (1994). Living Poor: Family Life among Single Parent, African-American Women. *Social Problems*. 41, 30–49.

Jones, Edward Ellsworth, and Richard E. Nisbett. (1972). The Actor and the Observer: Divergent Perceptions of the Causes of Behavior. In Edward E. Jones, David Kanouse, Harold Kelley, Stuart Valins, and Bernard Weiner (Eds.) *Attribution: Perceiving the Causes of Behavior*. New York: General Learning Press.

Kahn, Alfred J., and Shelia B. Kamerman. (1975). *Not for the Poor Alone: European Social Services*. New York: Harper and Row.

Kaplan, April. (1997a). *Domestic Violence and Welfare Reform*. Welfare Information Network, HN 5449, Vol.1, No. 8, September [Online] Available: *http://www.igc.apc.org/handsnet2/welfare.reform/Articles/art/874022785.htm*

Kaplan, April. (1997b). *Domestic Violence and Welfare Reform*. The Welfare Information Network.

Kaplan, April. (1998). *Transportation and Welfare Reform*. [Online] Available: *http://www.welfareinfo.org/transita.htm*

Karger, Howard J. (1992). Income Maintenance Programs and the Reagan Domestic Agenda. *Journal of Sociology and Social Work*. XIX, 45–61.

Katz, Michael. (1986). *In the Shadow of the Poorhouse: A Social History of Welfare in America*. New York: Basic Books.

Kaus, Mickey. (1992). *The End of Equality*. New York: Basic Books.

Kelley, Harold H. (1973). The Process of Causal Attribution. *American Psychologist*. 28, 107–128.

Kessler-Harris, Alice. (1982). *Out to Work: A History of Wage Earning Women in the United States.* New York: Oxford University Press.

Kluegel, James R., and Eliot R. Smith. (1982). Whites' Beliefs about Blacks' Opportunity. *American Sociological Review.* 47, 518–532.

Kozol, Jonathan. (1991). *Savage Inequalities.* New York: Crown Publishers.

Leadbeater, Bonnie J., and Sandra J. Bishop. (1994). Predictors of Behavior Problems in Preschool Children of Inner-City Afro-American and Puerto Rican Adolescent Mothers. *Child Development.* 65, 638–648.

Lerman, Robert. (1995). Increasing the Employment and Earnings of Welfare Recipients. In Isabel V. Sawhill (Ed.) *Welfare Reform: An Analysis of the Issues.* The Urban Institute. [Online] Available: *http://www.urban/org/welfare/overview.htm*

Lewin, Tamar. (April 28, 1991). The Ailing Health Care System: A Question of Access. *The New York Times.* pp. 1, 28.

Lewis, Oscar. (1966). The Culture of Poverty. *Scientific American.* 215, 19–25.

Lipset, Seymour Martin. (1990). *The Continental Divide: The Values and Institutions of the United States and Canada.* London: Routledge.

Lino, Mark. (1996). Income and Spending of Poor Households with Children. *Family Economics and Nutrition Review.* 9, 2–13.

Lloyd, Susan. (1997). The Effects of Violence on Women's Employment. Joint Center for Poverty Research. MacArthur Fundation. Chicago, IL [Online]. Available: *http://www.uchicago.edu/PovertyCenter/violence.html*

Loprest, Pamela, and Gregory Acs. (1996). *Profile of Disability Among Families on AFDC.* Washington DC: Urban Institute Report to the Henry J. Kaiser Family Foundation.

Lott, Bernice. (1994). *Women's Lives: Themes and Variations in Gender Learning*, 2nd ed. Pacific Grove, CA: Brooks/Cole.

Lutz, Steven, Janet R. Blaylock, and David M. Smallwood. (1993). Household Characteristics Affect Food Choices. *Food Review* Vol. 16, No. 2, p. 12 (6).

Mackie, Gerry. (1996). Ending Footbinding and Infibulation: A Conventional Account. *American Sociological Review.* 61, 999–1017.

Marx, Karl, and Friedrich Engels. (1959). Manifesto of the Communist Party. In L. S. Feuer (Ed.) *Marx and Engels: Basic Writings on Politics and Philosophy.* Garden City: Doubleday.

————. (1968). *Selected Works.* New York: International Publishers.

Mayer, Susan E., and Christopher Jencks. (1989). Poverty and the Distribution of Material Hardship. *Journal of Human Resources* 24, 88–113.

McElroy, Susan Williams, and Kristin Anderson Moore. (1997). Trends over Time in Teenage Pregnancy and Childbearing: The Critical Changes. In R. A. Maynard (Ed.). *Kids Having Kids: Economic Costs and Social Consequences of Teen Pregnancy.* New York: Urban Institute.

McGuire, Merideth B. (1992). *Religion: The Social Context*, 2nd ed. Belmont, CA: Wadsworth.

McLanahan and Sandefur. (1994). *Growing Up with a Single Parent.* Cambridge: Harvard.

Mead, Lawrence M. (1986). *Beyond Entitlement: The Social Obligations of Citizenship.* New York, NY: The Free Press.

————. (1992). *The New Politics of Poverty: The Non-Working Poor in America.* New York: Basic Books.

Meyer, Carol. (1994). The Latent Issues of Welfare Reform. *Affilia.* 9, 229–231.

Meyers, Judith, and John E. Kyle. (1996). *Critical Needs, Critical Choices: A Survey on Children and Families in America's Cities.* Washington, DC: National League of Cities. March.

Meyers, Marcia K., Anna Lukemeyer, and Timothy M. Smeeding. (1996). Work, Welfare, and the Burden of Disability: Caring for Special Needs Children in Poor Families. Syracuse,

NY: Center for Policy Research, Maxwell School of Citizenship and Public Affairs, Syracuse University, Income Security Policy Series, Paper No. 12.

Miller, Dorothy C. (1992). *Women and Social Welfare: A Feminist Analysis*. New York: Praeger.

Mills, C. Wright. (1956). *The Power Elite*. New York: Oxford University Press.

Mills, Frederick B. (1996). The Ideology of Welfare Reform: Deconstructing Stigma. *Social Work*. 41, 391–396.

Mink, Gwendolyn. (1995). *The Wages of Motherhood: Inequality in the Welfare State, 1917–1942*. Ithaca, NY: Cornell University Press.

Moffitt, Robert. (March, 1990). *Incentive Effects of the U.S. Welfare System: A Review*. (Special Report, Series No. 48). Madison: University of Wisconsin, Institute for Research on Poverty.

Moody, Anne. (1968). *Coming of Age in Mississippi*. New York, NY: Laurel.

Moore, Kristen A., Martha J. Zaslow, Mary Jo Coiro, Suzanne M. Miller, and Ellen B. Magenheim. (1995). *The JOBS Evaluation: How Well Are They Fairing? AFDC Families with Preschool-Aged Children in Atlanta at the Outset of the JOBS Evaluation*. Washington DC: U.S. Department of Health and Human Services. Office of the Assistant Secretary for Planning and Evaluation.

Morrow, Lance. (1993). The Temping of America. *Time*. March 29, pp. 40–41.

Moynihan, Daniel P. (1965). *The Negro Family*. Washington DC: U.S. Department of Labor.

Murray, Charles. (1984). *Losing Ground: American Social Policy, 1950–1980*. New York: Basic Books.

_____. (1988). *In Pursuit of Happiness and Good Government*. New York: Simon & Schuster.

National Center for Health Statistics. (1995). *Advance Report of Final Natality Statistics. 1993. Monthly Vital Statistics Report. Vol. 43, No. 3 (supplement)*. Hyattsville, MD: U.S. Public Health Service.

National Governors' Association Center for Best Practices. (1997). *Current Trends and Emerging Issues in Welfare-to-Work*. [Online] Available: *http://www.nga.org/Pubs/IssueBriefs/1997/971204WelfareWork.asp*

National Opinion Research Center. (1993). *General Social Surveys, 1972–1993: Cumulative Codebook*. Chicago: National Opinion Research Center.

Needleman, Herbert L., Alan Schell, David Bellinger, Alan Leviton, and Elizabeth N. Allred. (1990). The Long-Term Effects of Exposure to Low Doses of Lead in Childhood. *New England Journal of Medicine*. 322, 83–88.

Nightingale, Demetra S., Regina Yudd, Stacey Anderson, and Burt Barnow. (1991). *The Learning Disabled in Employment and Training Programs*. Washington, DC: U.S. Department of Labor.

Nitz, Katherine, Robert D. Ketterlinus, and Linda J. Brandt. (1995). The Role of Stress, Social Support, and Family Environment in Adolescent Mothers' Parenting. *Journal of Adolescent Research*. 10, 358–382.

Oliker, Stacey J. (1995). The Proximate Contexts of Workfare and Work: A Framework for Studying Poor Women's Economic Choices. *The Sociological Quarterly*. 36, 251–272.

Olson, Krista, and LaDonna Pavetti. (1998). *Personal and Family Challenges to the Successful Transition from Welfare to Work*. [Online] The Urban Institute. Available: *http://www.urban.org/welfare/report1.htm*

Panzarine, Susan, Elisa Slater, and Phyllis Sharps. (1995). Coping, Social Support, and Depressive Symptoms in Adolescent Mothers. *Journal of Adolescent Health*. 17, 113–119.

Passell, Peter. (July 31, 1997). Economic Scene: Report Shows How Hard It Is to Break Welfare Dependency. *New York Times*. [Online] Available: file:///A|/Passell-hardtobreak.htm

Pavett, LaDonna, and Amy-Ellen Duke. (1995). *Increasing Participation in Work and Work Re-*

lated Activities: Lessons from Five Welfare Reform Demonstration Projects. Report Prepared for the Office of the Assistant Secretary for Planning and Evaluation, U.S. Department of Health and Human Services. Washington, DC: The Urban Institute.

Pear, Robert. (March 25, 1995). House Backs Bill Undoing Decades of Welfare Policy. *New York Times.* Section I, p. 1.

Peterkin, Betty. (1964). Family Food Plans, Revised, 1964. *Family Economics Review.* October 3, 12.

Peterkin, Betty, and Richard L. Kerr. (1982). Food Stamp Allotment and Diets of U.S. Households. *Family Economics Review.* Winter 1, 23–26.

Petersen, Carol D. (1995). Female-Headed Families on AFDC: Who Leaves Welfare Quickly and Who Doesn't. *Journal of Economic Issues.* 29, 619–628.

Peterson, Paul E., and Mark C. Rom. (1990). *Welfare Magnets.* Washington, DC: Brookings Institution.

Peterson, Richard R. (1996). A Re-Evaluation of the Economic Consequences of Divorce. *American Sociological Review.* 61, 528–536.

Posner, Jill, and Deborah Lowe Vandell. (1994). Low-Income Children's After-School Care: Are There Beneficial Effects of After-School Programs? *Child Development* 65, 440–456.

Presser, Harriet B., and Amy G. Cox. (1997). The Work Schedules of Low-Educated American Women and Welfare Reform. *Monthly Labor Review.* April, 25–33.

Quadagno, Jill. (1994). *The Color of Welfare. How Racism Undermines the War on Poverty.* New York: Oxford.

_____. (1988). *The Transformation of Old Age Security: Class and Politics in the American Welfare State.* Chicago: University of Chicago Press.

Quint, J., H. Bos, and H. Polit. (1997). *New Chance: Final Report on a Comprehensive Program for Young Mothers in Poverty and Their Children.* New York: Manpower Demonstration Research Corporation.

Rank, Mark Robert. (1994). *Living on the Edge: The Realities of Welfare in America.* New York, NY: Columbia University Press.

_____. (1989). Fertility among Women on Welfare: Incidence and Determinants. *American Sociological Review.* 54, 269–304.

Raphael, Jody, and Richard M. Tolman. (1997). *Trapped by Poverty, Trapped by Abuse—New Evidence Documenting the Relationship between Domestic Violence and Welfare.* Taylor Institute and University of Michigan School of Social Work. April. 773-342-5510. Ann Arbor, MI.

Rausch, Paula. (February 19, 1997). Welfare Job Needs Worry Officials. *The Gainesville Sun.* pp. 1A, 7A.

Reagan, Ronald, Home Page. (1997). *Social Welfare Expenditures under Public Programs.* [Online] Available: *http://www.dnaco.net/~bkottman/social_spending.htm*

Regan, Edward V. (1994). *Infrastructure Investment for Tomorrow.* Public Policy Brief, no. 141, Jerome Levy Economics Institute, Barol College.

Resnick, M. D., L. J. Harris, and R. W. Blum. (1993). The Impact of Caring and Connectedness on Adolescent Health and Well-Being. *Journal of Pediatric Child Health.* 29 (Supplement 1), S3–S9.

Roberts, Paula. (1997). *Pursuing Child Support: More Violence?* The Center for Law and Social Policy [Online] [May]. Available: *http://epn.org/clasp/970916.htm*

Rogers-Dillon, Robin. (1995). The Dynamics of Welfare Stigma. *Qualitative Sociology.* 18, 439–456.

Rosier, Katherine Brown, and William A. Corsaro. (1993). Competent Parents, Complex

Lives: Managing Parenthood in Poverty. *Journal of Contemporary Ethnography*. 22, 171–204.

Rubin, Lillian B. (1994). *Families on the Fault Line*. New York: Harper Collins.

Ruggles, Patricia. (1990). *Drawing the Line: Alternative Poverty Measures and Their Implications*. Washington, DC: Urban Institute Press.

Saluter, Arlene F. (1989). *Singleness in America*. U.S. Bureau of the Census, Current Population Reports, Special Studies, Series P-23, no. 162. Washington DC: U.S. Government Printing Office.

San Francisco Chronicle. (February 22, 1993). "A Different Kind of Chicago Housing Project: Urban Blacks Find New Hope and Pain in Suburbs." p. A1.

Schlein, Michael. (September 28, 1997). Fraternity Life Today. *Gainesville Sun*. pp. D1, D5.

Scott, Marvin B., and Stanford M. Lyman. (1968). Accounts. *American Sociological Review*. 33, 46–61.

Seccombe, Karen. (1995). Health Insurance Coverage and Use of Services among Low-Income Elders: Does Residence Influence the Relationship? *The Journal of Rural Health*. 11, 86–97.

Seccombe, Karen. (1993). Employer Sponsored Medical Benefits: The Influence of Occupational Characteristics and Gender. *The Sociological Quarterly*. 34, 557–580.

Seccombe, Karen. (1996). Health Insurance Coverage among the Working Poor: Changes from 1977–1987. *Research in the Sociology of Health Care*. Vol. 13, 199–227. Greenwich, CT: JAI Press.

Seccombe, Karen, Delores James, and Kimberly Battle-Walters. (1998). "They Think You Ain't Much of Nothing": The Social Construction of the Welfare Mother. *Journal of Marriage and the Family*. Forthcoming.

Seccombe, Karen, and Cheryl Amey. (1995). Playing by the Rules and Losing: Health Insurance and the Working Poor. *Journal of Health and Social Behavior*. 36, 168–181.

Segura, Denise. (1994). Working at Motherhood: Chicana and Mexican Immigrant Mothers and Employment. In E. Nakano Glenn, G. Chang, and L. R. Forcey (Eds.). *Mothering: Ideology, Experience, and Agency*. New York: Routledge.

Sexton, Joe. (March 19, 1997). In Brooklyn Neighborhood, Welfare Fraud Is Nothing New. *New York Times. (web)*

Singh, Gopal K., T. J. Mathews, Ally C. Clarke, Trina Yannicos, and Betty L. Smith. (1995). Annual Summary of Births, Marriages, Divorces, and Deaths: United States, 1994. *Monthly Vital Statistics Reports*. Hyattsville, MD: National Center for Health Statistics. 43, 13.

Smeeding, Timothy M. (1992). Why the U.S. Antipoverty System Doesn't Work Very Well. *Challenge*. 35 (January/February), 30–35.

Smith, Dorothy E. (1993). The Standard North American Family: SNAF as an Ideological Code. *Journal of Family Issues*. 14, 50–65.

Smith, Kevin B., and Lorene H. Stone. (1989). Rags, Riches, and Bootstraps: Beliefs About the Causes of Wealth and Poverty. *The Sociological Quarterly*. 30, 93–107.

Smock, Pamela J., and Wendy D. Manning. (1997). Nonresident Parents' Characteristics and Child Support. *Journal of Marriage and the Family*. 59, 798–808.

Sonenstein, Freya L., Joseph H. Pleck, and Leighton C. Ku. (1989). Sexual Activity, Condom Use, and Aids Awareness among Adolescent Males. *Family Planning Perspectives*. 21, 152–158.

Sorensen, Elaine. (1997). A National Profile of Nonresident Fathers and Their Ability to Pay Child Support. *Journal of Marriage and the Family*. 59, 785–797.

Spalter-Roth, Roberta, Heidi Hartmann, and Beverly Burr. (1994). *Income Insecurity: The Failure of Unemployment Insurance to Reach Working AFDC Mothers*. Washington, DC: Institute for Women's Policy Research.

Stack, Carol B. (1974). *All Our Kin: Strategies for Survival in a Black Community*. New York: Harper and Row.

Sterner, Richard. (1943). *The Negro's Share: A Study of Income, Consumption, Housing, and Public Assistance*. New York: Harpers and Brothers Publishers.

Straus, Murray A. (1991). Physical Violence in American Families: Incidence, Rates, Causes, and Trends. In Dean D. Knudsen and JoAnn L. Miller (Eds.). *Abused and Battered: Social and Legal Responses to Family Violence*, pp. 17–34. New York: Aldine de Gruyter, 1991.

Straus, Murray A., and Richard Gelles. (1988). How Violent Are American Families? Estimates from the National Family Violence Resurvey and Other Studies. In Gerald T. Hotaling, David Finkelhor, John T. Kirkpatrick, and Murray A. Straus (Eds.). *Family Abuse and Its Consequences: New Directions in Research*, pp. 14–36. Newbury Park: Sage.

Straus, Murray A., and Richard Gelles. (1986). Societal Change and Change in Family Violence from 1975 to 1985 as Revealed by Two National Surveys. *Journal of Marriage and the Family*. 48, 465–479.

Super, David A., Sharon Parrott, Susan Steinmetz, and Cindy Mann. (1996). The New Welfare Law—Summary. The Center on Budget and Policy Priorities. [August 13]. [Online] Available: *http://www.cbpp.org/WCNSUM.HTM*

Swanson, Mark C. A., Mahendra K. Agarwal, and Charles E. Reed. (1985). An Immunochemical Approach to Indoor Aero-Allergen Quantitation: Studies with Mite, Roach, Cat, Mouse Allergens. *Journal of Allergy and Clinical Immunology*. 76, 724–728.

Swarns, Rachel L. (1997). "Welfare Mothers Prep for Jobs, and Wait." *New York Times* [August 31]. [Online] Available: file:///A1/swarns~job prep.htm

Szanton, Peter L. (1991). The Remarkable Quango: Knowledge, Politics, and Welfare Reform. *Journal of Policy Analysis and Management*. 10, 590–602.

Tanner, Michael, Stephen Moore, and David Hartman. (1997). The High Value of Welfare Benefits Keeps the Poor on Welfare. pp. 75–82. In C. P. Cozic and P. A. Winters (Eds.). *Welfare: Opposing Viewpoints*. San Diego, CA: Greenhaven Press.

Teti, Douglas M., Michael E. Lamb, and Arthur B. Elster. (1987). Long-Range Socioeconomic and Marital Consequences of Adolescent Marriage in Three Cohorts of Adult Males. *Journal of Marriage and the Family*. 49, 499–506.

Thomas, Susan. (1995). Exchanging Welfare Checks for Wedding Rings: Welfare Reform in New Jersey and Wisconsin. *Affilia*. 10, 120–137.

Thompson, Linda. (1992). Feminist Methodology for Family Studies. *Journal of Marriage and the Family*. 54, 3–18.

Thurer, Shari L. (1994). *The Myths of Motherhood: How Culture Reinvents the Good Mother*. Boston: Houghton Mifflin.

Trattner, Walter I. (1989). *From Poor Law to Welfare State*, 4th ed. New York, NY: The Free Press.

Trent, Katherine, and Kyle Crowder. (1997). Adolescent Birth Intentions, Social Disadvantage, and Behavioral Outcomes. *Journal of Marriage and the Family*. 59, 523–535.

U.S. Bureau of the Census. (1997a). *Poverty in the United States: 1996*. Current Population Report Series P-60. No. 198. Washington, DC: U.S. Government Printing Office.

U.S. Bureau of the Census. (1997b). *Statistical Abstract of the United States*. 117th ed. Washington, DC: U.S. Government Printing Office.

U.S. Bureau of Labor Statistics. (No date). *The Value of the Federal Minimum Wage, 1954–1996*. [Online]. Available: *http://www.dol.gov./dol/esa/public/minwage/chart2.htm*

U.S. Bureau of Labor Statistics. (1992). *Employment and Earnings* 39 (1 January). Washington, DC: U.S. Government Printing Office.

U.S. Congress, Office of Technology Assessment. (1992). *Does Health Insurance Make a Difference?—Background Paper.* (OTA-BP-H-99) Washington, DC: U.S. Government Printing Office.

U.S. Department of Education. (1994). *The Condition of Education: 1993.* Washington, DC: National Center for Education Statistics.

U.S. Department of Health and Human Services. (July 1997). *Health United States, 1996–97.* Washington, DC: U.S. Government Printing Office.

U.S. Department of Health and Human Services, Administration for Children and Families. (January 1998). *Changes in Welfare Caseloads.* [Online] Available: *http://www.acf.dhhs.gov/news/case-fam.htm*

U.S. Department of Justice. (1994). Violence Between Intimates. *Bureau of Justice Statistics Selected Findings: Domestic Violence.* Nov. No. NCJ-149259. Washington, DC: U.S. Department of Justice, Office of Justice Programs.

U.S. Department of Labor. (1994). *Employment and Earnings.* 30 (4) Washington, DC: U.S. Department of Labor.

U.S. Federal Bureau of Investigation. (1995). *Crime in the United States 1994.* Washington, DC: U.S. Government Printing Office.

U.S. House of Representatives, Committee on Ways and Means. (1996). *1996 Green Book.* Washington, DC: U.S. Government Printing Office.

U.S. News Online. (October 20, 1997). Was Reagan Right? [Online]. Available: *http://www.usnews.com/usnews/issue/971020/20chea.htm*

U.S. News Online. (August 18, 1997). Fast Food and Welfare Reform. [Online]. Available: *http://www.usnews.com/usnews/issue/970818/18burg.htm*

U.S. News Online. (April 29, 1996). Raise the Minimum Wage? [Online]. Available: *http://www.usnews.com/usnews/ISSUE/WAGE.HTM*

U.S. Social Security Board. (1940). *Social Security Yearbook 1939: Annual Supplement to the Social Security Bulletin.* Washington, DC: U.S. Government Printing Office.

USA Today. (September 16, 1997). "Call of the Road." p. 3A.

USA Today. (July 2, 1996). "Welfare Mistrust." p. 1A.

Weitzman, Lenore. (1985). *The Divorce Revolution: The Unexpected Social and Economic Consequences for Women and Children in America.* New York: The Free Press.

White House Working Group on the Family. (1986). *The Family: Preserving America's Future.* November 13, 1986.

Williams, Dave. (December 17, 1997). State's Rich-Poor Gap among the Widest. *The Gainesville Sun.* Page 3B.

Wilson, Mark. (1996). *The Folly of Increasing the Minimum Wage.* Backgrounder Update, No. 275. April 22. The Heritage Foundation. [Online] Available: *http://www.nationalsecurity.org/heritage/library/categories/theory/bgup275.html*

Wilson, William J. (1987). *The Truly Disadvantaged: The Inner City, the Underclass, and Public Policy.* Chicago: University of Chicago Press.

_____. (1993). *The New Urban Poverty and the Problem of Race.* The Tanner Lecture, University of Michigan, Ann Arbor.

_____. (1996). *When Work Disappears: The World of the New Urban Poor.* New York: Alfred A. Knopf.

Woolsey, Lynn. (January 22, 1994). Reinvent Welfare, Humanely. *New York Times.* p. 21.

World Values Survey. (1994). *World Values Survey, 1990–1993.* Ann Arbor, MI: Inter-University Consortium for Political and Social Research.

Yaniv, Gideon. (1997). Welfare Fraud and Welfare Stigma. *Journal of Economic Psychology.* 18, 435–451.

APPENDIX

Our interview instrument is provided as follows. Because we tried to conduct the interviews more as a conversation rather than as a structured survey, the questions were often asked out of order. We did, however, collect the following information from each of our respondents.

Introduction:

    My name is _____. I am from the University of Florida and am working on a project to try to get a better understanding of what it is like to receive welfare. Our research team hopes that this information will be useful to people who create programs such as AFDC or food stamps. We will be interviewing approximately 50 different people about their experiences. The interview may last about an hour to an hour and a half. I wish that we had money to pay you for your time, but, unfortunately, we do not.

    Your answers are completely confidential. Your name will never be associated with your answers. And as you know, your participation is completely voluntary. We hope that you will answer all the questions, but you do not have to answer any question that you do not want to. Your AFDC, food stamps, or other aid is not tied to this research. Do you have any questions about the project?

    Here is a letter with my and my supervisor's names, addresses, and phone numbers on it. Please feel free to call us if you have any questions afterwards, or want to mention something else that we didn't cover here.

    If you do not object, I would like to audiotape record your answers. It is easier for me to use a tape recorder rather than try to write everything out right now. Later your answers will be typed out so that we can analyze all 50 interviews for ideas. We will not use your name on this audiotape—we will just give you and this interview an ID number. No one outside this project will ever hear your tape. It will be kept in a locked file in my supervisor's office.

    Before I begin, let me ask you for the record, would you like to participate in this research?

    Okay, to start off, I'd first like to ask you some general questions about your daily life. . . .

I. Daily Life

I'd like to find out what an average day is like for you.

    1. Do you have a regular schedule to a typical day (i.e., get up at about the same time, eat at a certain time, etc.)?

(if yes)

    1a. What is that schedule like?

(if no)

    1b. What did you do yesterday? What did you do today?

  2. How many children do you have?

  3. Do you have any children living with someone else?

(if yes)

    3a. Why are they living there?

    3b. How long have they been living there?

    3c. Do anyone else's children live with you?

  4. Do the children have a regular schedule (i.e., homework, playtime, bedtime, etc.)?

(if yes)

    4a. In general, what is their daily schedule?

(if no)

    2b. What did they do yesterday? What did they do today?

  3. What are some of the things you enjoy doing when you're not working or taking care of your family?

  4. How often do you see family members who do not live with you? What kinds of things do you do with them?

  5. How often do you see friends? What kinds of things do you do with friends?

  6. What do you do when you just want to have fun?

  7. Do you belong to a church or other organizations?

  8. Do you do any type of volunteer work (i.e., At school, or helping neighbors or kin)?

  9. Do you have a phone in your home?

 10. Do you have a driver's license?

 11. Do you have a car?

II. Coping and Decision Making

Things often come up that break the daily routine or make it difficult to have a routine. I was wondering if any of these events have happened to you, and if so, how you dealt with them:

12. If one of the children gets sick or injured, what would you do?

13. If you were sick or injured, what would you do?

14. What would you do if a major appliance (like a refrigerator or washing machine) were to quit?

15. What if you had to go somewhere without the children—do you have someone you can call on short notice?

(owns a car)
   15a. If the car breaks down, what would you do?

(if no car)
   15b. How would you get somewhere in an emergency?

Let's talk about the things that have to be done. Let's say that this is the day you get your check.

16. What do you spend your money on first?

17. How much money do you have left after that?

18. How do you decide what other things to get?

19. What do you do if the children need something, such as shoes, but you do not have enough money left?

20. What about Christmas or other holidays?

21. If you had an extra $50 this month, what would you spend it on?

22. Do you save any money?

Sometimes when emergencies come up people have to put off paying some bills in order to pay others.

23. Has this ever happened to you?

(if yes)

    23a. How often does it happen?

    23b. Are companies/people willing to work with you?

24. Do you ever feel overwhelmed by all of these decisions?

(if yes)

24. What do you do to cope?

III. Food Stamps and Other Assistance

I'd like to ask you some questions about the assistance that you get.

25. First, could you tell me whether you receive the following kinds of assistance?

    25a. AFDC and how much each month?

    25b. Food stamps and how much each month?

    25c. Subsidized housing?

        25c.1. How much is your rent each month?

    25d. Medicaid?

        25d.1. How much do you spend on monthly medical bills?

    25e. Subsidized utilities?

        25e.1. About how much do you spend on utilities each month?

    25f. Subsidized day care for your children?

        25f.1. About how much do you spend for baby-sitting/day care each month?

    25g. Education or job training?

        25g.1. About how much does this cost?

    25h. WIC program?

25i. Anything else?

25j. Were you invited to participate in the Family Transition Project?

(if yes)

25j.1. Did you choose to participate? Why or why not?

26. Do you have any other regular expenses (e.g., car insurance)?

27. Who do you support with your welfare checks and food stamps?

28. If you could only get one kind of public assistance such as food stamps, AFDC, or Medicaid, which one would you choose, and why?

29. Do you get enough food stamps?

30. Have you ever run out of food stamps?

(if yes)

30a. What did you do?

31. When you are running short on food stamps, which foods do you stop buying?

32. Do you ever use food banks (e.g., Gainesville Harvest) or go to soup kitchens (e.g., St. Francis Shelter)?

33. Do you or your children ever go to bed hungry?

(if yes)

33a. How often?

34. Which foods do you usually treat yourself or your children to when you first get your food stamps?

35. How often do you eat out, and where do you usually go?

IV. Network and Social Support and Use of Other Social Services

Sometimes those of us who don't have a lot of money depend on others to help out when things get tough. I'd like to talk with you about the people who may help you out.

36. Right now, are you married, single, divorced, or widowed?

37. Were you ever married?

38. How do you get along with your children's father(s)?

39. What do you expect from the children's father(s)?

40. Does he/they pay child support or visit the children regularly?

41. Do you have friends, family, or anyone else that you can ask to help you out if you need it?

(if yes)
    41a. How important is this help to you?

42. Other than the people you already mentioned, is there any other group or organization that you get help from (e.g., civic organization, church, social agency)?

(if yes)
    42a. What kind of help do you get?

    42b. How comfortable do you feel asking these people/groups for help?

V. Transitions/Plans for Independence

Now I'd like to ask you some questions about the kinds of jobs that you may have had in the past, and about welfare. First,

43. Have you ever worked outside of your home for pay?

(if yes)
    43a. What type(s) of jobs did you have?

44. Do you do any kind of work for money now, either inside or outside the home (e.g., baby-sitting, doing hair or nails)?

45. How long have you been on welfare?

46. What circumstances made it necessary for you to first apply for welfare?

47. Have you ever gotten off welfare?

(if yes)

     47a. How did you manage to do so (resources, support, etc.)?

     47b. What made it necessary for you to reapply?

    48. Do you foresee a time when you and your children won't have to get by with the help of AFDC or food stamps?

(if yes)

     48a. How will you do this?

     48b. When do you think this may happen?

(if no)

     48c. Why not?

    49. Do you think that you will be on welfare five years from now?

(if no)

     49a. What type of work do you think you might do in the future?

    50. If you could have any job in the world, what would that be?

    51. Do you think you could do that?

VI. Stigma

Sometimes other people have opinions about people who receive welfare.

    52. What kinds of things have you heard said?

    53. Do you think these things are true?

    54. Have those things ever been said to you or your children?

    55. Have you ever felt that you or your children were treated differently or unfairly compared to someone not on welfare (e.g., refused service, made to wait a long time, treated rudely)?

VII. Self-Esteem

Now, if you don't mind, I'd like to ask you some questions about how you feel about yourself as a person.

56. What are some of your strengths, or things you are good at?

57. What are some things about yourself that you would like to change?

VIII. Health Needs and Health Insurance

We all would like to stay healthy all the time, but that doesn't always happen. In this section, I'd like to talk about your family's health and health care.

58. How is your and your family's health; do you have any particular health problems?

(if good)
58a. So, you feel good all the time?

59. Are you able to find a doctor and get the health care that you need?

IX. General Questions about Poverty and Welfare

Now we know about your situation pretty well. I'd like to ask you your opinion about some other issues—things about other people that you don't know.

60. Why are other people on welfare?

61. In what ways is your situation different from theirs?

62. Who's fault is it if people are poor?

63. Do you think the government should help poor people?

(if yes)
63a. What should the government do?

X. Strengths and Weaknesses of the Welfare System

Some people are talking about changing the AFDC program.

64. Do you think that someone on AFDC should be required to get a job for their check?

65. Do you think that AFDC payments should stop after two or three years?

66. Do you think that women who have children while on AFDC should have their monthly check stay the same or should it increase?

67. What do you see as the strengths of the welfare system as it is currently run (i.e., efficiency treatment of clients, services, etc.)?

68. What are the weaknesses?

69. If you could tell the president, Congress, the governor, and everybody else about women who receive AFDC, what would you tell them?

XI. Demographics

Finally, we are at the end of the interview. Just to make sure I have background information on everyone, let me do a quick check on a few things. Some of these may have been answered already.

70. How old are you?

71. Do you have a high school diploma or a GED?

72. Did your parent or guardian ever receive welfare when you were a child?

73. Were your parents married during all of your childhood?

74. Do you usually vote in elections?

75. Race/ethnicity? (Ask if not obvious.)

76. In conclusion, in just one word, how would you describe life on welfare?

77. Is there anything else we should know about what it's like living on welfare or is there anything we haven't talked about that you think is especially hard in your life . . . or anything that causes you stress?

That's it! Thank you so much for helping us out on our research project.

INDEX